# Practical Politics

# Practical Politics

## Five Principles for a Community That Works

**Michael K. Briand**

University of Illinois Press
Urbana and Chicago

1 2 3 4 5 C P 6 5 4 3 2

∞ This book is printed on acid-free paper.

Library of Congress Cataloging-in-Publication Data
Briand, Michael K. (Michael Keith)
Practical politics : five principles for a community that works /
Michael K. Briand.
p.   cm.
Includes bibliographical references and index.
ISBN 0-252-02460-5 (cloth : alk. paper) / 978-0-252-02460-3
ISBN 0-252-06766-5 (pbk. : alk. paper) / 978-0-252-06766-2
1. Politics, Practical—United States.
2. Political participation—United States. I. Title.
JK1764.B75   1999
324.7'0973—dc21   98-58010
CIP

# Contents

# Acknowledgments

Most of this book was written during the three years I served as director of the Community Self-Leadership Project, an undertaking of the Colorado Community College and Occupational Education System (CCCOES), funded by the W. K. Kellogg Foundation. The purpose of the project was to enhance the ability of communities throughout the state of Colorado to respond effectively to the problems, challenges, and opportunities facing them. It was designed to accomplish this by enabling the state's two-year colleges to become a resource and a catalyst for inclusive, deliberative, and collaborative public decision-making in the communities of their service areas.

Without the Kellogg Foundation's support, which afforded me the opportunity to refine the arguments in this book while working with real communities and real political issues, I simply could not have written it. I owe a special debt of gratitude to my Kellogg program officer, Dr. Betty J. Overton. Her faith in the project and in me personally, her experience and savvy, her patience and steadfast support, and her wise counsel kept the project, and me, afloat.

I would also like to thank Dr. Jim Raughton, CCCOES vice-president, for his commitment to the project and its success. Dr. Harold Deselms, president of Trinidad State Junior College, gave the project its first home and the chance to establish itself. Dr. James Weber, president of Arapahoe Community College, welcomed the project to the Denver area and provided a place for it to expand and mature.

Several people read the manuscript and offered immensely helpful comments and questions, beginning with the anonymous reviewers who did so at the request of the University of Illinois Press. Dr. David Lisman of the Community College of Aurora read the manuscript not once, but twice. He has been not only a colleague and fellow traveler, but a friend sine qua non. Harry Boyte, Frances Lappé, David Mathews, and Bill Sullivan also read the manuscript and not only offered helpful comments but found something nice to say about it as well.

The idea for the book and much of my thinking about it began to take shape during my tenure as a program officer with the Charles F. Kettering Foundation.

Ned Crosby gave me the early support I needed to begin work on it, and Suzanne Morse provided constant encouragement. The intellectual stimulation I received from my colleagues at Kettering, especially David Mathews and Bob Kingston, drove my thinking forward like a small boat in a brisk following wind.

"There is no new thing under the sun," said the author of Ecclesiastes. At least as far as this book is concerned, truer words were never spoken. Although I might have put the ideas together and expressed them in a unique way, by no stretch of the imagination are they original with me. I have been influenced greatly by the work of, among others, Robert Bellah, Harry Boyte, John Diggins, Richard Flathman, James Fishkin, John Gray, R. M. Hare, Christopher Lasch, Alasdair MacIntyre, J. L. Mackie, Harold Saunders, and Charles Taylor.

I am most grateful to my editor, Richard Martin, whose readiness to entertain my initial inquiry has endeared the University of Illinois Press to me, and whose erudition, professionalism, and patience got me through the endurance test of turning a manuscript into a book worth publishing. Thanks also to the Press's managing editor, Theresa L. Sears, and my copy editor, Carol Betts, who attended to a multitude of details—and forced me to do so, too.

Finally, my wife, Karen, and my children, Aaron and Alexandra, reminded me every day why it was important to try to write something useful, illuminating, and encouraging about democratic decision making in the communities of the late twentieth and early twenty-first centuries. As those communities go, so go our loved ones. It is for them we strive to build and sustain communities that work.

# Introduction: The Work of Democratic Communities

*Malcontentedness may be the beginning of promise.*
—Randolph Bourne

### Politics and Problems—and the Problem of Politics

We live most of our lives in communities—in neighborhoods, school districts, towns, and other collective entities that occupy the small geographical area we call home. In every community there is work to do. Streets must be repaired, children must be educated, waste must be disposed of, water and electrical power must be supplied, people and property must be protected, commerce must be conducted.

These aren't the only kinds of work a community must do. Over time, every community encounters new problems it must address, needs it must fill, issues it must resolve, disputes it must settle, challenges it must meet, and opportunities it should seize. In turn, each of these tasks generates still more work that a community must do before it can act: information must be obtained, study and analysis must be undertaken, options should be identified and evaluated, and decisions must be made.

The work facing our communities today differs from place to place, varying in nature and degree. But rare is the community that, in addition to its routine tasks, does not have at least one substantial problem or challenge. Many have crumbling roads, an aging water and sewage system, or an overflowing landfill. Some are losing population, others are gaining too much. The volume of traffic is an irritation in all but the smallest communities. Too many communities have high levels of violent crime, homelessness, or drug abuse. In most, people are struggling to keep up with rising costs and the social changes that trail in the wake of economic and technological change. In many, people are concerned about whether their children are being educated well. Throughout the country there are communities where people are unemployed or underemployed, where families break apart, where children are abused and neglected. Particularly in large cities, juvenile detention facilities, jails, and prisons fill up faster than new ones can be built, as young men (and, increasingly, women) with no prospects and no stake in widely shared values and the institutions that uphold them act out their frustration and despair.

Trying to solve problems such as these, many of which are complex and deep-rooted, is work indeed, especially in today's political climate. Politically fraught in addition to being inherently difficult, such problems often occasion bitter disputes that leave people feeling frustrated and angry, in no mood to cooperate—hence the well-remarked "NIMBY" ("not-in-my-backyard") and "BANANA" ("build absolutely nothing anywhere near anything") phenomena. Distressed by the apparent impotence of their communities' political leaders and institutions, people turn to obstruction. According to Lawrence Susskind and Jeffrey Cruikshank, professors at MIT, almost every effort to build prisons, highways, power plants, mental health facilities, and low-income housing is blocked by people who live nearby. For example, not a single hazardous waste treatment plant has been built in this country since 1975, even though everybody knows we need such plants.[1] Yet even when policy decisions are made, they are often ineffective because public support for them is not strong enough or cannot be sustained long enough for them to succeed. As Susskind and Cruikshank have observed, "we are at an impasse. . . . Whenever [our] leaders try to set standards, allocate resources, or make policy . . . we can expect a fight. . . . The 'laws' of public policy making tend to parallel the laws of physics: for every imposed action, there is an equal and opposite reaction."[2]

These examples help explain why Americans today are disillusioned with their public institutions, especially government but also the news media, schools and universities, and the legal system: those institutions—government in particular—seem unable to respond effectively to the problems and challenges facing their communities. Writing in the *Atlantic Monthly* in 1996, Robert A. Levine asserts that "most Americans . . . just want solutions to the nation's problems."[3] The political analyst William Schneider agrees. He contends that most Americans are "pragmatists"—they believe that what works is right.[4] They support policies and policy makers that produce results.

To be sure, much of the public's dissatisfaction with politics in the United States today stems from unrelieved exposure to national political debate about problems and issues that the federal government must address. Whether it is justified or not—and in many cases, I believe, it is not—there is a profound perception that our political decision-making process doesn't work. This pervasive perception owes much to the sense that politics at the national level is too partisan, too narrowly "political," too ideological, and hence too adversarial.[5] Our attitudes toward politics are shaped by what we hear, see, and read in the news media. And what we hear, see, and read is not encouraging.

The excesses committed during an election campaign are not typical of our public political discourse. But as national politics takes on the character of what Sidney Blumenthal has called a "permanent campaign,"[6] those excesses become increasingly representative. Political discourse at the national level too often amounts to little more than impugning the motives of unbelievers, on the one hand, and preaching to the converted, on the other. Through the media, political partisans sermonize like rival evangelists, exhorting the faithful to greater vigilance while damning those lost souls who refuse to see the light.

We accept this mode of discourse as normal, so much so that we tolerate even the grossest errors of reasoning and breaches of courtesy. As a result, productive discussion of divisive issues has been rendered virtually unobtainable. As Alasdair MacIntyre has observed, most public argumentative debate is sterile: "We have lost forums of genuine, extended public debate. Ask yourself when last the United States Senate assembled with senators ready to have their opinions formed *through* debate, rather than bringing intransigent opinions *to* debate."[7]

As rhetorical sloppiness and immoderation spread and worsen, the prospect of achieving effective, widely supported responses to the problems and challenges facing us recedes even further into the distance. The news media are of little help. James Fallows, former editor of *U.S. News and World Report,* observes that newspaper and television reporters "present every public issue as if its 'real' meaning were political in the meanest and narrowest sense of that term—the attempt by parties and candidates to gain an advantage over their rivals." In contrast, Fallows says, "when ordinary citizens have a chance to pose questions to political leaders, they rarely ask about the game of politics. They want to know how the reality of politics will affect them." This "relentless emphasis on the cynical game of politics threatens public life itself, by implying day after day that the political sphere is nothing more than an arena in which ambitious politicians struggle for dominance, rather than a structure in which citizens can deal with worrisome collective problems."[8]

The result, says Jonathan Schell, is a level of public disdain for "the media" that approaches that directed at politicians: "If the voters I met on the campaign trail are any indication (and poll data suggest they are), much of the public has lumped news people and politicians together in a single class, which, increasingly, it despises. More and more the two appear to be an undifferentiated establishment—a new Leviathan—composed of rich, famous, powerful people who are divorced from the lives of ordinary people and indifferent to their concerns."[9] In this climate, who could blame Americans for their frustration and dismay over politics? They feel bombarded with bad news, plagued with interminable disputes, assaulted with partisan bickering, and elbowed aside by self-interested competition for private advantage.

Unfortunately, it is in this partisan, ideological, and adversarial national political sea that citizens and communities have to swim. We take our cues about politics from the national political elite identified by Schell.[10] When most of what we hear about and see of politics is the jousting of prominent national political figures, it becomes hard for politics even at the local level to avoid being tarred with the same brush. According to Dirk Johnson of the *New York Times,* "what is perhaps most striking about the rancor [in local politics] is that it flares so explosively . . . [in] the very places said to be more capable than faraway Washington of solving issues with common sense and consideration for neighbors." Johnson says "there are several factors contributing to ever-rougher local politics: the stakes are higher as Washington kicks more issues back to local governments. Open-meeting laws are exposing dissent that was previously kept behind closed doors, and the presence of television cameras often encourages the high drama. Moreover, the mobility of American society means that town meetings are more often a collection of strangers than a comfortable gathering of old friends scripted by Thornton Wilder."[11]

Perhaps most important, however, few communities remain untouched by the larger world they inhabit. Many of the social, cultural, and economic changes occurring in the country (indeed, in the world) are producing repercussions that manifest themselves in the political life of our communities. Dirk Johnson quotes Don Eberly, the director of the Civil Society Project, as saying that "there was a romantic view that local institutions would reflect the local consensus. In fact, they tend to reflect a devolution of society's culture wars."[12] The problems and issues that arise in consequence of "society's culture wars" are ones that communities have not had to deal with before, and that in consequence have caused divisions within the community that either did not exist previously or existed well beneath the surface of political life.

For example, the question of bilingual public education was not an issue in communities even in states such as California until increased immigration and growth in the native-born Spanish-speaking population forced people to confront the challenge of educating children whose first language is Spanish. Another example, also from public education, is the debate surrounding the pressure on schools to go "back to basics." There was no perception of a need to "go back to basics" before public school teachers and administrators began to depart from traditional curricula and teaching methods in response to a variety of new circumstances, ranging from recognition of different learning styles to awareness of and respect for cultural differences to acceptance of responsibility for meeting the needs of the increasing number of children whose home life prevents them from coming to school "ready to learn."

Communities can no longer shut out the world. New, difficult issues are dividing people along new lines. Along with social phenomena such as the isolation abetted by the suburban way of life, these troublesome issues have strained our civic relationships—or what remains of them. With considerable justification, many Americans believe that their relationships with each other as citizens and as members of their communities have broken down. They feel disconnected and isolated from each other.

Few communities have dealt easily with the double whammy of tough new problems and a disjointed, civically de-skilled citizenry. Most have too few members with the experience, interpersonal skills, and energy required to tackle difficult new problems and issues in a context of weakened civic relationships. Even when they are disposed to conciliation and collaboration, few community leaders are adept at the arts of communication, facilitating change, and managing conflict, which they need in order to strengthen relationships and encourage productive citizen participation in the decision-making process.

Moreover, few communities possess the kind of political structures, processes, and habits they now require. As I will explain in chapter 1, our political institutions—local as well as national—governed as they are by the principle of majority rule and designed to produce winners and losers, are ill-suited to the task of generating results that elicit deep and broad support. Our communities need political processes that encourage participation, personal responsibility, cooperation, and joint action. At the very least, the activity of existing community decision-making bodies—city councils, county commissions, and other structures of local government—needs to be supplemented by community political activity in forums and other venues that encourage and enable citizens to work toward results that more closely resemble consensus than victory.

The need to supplement the workings of existing community political institutions means that the job of responding to problems and issues cannot be left to public officials alone. The long-standing practice of leaving it to elected and career officials to identify the matters to be addressed, to devise appropriate policies, and to implement those policies no longer works well. We must resurrect and give concrete expression to the idea that governing in a democratic community is a task of and by the people as well as for them.

There is one crucial respect in which the prevailing practice of community decision making resembles, to everyone's misfortune, the practice of politics at the national level: the assumption, shared by political elites and citizens alike, that government is the chief or even sole agent by which a community can respond to the problems and challenges it encounters. Just as we have often asked the public schools to act *in loco parentis* with respect to the various needs of our children, so we have asked government to act *in loco civitatis* with respect to the various needs of citizens.

Although our readiness to look to government for solutions to community problems has diminished precipitously in recent years, we continue to feel that, if government must exist, it must exist to serve us. Our attitude is, we pay good money for its services, and we expect the persons in official positions to use their power, expertise, resources, and political authority to do the work that needs to be done. Clearly, this expectation isn't being met; as a nation, we believe we aren't getting from our governmental institutions the sort of performance and service that we believe we have a right to expect in return for our support of those institutions. We are inclined to think that obtaining good government is like buying a car or a house. If government officials don't produce good "social products," then just as in the marketplace, we have to look elsewhere. During the 1970s and into the 1980s, many of us grew dissatisfied with the automobiles produced by Ford, General Motors, and Chrysler. So we turned to Japanese and European auto makers, who offered products we wanted to buy. Analogously, we have become dissatisfied with the "product" of government. We say, in effect, "If you can't solve our problems, then at least quit spending money on them." Unfortunately, the only alternative that most of us can conceive is the absence of government. Hence the calls to "limit government" and to "get government off our backs."

The sort of relationship between citizen and government implied by this outlook is that between a buyer and a seller.[13] We view ourselves as essentially *consumers* of what we expect government to provide. The point here is not that government is unnecessary, or that it should be smaller, or less active, or more restricted in its reach. Quite the contrary—government is indispensable. The point is, expecting government to succeed by itself—without the active, deliberate support, assistance, and guidance of the public—is setting government up for failure, and ourselves for disappointment.

### The Public to the Rescue?

Americans today are especially unhappy with their political system. They feel that something fundamental has gone wrong. They suspect that public officials have betrayed them, that persons in positions of power and authority have "broken the compact" with ordinary citizens. They worry that their representatives' primary loyalties are no longer to the people they represent. For many Americans "the deal is off, the social contract has been broken." People feel "it's slipping away." They feel that they're losing control over the conditions in which they have to live their lives. They feel shut out of the process by which they decide what sort of communities they will have.

Fortunately, the news is not all bad. Anger has not yet given way to despair. People are not yet demoralized to the point of paralysis, particularly with respect to matters of local concern, over which they feel they have greater control. Americans want to work together. And they're beginning to do so. Writing in the *San Jose Mercury News* and other newspapers, Holly Heyser observed in late 1996 that citizens are starting to take back control over their affairs: "Fueled by disenchantment with political gridlock and alarm over citizen alienation, people all over the country are finding innovative ways to tackle problems that government seems incapable of solving by itself."[14]

People want to do their part. Americans' response to disasters such as the San Francisco–area earthquake of 1989, hurricane Andrew in Florida, and flooding in the Midwest in the summers of 1993 and 1997 demonstrates their willingness to pitch in when they think they can make a contribution, when they see a need that government alone cannot respond to adequately, and when people are suffering through no fault of their own. These examples suggest that in the right conditions (for example, when it appears that a burden will be shared equally, when people are harmed by forces beyond their control) people will make sacrifices. They are willing to do more. But they want a real discussion about new priorities and new policies. And they don't want to follow—they want to be full partners in getting things done. They're not going to take risks unless they think others will join them and there's a chance of succeeding. They want a reason to believe that progress is possible. That's why, when asked, many say they want to "de-politicize" politics—turn it from partisan competition and institutional policy making into a problem-oriented, practical public undertaking.

Eventually, and one way or another, Americans will reinsert themselves into— and reassert control over—the process of responding to the problems and issues that trouble their communities. The Bradley Foundation's Michael Joyce may be correct in asserting that "Americans are sick and tired of being told that they are incompetent to run their own affairs. . . . [They] are clearly willing and eager to seize control of their daily lives again—to make critical choices for themselves, based on their own common sense. . . . In short, Americans are ready for what might be called 'a new citizenship.'"[15] In a similar vein, the 1991 Kettering Foundation report *Citizens and Politics* revealed that although people are angry about being shut out of the process in which they supposedly have the right and the responsibility to govern themselves, they remain active in trying to make their communities better places to live.[16] Americans care about the places they call home. Despite the obstacles they face, they go on trying to make their neighborhoods and cities the homes of their aspirations.

### We, the Community

Communities that respond effectively to the problems, challenges, and opportunities that come their way are likely to be genuinely democratic. In such a community, people accept responsibility for its well-being. They know that, as individuals, their power to effect change is limited. Even Thomas Jefferson, an extraordinary man, did not by himself make the state of Virginia the kind of democratic republic he envisioned. Nor did Martin Luther King Jr. by himself make Alabama, or even Selma, a place in which all people have equal civil rights. But by acting together, people can accomplish extraordinary things. "Never doubt," Margaret Mead said, "that a small group of committed citizens can change the world. Indeed, it's the only thing that ever has." *We* can "change the world" of our communities, not by acting alone—and certainly not by acting at odds with each other—but by acting together.

And that means coming to a decision—together—about what to do. If together we cannot reach a decision that most of us can at least live with, even if we do not agree completely, then *as a community* we will not be able to act effectively. Making decisions together is not easy. Working with others that we disagree with, that we do not understand, that we do not have much respect for, or that we might even dislike is just plain hard. Much of the difficulty we encounter in trying to make collective decisions stems from the inescapable fact that people are different—they have different views, different perceptions, different beliefs and attitudes, different sensitivities and feelings, different interests, and different priorities. But in addition, we are impatient with talk—we want results, and we want them now. Too often, we think the problem is obvious and the solution is clear. We think we know what should be done, and we do not want to listen to other people's views. Conversely, we might want to do nothing but talk, so we can feel that we are doing something without actually risking anything. Or we might be afraid to make a mistake or to incur someone else's displeasure. Or perhaps we don't want to take responsibility.

All of these are very understandable reactions. The trouble is, in the long run they get in the way of effective community action. When we work together, we're much stronger, wiser, better informed, less short-sighted and narrow-minded, and as a result more effective than we could ever be as individuals acting alone.

## Practical Politics

Although it might be difficult to imagine how politics could be other than it is, the kind of politics we have is up to us. We are not stuck with any particular kind. We made politics what it is today. We can remake it.

At the beginning of this introduction I observed that, in every community, there is work to do: streets to be repaired, children to be educated, waste to be disposed of, water and electrical power to be supplied, people and property to be protected, commerce to be conducted. As communities go about performing these tasks, they encounter problems that must be addressed, needs that must be filled, issues that must be resolved, disputes that must be settled, challenges that must be met, and opportunities that should be seized. In turn, each of these generates still more work that must be done before action can be taken: information that must be obtained, study and analysis that must be undertaken, options that must be identified and evaluated, and decisions that must be made.

In the book that follows, I recommend a pragmatic approach to the work of democratic communities. What I call "practical politics" can be summed up in five basic principles: inclusion, comprehension, deliberation, cooperation, and realism.

### FIRST PRINCIPLE: INCLUSION

"Inclusion" means that the process of deciding how to respond to public problems requires the active participation of a broad range and large number of ordinary persons, not just those with formal decision-making authority. Although the moral arguments for including such persons in the decision-making process are compelling, the argument in this book is that the consent and contribution of the entire community is a *practical* requirement for identifying and implementing effective public policies. People who are not brought into decision making may not support the decision that is made or, worse, may actively oppose it. If they have any influence or any interest in the problem under consideration, they must be included. If this is not feasible (and often it is not), at the very least their viewpoints must be well represented. Communities will not succeed until they accept that every segment of the community, and as many of its members as possible, must take responsibility for the work the community must perform. A "practical" approach to community decision making emphasizes that all members of the community have a personal stake in doing this work and doing it well, and hence that it is in their interest as well as their responsibility to contribute their energy, ability, and experience to the task of performing it.

### SECOND PRINCIPLE: COMPREHENSION

"Comprehension" means that the decision-making process must begin with a profound and comprehensive political understanding of the matter to which the community must respond. The usual way of conducting our political business—proposing solutions, debating arguments for them, and then voting on them—just doesn't work very well anymore. Instead of sound decisions and effective actions we get "solution wars" that nobody wins. The only way out of this dead-end is to go back to the situation that occasions a debate over solutions, examine every one of its facets and probe the depths of every one of its sources, and then generate a range of possible responses to the situation as it is now understood. This offers no guarantee of agreement. It is not agreement that we need, however, but rather mutual understanding. If we take the trouble to look behind the words and beneath the positions of our fellow citizens, we will find needs, desires, and feelings we can understand and appreciate. By acknowledging that we understand and appreciate these needs, desires, and feelings, we give one another the chance to let go of the positions we have staked out, which otherwise give rise to the perception of "zero-sumness." The principle of comprehension encourages us to work together at the level of the underlying, "non-zero-sum" sources of our differences. The ability and willingness of people to comprehend each other's motivations is the key to dispelling the perception of zero-sumness.

### THIRD PRINCIPLE: DELIBERATION

"Deliberation" means recognizing and accepting that every political situation presents us with a hard choice between good things about which people understandably care deeply. There are always multiple responses to any situation. Although they might not be equally desirable, each of them will offer advantages and disadvantages. Any one of them, if adopted, would have both negative and positive consequences. Moreover, because every set of circumstances is unique, we can't know *in advance* how well different responses will "fit" our situation. These two facts—the mixed consequences of every option we might consider, and our inability to foresee how those consequences will play out in practice—mean that the question of what we should do has no objectively correct answer that can be known in advance or by persons standing outside the political decision-making process. There are no authorities or experts to tell us what to value or what priority to assign what we value. All we have at our disposal is our best political judgment, achieved through democratic deliberation.

### FOURTH PRINCIPLE: COOPERATION

"Cooperation" means working together for mutual benefit. Cooperation should be distinguished from "collaboration," which is a stronger form of cooperation made possible by a shared or common purpose. The distinction is important because it reminds us that in politics the goods we seek and our interests in obtaining them can conflict, and often do. It reminds us that we can, and often must, work together because it is in our own interest to do so—not because we want exactly the same thing as the folks we disagree with, but because we stand to gain more from a pragmatic decision to work together than from a mutually harmful competition. Cooperation has become more and more difficult to achieve, however, because the political fragmentation of our communities has obscured and attenuated our civic relationships with one another. Recognizing the existence of such relationships and working to strengthen them is essential to encouraging cooperation.

### FIFTH PRINCIPLE: REALISM

"Realism" means understanding and accepting that a number of obstacles—some small, some large—stand in the way of a widespread, durable, productive practice of practical politics. We should have no illusions about the ease of overcoming these obstacles. Accordingly, we should have no illusions about the ease of solving the problems, meeting the challenges, and resolving the issues that confront us today. Realism in the face of the difficulties that lie ahead will dissipate any naïve optimism we might have. It will permit us to proceed without expectations of swift and dramatic change. But it will help us acquire something that will serve us better in the long run—hope.

The five principles I recommend are practical in four respects:

First, in the United States (and elsewhere) we have accumulated an abundance of experience and evidence suggesting that "communities that work"—that is, communities that respond effectively to the problems, issues, challenges, and opportunities they encounter over time—make decisions in a way that is characterized by the five principles. Following these principles greatly enhances a community's prospects for addressing successfully and satisfactorily the conditions that elicit a response from them. Although the citizens of communities that follow the five principles do not always hold them consciously, and seldom do so in precisely the way they are presented in this book, it is clear that citizens in these communities think, talk, and act *as if* they were following them. The five principles represent a distillation from and an idealization of the actual habits and practices of "communities that work." For this reason we may feel confident that allowing them to guide the decision-making process in our communities will produce results that are more effective—and hence more satisfactory—than the results we would otherwise achieve.[17]

Second, the five principles are practical in the sense that they are more usable and useful than any set of detailed instructions. Our communities are too different, our public life too complex, the situations we encounter too varied, to permit a "cookbook" approach to a community's work. There is no "recipe," no "formula," no "blueprint," that can be applied mechanically to a community's problems, challenges, and opportunities. In contrast, precisely because they are general and have been inductively extracted from the experience of successful communities, the five principles can be applied in most communities at most times in most situations. They cannot be so applied in *every* community at *every* time in *every* situation. It would be foolish to treat them as scientific laws rather than as what they are: generalizations from experience. The five principles represent wisdom, not science. They must be applied using good judgment, not pseudoscientific precision.

Third, the five principles are practical in the sense that the arguments I offer in support of them appeal to our desire to see our communities make progress toward solving problems, meeting challenges, and seizing opportunities. Other arguments—moral ones, for example—can be made for each principle individually and for the five taken together. Occasionally, I invoke such justifications. For the most part, though, I rely on an appeal to consequences—not because other justifications are not compelling, but because I wish to take advantage of what I presume to be a widely shared interest in "getting results." Americans are divided deeply over many things, but most of us readily assent to the proposition that chief among the purposes of democratic politics is to solve problems, meet challenges, resolve issues, and seize opportunities for the good of all. This is important common ground, and I take it as my starting point.

Finally, the five principles are practical in the sense that they rest on assumptions that are philosophically pragmatic. This will become clear in chapter 7. For now it is enough to note that such knowledge as we may have in political matters can be no more—though it should also be no less—than a sound collective judgment. Consider this analogy from our legal system. In criminal cases neither the judge nor the attorneys nor the jury know whether the defendant has committed the crime he or she is charged with. Because they are not eye witnesses, they cannot know whether the accused is guilty. So we have devised a set of rules and procedures, refined through experience and over time, that give us a high level of confidence that, if they are followed carefully and applied judiciously, the resulting decision will be for all practical purposes correct. We cannot know the truth. We can only trust that the process by which we endeavor to ascertain the truth is sound, and that in consequence the judgment we arrive at is (in criminal cases, at least) beyond a reasonable doubt the same as the truth. This (practical) reliance on process to produce a stand-in for (unknowable) truth lies at the heart of what I call "practical politics."

## About This Book

*Practical Politics* is not a "how-to" guide for achieving desirable political outcomes,[18] but rather an explanation of and an argument for the five principles, which are "practical" in the four senses just discussed: They improve the ability of communities to respond effectively to problems, challenges, and opportunities. They are more useful and usable than detailed instructions, strategies, or techniques. They are based on arguments that appeal primarily to our shared interest in seeing our communities make progress toward solving problems, meeting challenges, and seizing opportunities. And they rest on the philosophically pragmatic contention that in political matters the most we may aspire to is a sound collective judgment about what is good, best, or right.

*Practical Politics* offers you a place to begin making a contribution to the transformation of the public decision-making process where you live. The ideas and principles described here are sound as far as they go. But you will have to work out the details for yourself. You will have to draw on your own abilities, skills, and experience. No matter what you do, no matter how well prepared you are, you will make mistakes. Practical politics is an art, not a science. Like learning to play the piano or drive a car, we have to learn practical politics by doing. In a sense, we teach ourselves the art of practical politics by repeatedly trying—and sometimes failing—to follow general principles and achieve effective results. If we don't give up, if we reflect on the results of our efforts, if we continually revise our thinking and try again, in the long run we will make progress.

Practical politics comes at a price. It might not require blood, sweat, and tears, but it certainly demands intense and sustained effort. Most of us are impatient and we tire easily. We're not in shape for the hard work our communities need to do. Responding to a problem, challenge, or opportunity with a lot of talk might strike us as trying to cut steel with a flashlight when what we need is an acetylene torch. But the answer is not to throw away the flashlight. The answer is to focus the light until it penetrates like a laser. We can cut through any situation if we focus our collective energy into a tight, precise beam.

Working together as members of a community is a job for people who understand that this is not a perfect world, that there are no ideal solutions, and that we cannot have everything. It is not a job for the faint of heart, the undisciplined, or the self-absorbed and self-indulgent. We shouldn't expect people to compromise just for the sake of compromise or to reach agreement. We shouldn't ask them to sacrifice beliefs or values or interests that they honestly consider central to their lives. But we shouldn't let people off the hook, either. As citizens of our communities, each of us has a civic duty to perform, one that's every bit as serious as the one that a member of a jury has in a court of law. We have to be willing to take this responsibility seriously and put everything we've got into it. Democratic politics has to be a team effort. Every member of our community has an indispensable role to play. We owe it to ourselves and to each other to work together in good faith with our fellows.

That's what this book can help you do. Do you want your community to take effective action? Do you want your fellow citizens to cut through the tangle of obstacles and start making progress toward solutions? If so, you're going to have to put your shoulder to the wheel and push, without letting up, until the problem budges. But we have to push together, not against each other. As Benjamin Franklin said at the time of the American Revolution, either we hang together or we hang separately. That's as true today as it was then, though fortunately not so literally. We succeed together, or we fail individually.

What's it going to be?

# 1

# Impractical Politics

*Politics, n. strife of interests masquerading as a contest of principles. . . . The conduct of public affairs for private advantage.*
—Ambrose Bierce

## A Misleading Metaphor: Politics as a Consumer's Market

Americans today are critical of politics in large measure because it doesn't produce effective results—it "doesn't work."[1] In August 1996, just before the general elections, Jonathan Schell wrote in the *Atlantic Monthly* that "the political process today . . . is doggedly devoted to ascertaining and satisfying the desires of the voters. The candidates have long since learned that the path to power is far smoother if one gives the people what they already believe they want than if one undertakes the business of persuading them to want something else."[2] But if politicians and their strategists seek nothing more than to please the voters, Schell asks, why do the voters feel so estranged from and dissatisfied with politics? Why are voters so displeased despite the extravagant lengths to which politicians go to find out what they want? Schell writes: "Technically, the system appears to be in working order. . . . And yet no mandate is produced. . . . The government . . . is paralyzed. Paralysis, of course, breeds disillusionment with . . . 'the politicians.' The politicians have been sent . . . to solve problems. [People ask,] *Why don't they do so?*" (emphasis added).[3]

Why indeed? The reason politics "doesn't work" lies in the way most of us—political and policy professionals, journalists and commentators, scholars, and ordinary citizens alike—usually think of politics. We think of politics as the process by which groups and individuals pursue their various visions of what's desirable. For example, to young families a community might be primarily a place to raise and educate children. To teenagers it might be mainly a place to have as much fun as possible until they can move away from home. To a merchant it might be chiefly a place to earn a living. To a retired couple it might be largely a place to enjoy life quietly in pleasant, safe surroundings. To a property owner it might be the place where he has an investment he wants to protect and enhance. Each of these visions of what's desirable gives rise to interests, which may conflict.[4]

An *interest* is the stake a person has in obtaining a favorable political result. The favorable result itself constitutes a *political good*. In a consumerist understanding of democratic politics, political goods are essentially individual in nature—they are goods for particular persons and groups.[5] However, they are goods that people cannot obtain, or obtain as readily, on their own. In order to obtain them, people require the assistance, or at least the acquiescence, of their fellows. That is why (in this view) we have a political process. Democratic politics is the mechanism by which groups and individuals try to obtain the political goods that serve their interests. As Harold Lasswell put it, politics is the process of determining "who gets what, when, and how."[6]

The institutional arena of politics (that is, government) is where people attempt to answer the question of "who gets what, when, how" in a way that yields favorable results, results that get for them what they consider politically desirable. Government has the authority and the power to produce those results—it can "deliver the (political) goods." Government in the political "market" is like a producer of goods and services in an economic market.[7] It has "products"—laws, policies, regulations, rulings, subsidies, tax breaks—and "customers"—constituents, interest groups, voters—who want those products. The political activity of seeking political goods from government is analogous to the economic activity of purchasing material goods. In a sense, people seek to "buy" the political goods they want from government, which is the only "producer" of such goods they know. The assumptions that political goods are essentially individual in nature, and that government is the entity having the authority and power to produce and bestow those goods, have led us to think of politics as a quasi-economic activity.[8] We have come to think of ourselves, not as citizens, but as *consumers* of what government can deliver. Hence the readiness and frequency with which we describe ourselves as "taxpayers." Taxpayers are persons whose chief concern is how much money they are spending for the goods and services their tax dollars buy. Taxpayers are the consummate political consumers.

Political consumers expect public officials to do things for them.[9] They see their own role as confined to alerting officials to their desires and opinions, and advocating actions and policies they believe will benefit them. In contrast, the "republican," or "civic," tradition of democratic politics, which stretches from the great figures of classical Athens to their counterparts at the founding of the United States, sees citizens not as consumers but as politically responsible, politically active masters of their own civic house. According to the Harvard philosopher Michael Sandel, "central to republican theory is the idea that liberty depends on *sharing in self-government,* . . . deliberating with fellow citizens about the common good and helping to shape the destiny of the political community" (emphasis added).[10]

The consumerist approach to democratic politics has four major shortcomings. Each is a symptom of its failure to enable and encourage us to deliberate together, *as a public,* for the purpose of reaching a shared judgment and making a genuinely collective decision about what to do. First, it often produces results that are (by nonpolitical standards) unacceptable or irrational. Second, it frequently paralyzes or nullifies our efforts, thereby preventing us from taking effective action. Third, precisely for this reason it tends to push us toward decision-making methods that are ill-suited to the problems or issues to be addressed. Finally, consumerist politics undermines the taking of personal responsibility for the difficult decisions that inevitably arise in our public life.

## MIGHT DOESN'T MAKE RIGHT—OR RATIONAL

Instances of morally objectionable political outcomes abound. The most glaring examples involve "democratic" (in the sense of majoritarian) political "decisions" that have, as in the case of African Americans, enslaved, disfranchised, stigmatized, or discriminated against an entire category of human beings. But there are less-extreme examples as well. The recent California referendum authorizing the state government to deny benefits and services to the children of illegal immigrants was institutionally "democratic," even though it provoked intense opposition from a great many Californians. Political scientists rationalize such "decisions" by arguing that democratic politics works so long as no one is consistently on the losing side, and provided that minorities enjoy certain rights that protect them from certain types of action that the numerical majority might otherwise take against them. Yet anyone familiar with the history of relations between Native Americans and the federal government, or between Catholics and the Unionist (Protestant) government of Northern Ireland, will realize that it's possible to be a perpetual loser in a democracy. The practice of simply adding up the electorate's political preferences (that is, their votes for and against a particular proposition) *by itself* does nothing to ensure that the resulting policy is right or just.

Nor does it ensure that the outcome is sensible or rational. For something like ten years, opponents of a plan to build a nuclear reactor on the Clinch River in Tennessee fought attempts by its supporters to appropriate enough federal money to complete construction and bring the plant on line. The problem was, neither side had enough votes to win outright. So they compromised. And every year enough money was spent to keep the project going—but never enough to finish it. In the end, after a decade of money disappearing down a hole, the project was written off. The plant's opponents finally "won"—if that's the right word for it. For in truth, everyone lost. As this example shows, coming out on the short end of a vote or a poll isn't the only way we can lose in the game of consumerist politics. Everybody can lose when no side in a dispute is strong enough to win outright. For example, for years we ran up ever-larger federal deficits and accumulated a growing mountain of total debt because neither the proponents nor the opponents of government spending were strong enough to impose their will.

But there's yet another way we can lose when we rely on the political market instead of making a genuine collective decision. And that's by "winning." This sounds paradoxical, but here's what I mean. Suppose in your state there's a proposal to allocate a few million dollars to widen the expressway that runs through the center of the state capital. Being a capital city commuter, you'd like that. Despite opposition from your fellow citizens in the hinterland upstate, who see only costs and no benefits to relieving traffic congestion for folks like you, a legislative majority prevails over the opposition, which was unable even to force a compromise. So over the next five years the expressway is widened. The result? In year one, there is considerably better traffic flow. But what about ten years on? Probably, it will be just as bad as it is today, maybe even worse. Why? Because adding capacity can allow the number of commuters to grow. There's a sort of spatial corollary to Parkinson's Law: the number of commuters tends to expand to fill the amount of highway surface available for commuting. Maybe the money should have been spent on mass transit.

My point here is not to make a case for mass transit, any more than it is to argue for (or against) nuclear reactors. Rather, it is to illustrate that

— The mechanism of majority rule, which consumerist politics relies on, isn't necessarily a fair way to devise policy. On the merits, the case submitted by the folks in the numerical minority might be stronger.
— Even those in the majority lose when the opposition is strong enough to impose a compromise.
— Everyone can lose because consumerist politics often produces outcomes that no one wants or intends.[11]

### CHECKMATE

The consumerist approach to public decision making often turns even well-intentioned efforts to solve problems and meet challenges into unproductive competitions to protect and advance narrow interests, resulting in protracted fights over different preferred solutions. In such "solution wars," people's efforts may cancel each other out, leading to paralysis and collective impotence. This pushes people toward methods, such as popular initiatives, that are ill-suited to making sound decisions about the problems or issues that need to be addressed. Worse, it further damages already weakened relationships, driving people farther apart and rendering agreement even more elusive.

For example, in an article in the fall of 1997, Eric Dexheimer described how people in Colorado had turned to popular initiatives to slow or halt growth and development:

> Fed up with a government that seemed to be growing out of control, in 1992 Colorado residents struck back, voting in favor of Amendment 1. Also known as the Taxpayer's Bill of Rights, the initiative aimed to slim down government bureaucracy by reining in the amount of taxes it could collect. Now Coloradans are starting to use the same grass-roots approach to check the state's phenomenal growth. . . . This year, residents of [two cities] voted on whether to stop development projects that had already successfully gone through the normal government planning processes but were opposed by some citizens. Prisons, another barometer of growth, have been the topic of three more initiatives in the past two years.
>
> [Of course, initiatives often aren't successful. A senior planner in one city says that when development issues are dealt with by initiative or referendum, the entire city is asked] "to make a decision on a specific piece of property. Most people have no idea what the issues are or even where the property is." Indeed, a good argument against using initiatives as a tool to slow growth is that they don't always work. Because the residents of an entire town or county must vote on a land-use decision [concerning property] that may be miles away, generating anti-growth sympathy for a single development can be an uphill battle. [Several initiatives have lost by large margins.]
>
> [Initiatives can prove counterproductive as well. According to officials of a large Denver suburb that is facing an initiative this fall, if the initiative passes, the developer] "has promised he will sue [the city] for up to $40 million. . . . To pay off a judgment that size, . . . either [city] property taxes would have to increase 1,000 percent, or the city's budget would have to be reduced by 80 percent." And [the initiative] could cost more than money: it could backfire and cost the city control. If [the developer's] proposed development is down-zoned in accordance with [the initiative's intent, the city] will lose much of its power over the project. With denser developments, city planners legally can make demands of developers—more public open space, buffer zones and parks—to ensure livable neighborhoods. With less dense projects, they can't. Which means that [the] initiative, if successful, might actually permit [the developer] to keep all his property private and off-limits to the public—the opposite of what [the authors of the initiative want].
>
> . . . [Former governor Richard Lamm says that the use of initiatives to resolve development issues is] "no way to make thoughtful land-use decisions. It's using a blunt instrument. There's got to be something better than this." [Lamm] guesses that anti-growth initiatives—and referendums forced

by public outcry—are the last resort of citizens frustrated by their elected officials' inability, or unwillingness, to hear their pleas to slow down growth. "It's a symptom of a problem that's bigger," he says.[12]

The "problem that's bigger" is the failure of consumerist politics to generate effective responses to the problems, challenges, and issues confronting American communities today. It's the failure of "the system" to deliver decisions that are both effective and widely regarded as fair. The frustration, anger, and divisiveness that consumerist politics produces can be seen on a small scale in the politics of education. A recent study by the Public Agenda Foundation of four public school districts illustrates how politics practiced as a market-like competition for individual advantage generates a counterproductive form of public interaction, one marked by miscommunication, misunderstanding and mutual suspicion, turf battles, factionalism, adversarial behavior, and narrowly partisan modes of thinking and acting. The study noted that

> the highly political nature of the education debate . . . was the most conspicuous characteristic observed in each of the four districts examined. . . . In each, the various factions—school boards, parent groups, teachers' unions, principals and administrators—were organized around narrow interests competing to influence policy and trying to deflect initiatives adverse to their own special interests. The . . . fragmentation meant . . . that the groups were in a perpetual tug-of-war over the issues. . . . The primary goal of the schools—quality education for students—had become peripheral to their day-to-day activity.[13]

Many of the participants caught up in the frustratingly inconclusive debates observed by the Public Agenda researchers lamented that no one seemed to be looking out for the common good. The "logic of the system" compelled people to act out of narrow self-interest for fear they would end up shouldering disproportionate burdens and sacrifices if they did not. Most participants seemed convinced that the best way to achieve their goals was to band together with like-minded persons to press for their particular interest. They were persuaded that organization and activism on behalf of their own interest was a necessary defense against the partisanship of others. In each of the four communities studied, people used the vocabulary and imagery of "hard ball" politics to describe how educational issues are dealt with. They characterized people's actions as "power plays." They believed that people's real motivations were "camouflaged" and that decisions were made in "back rooms." Not surprisingly, the Public Agenda researchers found deep feelings of estrangement, frustration—even fear and cynicism. Previous reforms failed, leaving people skeptical about the possibility of meaningful, sustainable change. In all four communities, groups that must work together in order for progress to occur were continually pulled apart by suspicion, prejudice, and fear of losing hard-won gains.

The Public Agenda study concluded that the difficulty the four communities encountered in achieving educational reform was not the result of malevolent persons or groups who deliberately stood in the way of progress. Rather, the difficulty lay in the fact that people were trapped in a *counterproductive decision-making process to which they could see no practical alternative* and which they felt powerless to change. The process that thwarted even the best-intentioned efforts in these four school districts is the consumerist approach to public decision making in action. Based as it is on the faulty assumption that the public interest emerges spontaneously from the competition of private interests, consumerist politics predictably degenerates into "solution wars" that, like many actual wars in this day and age, prove costly, unwinnable, and deeply divisive.

### JUST SAY NO!

The third major flaw in the consumerist version of democratic politics is that, because of results (such as those described above) that people consider objectionable, that are irrational, that prevent any real progress, or that damage our ability and willingness to work together, people gravitate toward forms of decision making that are essentially coercive. One form is the "power to block," or "NIMBY politics."

In one community where I lived, two instances of such "veto" politics occurred. In one case, prompted by the deteriorating condition and out-of-date design of the downtown exits from the interstate highway that runs through town, the state department of transportation proposed a plan for resiting and rebuilding the highway on- and off-ramps. Immediately a group of merchants whose businesses lie at the base of one off-ramp began circulating petitions and urging citizens to attend a public meeting to oppose any alteration in the existing exits. In the other case, in order to raise revenue to pay for the growing cost of the community trash and garbage disposal, the county commissioners and city council proposed a 3 percent tax on visitors staying in local motels and hotels. Immediately the local motel and hotel operators' organization swung into action, claiming that the tax would destroy tourism and hence one of the town's main sources of income.

The opponents of the government proposals in these two examples were not wrong. But their negative responses not only contributed nothing to the solution of the problem, they also further damaged their ability to work with public officials to find an effective solution that everyone could go along with. Although "blocking" action is perfectly within people's rights and we should not want to eliminate it, we have to concede that such action is essentially coercive, and hence often both ineffective and destructive of our ability to work together.

## IT'S YOUR PROBLEM, NOT MINE

The fourth (and, in my view, the fundamental) defect in consumerist politics is that it transfers conflict from where it originates—within the public—into formal institutional decision-making arenas such as public hearings, school board meetings, and regular sessions of city councils and county commissions, where we expect our elected officials to make our decisions *for* us. As a result, it undermines our willingness as citizens to take personal responsibility for the difficult decisions that inevitably arise in our public life.

To see how political consumerism weakens the sense of personal responsibility, we should look more closely at the "logic" by which conflict is transferred, or "displaced," onto elected officials. Suppose the town hall in your community is getting older and harder to maintain; it needs expensive repairs and it's increasingly inadequate for the uses it's being put to these days. One proposal is to construct a new town center. Another is to retain the exterior but to remodel the interior. Maybe 20 percent of the community favor new construction. Another 20 percent favor remodeling. Roughly 10 percent don't want to do anything at all. The remaining 50 percent don't know or don't care.

We can illustrate this situation by figure 1, which represents a typical political disagreement. The circles stand for the four factions, which are labeled B (for Build), R (for Remodel), N (for Neither), and U (for Uninterested). Faction B pursues goal B—it wants to build a new town center. Faction R pursues goal R—it wants to remodel the existing town hall. Faction U doesn't say or do or anything.

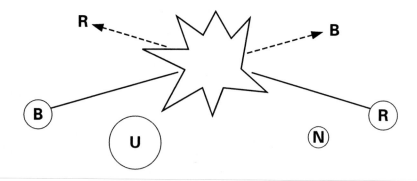

*Figure 1.* Public Factions in Political Disagreement

What about the fourth group, faction N (whose members don't like either alternative, and so want to do nothing)? Its adherents might participate in the public debate. Odds are, though, for the most part they will stay out of it—at least until it looks like a decision is about to be made. *Then* they will get busy trying to prevent either proposal from getting the upper hand. They might even wait until a decision has been made. Then, in good "*nimby*" fashion, they will set about blocking the action that's been decided upon. (At this point they may be joined by folks previously in the uninterested group who have suddenly awakened to find something is about to be done that they don't like.)

Notice the way political conflict is transferred from the public to the formal institutional decision-making arena—in this example, let's say, to a meeting of the city council. To the preceding diagram we can add a circle to represent city council (fig. 2). Inside it are three members of council, $C_1$, $C_2$, and $C_3$. The revised diagram shows faction B and faction R transferring, or "displacing," their disagreement onto city council. The arrows going from the symbol for a dispute to councilor 1 ($C_1$) show that both factions are putting pressure on that person to decide in favor of their respective positions. Councilors 2 and 3 are subjected to similar pressure. (In reality, the members of each faction might concentrate on the two who they feel are most likely to agree with them, or on the one who is not yet in their camp and who represents the "swing vote.")

In this simplified example, faction B and faction R believe that the authority

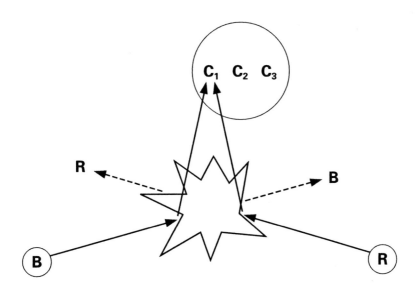

*Figure 2.* Political Disagreement Transferred to the Institutional Arena

and power to decide between their competing positions, B and R, resides with their representatives on council. In all likelihood, councilors 1, 2, and 3 believe this as well. So faction B demands that $C_1$, $C_2$, and $C_3$ decide in favor of building a new town center, and faction R demands that they decide in favor of remodeling the old town hall. $C_1$, $C_2$, and $C_3$ thus face a policy dilemma: Should they choose B or R? If they choose to build, they will frustrate and anger faction R. If they choose to remodel, they will frustrate and anger faction B. (And, of course, no matter what they do they will anger faction N.) Hence $C_1$, $C_2$, and $C_3$ face not only a policy dilemma but also a *political* dilemma: Is whose favor will they decide: faction B or faction R—or faction N?

Do factions B, R, and N help their councilors resolve the disagreements between them? Of course not. They pressure council to decide in favor of their own positions. So even when council makes its decision, the underlying conflicts between B, R, and N remain unresolved. And the political disagreements that B, R, and N have displaced onto council likewise remain unresolved. Council may make a decision in favor of one of the factions, and for a time the issue may seem settled. But this probably won't really be the end of the matter. The losing factions might seek redress in court. Or they might attempt to oust the councilors who voted against them and try to reopen the issue with a new council. Even if the issue is put to rest and the community goes ahead with one of the alternatives, relations might have been so strained and the political air so poisoned that the issue echoes down through the years, repeatedly rearing its ugly head under cover of other, completely unrelated issues.

How does consumerist politics undermine responsibility? If faction B and faction R believe that $C_1$, $C_2$, and $C_3$ have the authority to resolve the conflict between the different things they want (Building versus Remodeling), then $C_1$, $C_2$, and $C_3$ must have the *responsibility* to resolve it. Why? Because factions B and R believe that *they* lack the authority to do so. Their logic is simple: "'Ought implies can.' We can't. Therefore, we ought not." It doesn't occur to them that they might have a responsibility to choose between B and R, because they believe they "can't" (in the sense of "are not authorized to"). So instead, they transfer their responsibility to $C_1$, $C_2$, and $C_3$, who accept it. Faction B demands that $C_1$, $C_2$, and $C_3$ choose B. Faction R demands that $C_1$, $C_2$, and $C_3$ choose R. So $C_1$, $C_2$, and $C_3$ decide—to everyone's dissatisfaction. That is how consumerist politics undermines responsibility.[14]

How do we remedy this situation? For faction B not to demand that $C_1$, $C_2$, and $C_3$ choose B, and for faction R not to demand that $C_1$, $C_2$, and $C_3$ choose R, both factions must accept responsibility for resolving the conflict between the different political goods they wish to see realized. For them to accept this responsibility, they must have the authority to make the decision themselves. The factions must therefore reclaim from $C_1$, $C_2$, and $C_3$ the authority to decide. And $C_1$, $C_2$, and $C_3$ must return it to them—or at least share it with them.

## Consumers Do Not a Community Make

The consumerist conception of democratic politics treats the public as nothing more than a loose collection of individuals and groups, each with aims, opinions, interests, and positions that have to be reconciled in a way that (ideally) gives no one an unfair advantage over his or her fellow citizens. Consequently, as in an economic market, the best result is the one that comes closest to satisfying every individual's and group's desires. There is no room in consumerist theory (and hence none in consumerist practice) for the notion of genuinely collective decision making. In its stead the consumerist conception substitutes "preference aggregation" (that is, the toting up of what different folks want). The assumption that there are only particular desires of individuals and groups leads us to rely on procedures such as majority rule, which merely adds up people's preferences and bases policy on what the majority wants, on what gets the most votes.

In consumerist politics, we do not, *as a public,* make real decisions about how we should address the problems, challenges, and opportunities we encounter in the life of our communities. We do not inquire together into the nature and causes of the conditions that cause us concern. We do not talk with each other about the deep motivations that underlie the opinions we hold and the positions we take. We do not deliberate together—we do not weigh the consequences for what we value of the different courses of action open to us. We do not make the hard choices between conflicting values that would enable us to establish priorities. As a result, we do not come to genuinely collective decisions about what, as a public, we should do. Viewing politics as akin to a market reduces our interactions with each other to the question of "who gets what, when, and how." Not surprisingly, along with this outlook comes a preoccupation—indeed, sometimes a fierce obsession—with personal freedom and power.

In order to respond effectively, as communities, to the problems, challenges, and opportunities that come our way, we must become citizens again, producers of collective decisions and actions. Democratic self-government must be just that—we must do the governing ourselves. The work of communities cannot be accomplished simply by prevailing upon people in positions of official authority to meet our demands. We must take responsibility, individually and together, for the hard work of understanding the situation we are in, identifying and acknowledging the concerns we have, accepting the need for a collective response, evaluating the various options we might pursue, making the difficult choices that are necessary in order to establish priorities, and acting together in ways that move us, as a community, closer to where we want to be.

Consider an example that illustrates the importance of making genuinely collective decisions. It also shows that it's hard for us to recognize that our inability to make such decisions keeps us from truly solving the problems, meeting the challenges, and resolving the issues that cause us concern. In a provocative article on public education, Benjamin Barber remarks that "the social contract that obliges adults to pay taxes so that children can be educated is in imminent danger of collapse. Yet for all the astonishing statistics, more astonishing still is that no one seems to be listening. The education crisis is kind of like violence on television: the worse it gets the more inert we become."[15] Barber argues that the poor performance of so many of our country's public schools stems from a simple and fundamental source: "an absence of democratic will." Americans, he contends, are not serious about educational reform. We say we are, but our inaction makes clear that we're unwilling to pay the price for educational excellence. Barber points out that "America has historically been able to accomplish what it sets its mind to. When we wish it and will it, what we wish and will has happened. . . . Our failures seem to happen when will is absent. . . . Observe what we do badly and ask yourself, Is it because the challenge is too great? Or is it because . . . we aren't really serious? . . . To me, the conclusion is inescapable: we are not serious."[16]

Notice in Barber's remarks the use of the plural pronoun, "we." When Barber says "we" aren't serious about education, when he says "we" lack the will to do something about the educational crisis, he means we as a society, as communities. This is significant. Barber does not mean that we as individuals aren't serious, that we as individuals aren't willing to pay the price, that we as individuals aren't able to summon the will to act. The vast majority of Americans care deeply about education and are serious about wanting to improve it. But that's not the same thing as being serious and prepared to act as a society or a community.

## Our Problems Are OUR Problems

Just about any problem we can think of—drug abuse, economic stagnation, crime, lack of access to affordable health care, failing schools—is a *public* problem. By this I mean a problem that cannot be addressed successfully without a profound and comprehensive understanding of it, and a sustained and determined commitment to its solution on the part of our society or our community as a whole.

### "INDIVIDUAL" PROBLEMS THAT ARE REALLY PUBLIC PROBLEMS

AIDS is an example of a public problem that on its face appears to be a problem of and for individual persons. We have treated AIDS like other diseases: as a medical—and hence individual—problem that is susceptible, in principle, to a medical solution. But even if a miraculous breakthrough were discovered it would not necessarily translate into lives saved. A technical advance does not always constitute a solution to a problem. There are plenty of instances where researchers have answered a fundamental question about a disease only to have people's attitudes and habits get in the way of any good being done. AIDS may be another such instance. AIDS is a contagious disease that requires certain kinds of attitudes and behavior in order to spread. In other words, AIDS depends as much on social factors as it does on its underlying biology. We might effectively eliminate the threat of AIDS by approaching it as a collective problem that requires a collective response, not just a medical one applicable to individuals.

Examples abound of problems that seem to affect only some people but which turn out to be of genuinely collective concern. Consider the unsafe use of nuclear power in the former Soviet Union that resulted in the disaster at Chernobyl. The fallout from Chernobyl touched not just the inhabitants of Ukraine but people of other countries as well, as radiation drifted from the Soviet Union and settled on western Europe. Similarly, the destruction of the Brazilian rain forest ultimately will help degrade the quality of air available to all inhabitants of the earth.

To take an example closer to home, consider the reemergence of tuberculosis as a health menace. In recent years there has been a substantial increase in cases of active tuberculosis. What is especially worrying about this is the appearance of strains of TB resistant to all known antibiotics. An increasing number of reports indicate that people with no clear exposure or medical or sociological predisposition are contracting drug-resistant TB. Why?

One explanation is that people who have been diagnosed with drug-treatable TB aren't taking their medication properly. Effective treatment of tuberculosis requires several antibiotics taken daily without interruption. Intermittent use or premature discontinuation of the medication allows the disease to build tolerance to the drugs, leading to strains that are "multidrug resistant." This example shows that all of us may be endangered by the actions of a few persons. Yet we do not readily make the connection between what appears to be the personal problem of certain individuals and the good of the public as a whole. ᔕ૦૮ · immagination

## SOME PROBLEMS ARE PUBLIC IN THEIR VERY NATURE

Consider the current widespread concern with how well we are educating our children. At its most general, the purpose of education is to mold young people into the kind of young adults we believe they should become. It follows that educating our children requires that we—as a nation, as communities—decide what kind of adults (for example, responsible, independent, productive, prosperous) we wish them to be. Providing a good education requires that we as communities and as a society decide what "good" means—it requires that, as communities and as a society, we decide what is important for children to learn. As the widely known (and, lamentably, already politically debased) African proverb says, "it takes an entire village to raise a single child." This maxim points to the inescapably public—that is, social or collective—nature of education.

The contention that education is an irreducibly collective, or public, endeavor actually contains two assertions. First, as a practical matter, I can't fully educate a child by myself. Nor, for that matter, can teachers or schools. A young human being is exposed to a host of influences from a variety of sources, as any parent can attest. If we want to educate a child to be a particular sort of adult, we have to strengthen and reinforce what we consider the desirable influences and screen out or mitigate the undesirable ones. Only we, together, can educate a child, because the total environment that molds new adults is something that only we, together, can create.

Second, the product of education—a new adult—is inherently a collective or public good. Deciding how to educate a child is not like deciding what kind of new car to buy. It's more like deciding what good driving is. Should we set the speed limit at fifty-five or at seventy? Should we take turns going through intersections with four-way stops? Should we prohibit passing on curves and hills? Should we permit people to drink and drive? Should we dim our lights when another vehicle approaches? Should we require drivers to wear seat belts? These collectively determined rules make possible a collective good—the good driver. Without them, we would have neither good drivers nor agreement about what a good driver is. And if we lacked that agreement, we couldn't educate young people to become good drivers.

And so it is with education generally. In order to provide young people with a good education, we need to have widely agreed-upon, collectively determined criteria that specify what a well-educated adult must know and be able to do. Lacking as we currently do a shared conception of the well-educated adult, we can't know how to go about ensuring that our children receive a good education. Of course, different persons and different communities will have different views about the sort of adult citizens we should create, and hence about what's important for children to learn (and not learn). Conflicts are inevitable. But this is just the point. We can't avoid those conflicts. We shouldn't want to. Only by embracing them and, insofar as possible, resolving them—together—can we decide what a good education consists of. If we—as a nation, as communities—can't decide what constitutes a good education, it's futile to expect schools to do an effective job of providing one.

Consider another example: the problem of violent crimes committed by teenagers and, increasingly, preteens. This problem originates not in any single personal or institutional state of affairs, but in several mutually reinforcing ones— schools, families, the economy, the culture of poverty, and the general ethos of contemporary American society. If the conditions in which teenagers grow up are to be ameliorated, the problem must be attacked at its ultimate, hydra-headed source.[17] To wage such a campaign we need public policies to which we, as communities, are solidly committed. Like poor educational performance, teenage violence is a symptom of a deeper underlying problems. Its roots extend into virtually every aspect of a community's life. To respond effectively requires that we bring to the surface and discuss openly the conflicting concerns, needs, fears, and other motivations that lead people to hold different views of the problem and to prescribe different solutions for it.[18]

### Not Government—Government and Us

In 1831, the young French aristocrat and scholar Alexis de Tocqueville came to the United States to study democracy in America. The book he wrote on his return to France, *Democracy in America,* has become a classic. In many ways, it is still the most astute, most insightful analysis of public life in American communities ever written. In the United States of the 1830s, Tocqueville wrote, "Nothing [was] more striking . . . than the absence of . . . the government." He found this situation both understandable and admirable. In his view, no government could "administer the affairs of each locality better than the citizens could do it for themselves . . . when the people are as enlightened, as awake to their interests, and as accustomed to reflect on them as the Americans are." In the United States, Tocqueville went on to observe, "When a private individual meditates an undertaking . . . directly connected . . . with the welfare of society, he never thinks of soliciting the cooperation of government. . . . [He] courts the assistance of other individuals."[19]

Clearly, in the 1830s Americans were rather more self-reliant when it came to public matters than they are today. They didn't wait around for the experts or their official leaders to solve their problems for them. Instead, they talked with each other about what to do—and then they did it. In the towns and villages of the early nineteenth century, government wasn't just for the people—it was of them and by them as well. Americans were truly self-governing.

Granted, American communities of the late twentieth century are much bigger and more complex and exhibit greater cultural diversity than the communities Tocqueville observed. They must confront problems that are far-reaching and deep-rooted. Yet for all the obvious and important differences between our country then and now, it's worth asking ourselves whether the ultimate source of our frustration and dissatisfaction with politics isn't so much how our country has changed as how our view of democratic self-government has changed. Maybe the real trouble is that we've defaulted on our duty as citizens to take responsibility for the collective life of our communities and society. Maybe we should stop looking for leaders who will show us the way forward and instead start looking to ourselves for answers. Perhaps the question is not, How do we get effective leaders and good government? but How do we, as communities and as a society, begin to address the problems and challenges we're facing?

The real defect of American politics is not a "coup at the top," but corrosion of our democratic political culture. People say politics is irrelevant, that politicians are crooks, that ordinary folks don't have any influence. But the truth is more complicated. As Alan Ehrenhalt argues, "Our plight is not so much governmental as social; it is all around us in American life."[20] In essence, the problem with politics is a problem with the way we view ourselves and our relationships with one another. For the sad state of our public life together we have no one to blame but ourselves.

Ehrenhalt's view is echoed in a study by J. Mac Holladay, the former Mississippi state development director. Holladay contends that there is nothing more pernicious than the conventional wisdom that government should solve communities' problems for them. "Responsibility," he observes, "begins at home."[21] Home, in this case, means the community itself. Holladay points out, for example, that "communities that are dysfunctional in the economic development area are always dysfunctional elsewhere."[22] Holladay's contention finds support in the conclusions of studies showing that communities that succeed in solving their problems are ones whose members have developed the habit of talking together, of engaging each other in constructive civic conversation. For example, a study conducted by the Heartland Center for Leadership Development in 1986 revealed that communities that have coped well with fundamental restructuring exhibited (among other things) a participatory approach to community decision making; a cooperative community spirit; a problem-solving orientation to issues of public policy; and a belief in self-reliance—the conviction that, in the long run, "you have to do it yourself."[23]

In the communities studied by Holladay and the Heartland Center, it's clear that there's an established practice of cooperation. People are able and willing to work together to solve problems, meet challenges, and seize opportunities. They don't always see eye to eye. But they realize that they're all in the same boat and that any problem for the community is a problem for everyone. They succeed because they're able to find a way forward that everyone can live with, that everyone will go along with because his or her most important concerns and interests have been acknowledged and will be respected.

As Holladay observes, "If the community is alive and active, and responsibility and authority are shared, great things can happen."[24] But a community cannot make marked and sustained progress toward people's vision of the kind of community they want it to be until the public as a whole actively takes responsibility and shares authority for realizing that vision. We often don't get effective policies that everyone can go along with because we've forgotten what our forebears knew: that in a democracy government is supposed to be not only for the people, but of them and by them as well. Put another way, we have not only rights, but also responsibilities that we must be able and willing to shoulder. This is not to suggest that we should, or can, do away with government. But it is to recommend that we ask ourselves whether government can operate effectively in the absence of a form of public decision making that, unlike the consumerist version that prevails currently, places the responsibility for sound public decision making squarely on the shoulders of citizens.

## THE PUBLIC'S RESPONSIBILITY:
## TO COMMUNICATE, TO DELIBERATE, TO JUDGE, TO CHOOSE

Michael Kinsley has written that "the central problem of American politics [is] the inability of the electorate to deal with the hard reality we all had to learn as small children: that more of something usually means less of something else. . . . Our refusal to acknowledge that trade-offs are necessary—including, yes, the ultimate trade-off between money and human life—makes intelligent debate about intelligent trade-offs impossible."[25]

Jonathan Schell agrees: "Most people . . . have not thought deeply about the problems [we face], and their answers . . . reflect casual wishes. . . . When their wishes are granted, they bring unwanted consequences."[26] For example (and as President Reagan's budget director, David Stockman, discovered the hard way), "polls have for many years shown that the public wishes to balance the budget but does not wish to pay more taxes or endure steep cuts in government spending." The military buildup of the 1980s—strongly favored by a solid majority of Americans—produced the largest annual deficits and total public debt in the nation's history, which a solid majority of Americans strongly disapprove. Schell is exactly right when he remarks that, although promises such as balancing the budget while cutting taxes—made by politicians and not adequately criticized by journalists—continue to be politically popular, "the stage has been set for fiasco. Reality, though unconsulted, nevertheless imposes its price, and the bill has to be presented. Then a startled public feels either betrayed . . . or aggrieved. . . . Either way, faith in the political process is undermined."[27]

Democratic politics will do little to help us address effectively the conditions that cause us concern so long as we remain unable and unwilling to communicate, to deliberate, to make sound judgments, and to choose—together, as a public. The responsibility we bear for carrying out these tasks depends, in turn, on our ability and willingness to face up to and deal wisely with conflicts between the things we value. We need a public decision-making process that enables and encourages people to acknowledge the tradeoffs involved when conflicts arise between the things people value. Mechanical procedures such as majority rule do not suffice. Such devices cannot deal intelligently, wisely, and fairly with competing values and with the interests people have in realizing those values. They can aggregate people's desires—add them up—but they can't integrate them.[28] They can't reconcile the things that are important to people without compelling them to "win" or compromise. Only citizens can integrate desires for good things that conflict. By permitting us to escape taking responsibility, individually and collectively, for making the difficult choices that every problem, challenge, and issue invariably poses, consumerist politics keeps us from devising effective responses to them, and in so doing estranges us from our public institutions, from each other, and ultimately from the democratic way of life.

# 2

# The Inescapability of Choice

*To govern is to choose.*
—Pierre Mendès-France

## As in Life, So in Politics

Life being what it is, we frequently have to choose between different things that we consider good, valuable, or desirable.[1] The activities, states of affairs, and ways of life that we value, and that in turn motivate us to act, often conflict. They frequently prove incompatible in the sense that it's impossible to obtain or enjoy one thing without having to do with less of, or go without, something else that also has value.

Which should I assign greater importance: the pleasure I take from sparkling vistas and the continued good health that clean air makes possible, or the convenience and freedom that driving myself to work affords? The satisfaction of raising children or the freedom to lead my own life without having to be responsible for others who depend on me? The security of working for a well-established company or the independence that comes with self-employment? Should I buy an automobile that's economical and environment-friendly or one that's heavier and better able to protect me in an accident? In each case I face a dilemma—a hard choice.

Every matter of public concern raises such issues. Which should we give priority: the jobs that a new retail development would provide, or the green belt that shields our homes from the harshness of asphalt and skyscrapers? Should we spend more money on preparing three- and four-year-olds for school, or on providing training in job skills to high school dropouts? Should the principal aim of our criminal justice system be to prevent offenders from committing more crimes and to deter others from breaking the law, or should it be to rehabilitate offenders and prepare them for reentry into the community—or should it be simply to punish, to salve the victim's actual pain and our own vicarious pain by exacting retribution? In each case, we face a dilemma: which of two or more things, each valuable in itself, should we choose?

## TWO SOURCES OF CONFLICT

Things that are good or valuable, either in themselves or because they enable us to obtain other things that are good in themselves, can conflict for two basic reasons: One is "scarcity"—we don't have enough resources (e.g., money, time, technical knowledge) to have as much of both things at the same time as we would like. The other is the "qualitative distinctiveness" of the things in conflict. Goods that conflict because of scarcity are not invariably incompatible—it just happens that, in the circumstances, we don't have enough resources to "have our cake and eat it too." Good things that are qualitatively distinctive, however, by their nature are invariably incompatible. Even if we had unlimited resources, they would still conflict; it's impossible to choose one without sacrificing the other.

Conflicts resulting from scarcity occur in both our personal and our public lives. For example, I might face a choice between spending what money I have on buying a new car or on remodeling my house. In principle, I could do both things, provided I had enough money. As it happens, however, I don't, so I'm faced with a difficult choice. Similarly, I might have to choose between taking up the piano and learning karate—I just don't have the time and money to do both. Similarly, as communities and as a society, we might face a choice between spending money on social programs and cleaning up the environment. Or we might confront a choice between providing health care coverage for every ailment and type of treatment and ensuring that all persons are covered for certain common kinds of ailments and treatment. In principle, we could do both things. But as it happens, we don't have enough resources to do as much as we would like, so we have to make a difficult choice.[2]

Scarcity of resources isn't the only reason we face tradeoffs, however. Many of the good things that human beings value are qualitatively distinct from each other. They're as different as apples and computers. For example, I consider it good, both for myself and for others, to be honest with people. But there might be times when by being honest I would do serious harm—perhaps by hurting someone's feelings. In a case such as this, I face an inescapable dilemma. The good that I would realize by refraining from hurting someone else's feelings is inherently incompatible (in the circumstances) with being honest. Similarly, I might have to choose between accepting a job that pays well and provides job security, on the one hand, and taking one that, on the other hand, pays less and offers less security but more freedom and autonomy. In deciding where to live, I might have to choose which to give priority—climate, culture, or cost of living. Or I might face a hard choice between enjoying the freedom and pleasure of eating what I like and eating in a way that preserves my health. Or I might be forced to choose between a career and a family, or between my job and my spouse's career.

In our communities and nation as well as in our personal lives, we often confront difficult choices between valuable things that are qualitatively distinctive. For example, the value we place on national security might well conflict with the value we place on freedom of information, our right of free speech, and our right to know what our government is up to so that we can hold it accountable. Or the value of free expression may conflict with the value of mutual civility. For example, by choosing to protect the freedom of persons to speak freely, we unavoidably slight the value of being able to live without being exposed to disturbing or offensive talk. Similarly, we might face a choice between the value of allowing people to act however they wish and the value we place on public order. Or we might confront a choice between the quality of life (the enjoyment of mental clarity, freedom from pain, not having to be totally dependent on others) and the continuation of life. Again, some good things by their very nature can conflict; they are such that often we can't have one without giving up something with respect to another. It's impossible to choose without loss. As a result, we have to make a hard choice between them.

## VALUE CONFLICT AND PUBLIC POLICY DISPUTES: AN EXAMPLE

In an article about the Clinton administration's health care plan, Willard Gaylin, a Columbia Medical School professor, illustrates how conflicts between good things generate political dilemmas.[3] He argues that "no amount of tinkering with the process of delivery or payment . . . can resolve the fundamental contradiction . . . : if you promise everyone access to whatever medical care he or she needs or wants," we will be unable to stop the rising cost of health care. "We cannot do everything for everybody," Gaylin insists. We face a hard choice, in other words, between the value each of us places on his or her health (and hence on being able to obtain treatment for ailments that harm a person's health) and the value each of us places on the ability of everyone to maintain (or regain) his or her health. We confront this hard choice because, in current circumstances, we simply cannot afford to do both. (Scarcity of resources forces the choice upon us.) If we don't make the hard choice before us, costs will continue to rise, steadily consuming more and more of our currently available resources, forcing us into still tougher decisions about what to sacrifice in order to pay for health care, and ultimately bankrupting us.

Why aren't we facing up to this tough choice? In part, Gaylin believes, because "we don't want to hear about restrictions, especially on something like health care. . . . Americans refuse to believe there are limits—even to life itself." ("'Death with dignity,'" Gaylin contends, "really means death without dying," and "growing old gracefully" is "a related term that, on closer analysis, means living a long time without aging.") But equally important is the fact that the hard choices we face "are not medical choices; they are moral and ethical ones." We don't know how, as a public, to go about making such choices. Like our public officials and professional policy makers, we find it politically easier and safer "to talk about delivery systems, health-product-procurement procedures, and third-party payments than about what care to give a desperately ill child or whether a kidney patient over the age of fifty should be eligible for a transplant." Like our elected officials, we are "disdainful of the sticky dilemmas inherent in moral reasoning and terrified by the ambiguities inevitable when dealing with values." So we indulge "in the wishful thinking that we *can* have it all." We avoid the hard choices before us.

The first step in dealing successfully with the health care crisis, Gaylin argues, is "to admit to the cruel necessity of rationing health care"—to confront head-on the fact that we cannot guarantee everyone access to whatever health care treatment he or she wants. We will have to decide whether, for example, a desperately ill newborn who is unlikely to live past the age of one should be provided with every sort of treatment available in an effort to prolong his or her life for a year. We will have to decide whether an eighty-five-year-old suffering from a terminal degenerative disease should be kept alive for as long as our technology permits.

Gaylin commends the state of Oregon for facing up to the hard choice of how to allocate its scarce resources. Unlike the nation as a whole, "the state has addressed the uncomfortable truth that they cannot have equity in their health-care system without making anguished, even tragic choices. Even more important," he writes, "the people of Oregon have had a searching public conversation about . . . how much health care they can afford and what it really means to be healthy." Gaylin laments that "what could have been a wide-open, far-ranging [national] public debate about the deeper issues of health care . . . has been supplanted by relatively narrow quibbles over policy." He concludes that "unless we address . . . basic, almost existential questions" [such as] "our attitudes toward life and death, the goals of medicine, the meaning of 'health,' suffering versus survival, who shall live and who shall die (and who shall decide), . . . we stand little chance of solving our nation's health-care crisis."

## From Indeterminacy to Judgment

In instances of conflict between things we consider good, valuable, or desirable, it's distressing enough that we feel pulled in different directions. Choosing is made doubly tough by the fact that the question of which thing we should give priority has no answer that is clear, invariable, and decisive. When things that are desirable come into conflict, there is no one "right" or "correct" way to resolve the conflict. The solution is *indeterminate*.

Solutions to conflicts between things that are good, valuable, or desirable are indeterminate because the things in conflict are not "absolutes." An "absolute," as I use the term here, is a good, valuable, or desirable action or state of affairs that (a) has good consequences that always outweigh the good consequences of all other good, valuable, or desirable actions or states of affairs, and (b) has no significant downside, no negative consequences that offset the good consequences it would have. A good that is absolute would always "trump" or "defeat" every other good it might conflict with. No considerations could be brought to bear that would persuade us not to choose it. As a result, it would be always unquestionable and unchallengeable. It would "win out" in all situations, no matter what the consequences.

As I will argue below, however, there are no absolutes. And because there aren't, the question of how to resolve a dilemma between good things in conflict can have no predetermined answer. The answer to such questions is always indeterminate—there's no principle, no rule, no wise and benevolent authority that can tell us, "*this* is the right choice, *this* is the correct answer." For this reason, value conflicts do not have predetermined right or correct solutions. And if this is so, then no party to a political disagreement is justified in claiming, in advance, that his or her position with respect to that issue is *the* right or correct solution. Of course, it might turn out, upon reflection and examination, that this position is the best answer we can give to the matter in question. But we cannot know this in advance.

## THERE ARE NO ABSOLUTES

It might be thought that there are some rules, principles, or values that must always take precedence, that may never be subordinated to other considerations. But examples abound of ostensibly "hard and fast" rules that admit of exceptions. Perhaps the most frequently cited example of this sort is free speech. There is no absolute right of free speech because there are situations in which giving that right priority would have consequences that are unacceptable. No one has the right to yell "Fire!" in a crowded theater just for the sake of getting a reaction. We accept the ban on false advertising as a legitimate limitation on speech, as we do perjury, conspiracy to commit a crime, and attempted bribery. Is lying bad and wrong? "Absolutely." But it might be better to lie than to hurt someone badly. Is it wrong to kill another human being? "Absolutely." But sometimes it's excusable (e.g., when the killer is insane) or justifiable (e.g., in war and in defense of one's own life or that of another person).

Nor are the alleged "right to life" and "right to choose" exceptionless rules. For example, suppose there is a case of a pregnant twelve-year-old child who was raped repeatedly by her mentally defective and abusive father. The girl's mother died several years ago, and she has no other family. The emotional and physical trauma she's been through has put her into a psychotic state. In addition, she has a serious heart defect that virtually guarantees that she won't survive childbirth. As if that weren't enough, tests on the sixteen-week-old fetus show that it suffers from a congenital disease that in all known cases has brought death before the child's first birthday, and that tortures the infant with inconceivable pain during its brief existence. So, is there an absolute right to life? Even in a case like this? Is it clear that applying a policy of strict prohibition on abortion would be the right thing to do? Isn't there room for reasonable doubt about the wisdom of allowing the girl's pregnancy to continue?

Equally, the "right to choose" cannot be absolute. For example, we could imagine a situation in which a well-educated, happy, and healthy thirty-year-old professional woman wants to begin a family with her husband. Five months into the pregnancy the couple learns that the child will be a boy. Both prospective parents prefer a girl. So they want to terminate the pregnancy. In these circumstances, is it clear beyond any reasonable doubt that applying a strict policy of free choice would be the right thing to do? In such a case isn't there room for reasonable doubt about the wisdom of permitting abortion at will? It does not matter for present purposes whether such a situation has ever arisen or is ever likely to. The point is, it could. And that's all we need to establish that no value, no principle, no rule can ever be absolute.

There are no absolutes because our beliefs about what is good and bad, right and wrong, are *generalizations.* No matter how firmly we believe something, no matter how many times a belief has been reinforced, no matter how obviously and absolutely without exception it might seem, it remains a generalization. It does not cover—it cannot and will not ever cover—every situation that could or will arise. Every one of my beliefs about what's good or valuable is based on a large, but nonetheless limited, number of experiences that I or other human beings have already had—not on ones I might or will have. I might be as convinced that three thousand calories a day is good for me as I am that the sun will come up tomorrow. But like my conviction that tomorrow will come, my belief in the value of three thousand calories could be mistaken. There might be a situation or circumstance, not yet encountered by me or anyone else, that would throw my conviction into doubt.

If there are no absolutes, I can't *know* how to resolve a dilemma between good things in conflict. In a particular case or set of circumstances, an "absolute" rule might indicate a response that is in fact not the best one. For this reason, the ethical, moral, and legal rules, principles, and convictions that are available to me as I try to resolve a conflict between values are binding only *prima facie*—that is, they're valid only "on first viewing," upon initial examination. They do not determine fully, in advance, what's best, or right, or most rational. And they never will, because every situation to which I might apply them will be to some substantial and significant extent unique. They're valid only *prima facie* because they hold only *ceteris paribus*—"other things being equal." Put another way, what is best to do depends on the circumstances: on what good things are involved, on who is affected, on the consequences of favoring one thing over another.

When we encounter situations in which good things conflict, we can't rely on our "knowledge" of what's good and bad, right and wrong. We can't count on logic and facts to tell us what to do. We can't simply deduce or "observe" the answer. The best we can do is exercise our *judgment* about which is more important in the circumstances and all things considered. In effect, we have to "make (or at least refine) the rules as we go." We have to think our way through the conflict, consider the advantages and disadvantages of the various courses of action open to us, weigh the consequences, form a judgment about which seems to be wisest, all things considered, and then choose what to do on the basis of that judgment. General rules—even the ones we hold to most unshakably—give us only a starting point for our deliberations. That's why we should treat our beliefs about what is good and bad, right and wrong, as *presumptions*. It's all right to treat a belief as if it's absolute, provided we realize that a situation might arise in which our judgment will recommend that, in a given particular case, it should be modified.

### BY MYSELF, I CAN'T KNOW WHAT'S GOOD OR RIGHT

My conviction that something is good or right cannot, by itself, be a conclusive answer to the question of what I should believe or do. It can't be conclusive because its object—the action or state of affairs I desire or consider desirable—might conflict with some other good thing that I haven't yet weighed it against. The most I'm entitled to is a presumption—refutable upon further thought and consideration—that my conviction is justified.

Yet even if I could somehow weigh my conviction against every potential offsetting or contrary consideration that my imagination can conjure up, I still wouldn't be entitled to say that I *know* that what I desire or believe is good or right. No matter how sincerely or strongly I feel about the matter, the object of my conviction is something that, by myself, I cannot know.

To see what I mean, consider this fanciful scenario: Imagine that one April Fool's Day I'm sitting at home in the evening watching television. It's a program I've been looking forward to, so I'm taping it on my VCR. About halfway through, the program is interrupted for a special news bulletin. Peter Jennings (or Tom Brokaw or Dan Rather) appears on screen to report that Earth is being invaded by beings from another planet. Well, I can scarcely believe my ears. I must be imagining things. So after the report ends I turn on the VCR and play the tape back. Did I hear what I thought I heard? Yes, I did. Peter (or whoever) is right before my eyes, in living color, telling me again what he just got through telling me. So now I believe the report, right? Well, not if I'm wise I don't. At the very least, I ought to switch to one of the other networks for confirmation. Or I should call the police, or maybe go out and search the skies for direct evidence of my own.

The point of this imaginary example is that, to know something—including what's good or right, even for myself—I can't rely on a single source of information. If I rely exclusively on a single source, I'm as likely to be taken in as I would be if I relied solely on my videotape of Peter Jennings's April Fool's Day report. Replaying in my own mind what I already desire or believe, without seeking the confirmation or disconfirmation others can provide, is like replaying that videotape. That's why a desire or belief I happen to have can't be conclusive evidence of what is good or right, even for myself. It's important evidence, of course. But by itself it doesn't suffice. I need to test it by exposing it to other sources of information.

Given my own limited experience and information, the only place I can turn is to other people. By considering their views, I obtain information and the benefit of different perspectives that will help me weigh my initial disposition against alternatives, including ones that I might not even know exist. Genuinely to judge and choose implies that I need to engage others in a process that provides for exchange of information, experiences, insights, reasons, and so forth. If I act solely on the basis of what I feel at the moment I should do, it's possible that I'll end up realizing less value than I would if I chose otherwise. If I don't stop to reconsider my beliefs and desires, if I don't weigh the alternatives, if I go along unreflectively with my first inclination, I could very well end up kicking myself for not having thought through my decision more carefully. In short, it could turn out that I didn't really know what I thought I knew. The indeterminacy that characterizes conflicts between good things thus makes it rational and prudent to turn to others for their assistance in making decisions.

What's true for me as an individual applies with even greater force to us collectively. If indeterminacy makes it impossible for anyone to know for sure which of several good things he ought to give priority, it's even "more impossible" (if that's possible) for a community or society to know what it should do. In the absence of absolute rules for establishing priorities, and given the variability of constitution and experience among individuals, it's not surprising that people differ considerably in their personal views about what good things ought to be favored in instances of conflict. Interpersonal differences over how to resolve conflict between the things we care about and that motivate us—conflict that has no determinate solution—frequently underlies the disagreements that arise between us. True, we can end up in disagreements for all sorts of reasons—personality conflicts, injuries done by one person to another, miscommunication, and so forth. But an important source of conflict between persons (and hence between groups of persons) is conflict between things human beings can, and do, value. Disagreements about how to resolve a conflict are inevitable because no one can be absolutely certain what's best to do, even for himself, let alone for everyone affected. Public problems are political problems, problems that in their very nature elicit diverse and conflicting responses. Political conflict—disagreements between persons or groups of persons about how to respond to public problems—thus stems from the indeterminacy and uncertainty that each of us encounters when good things conflict.

## PERSONAL JUDGMENT AND PUBLIC JUDGMENT

The need to choose, both individually and collectively, between good things in conflict lies at the heart of politics. But how, as a community or society, do we combine our individual judgments to arrive at a public judgment that everyone can assent to? In particular, how do we resolve disagreements between persons who reach different *individual* judgments?

We don't. Disagreements that arise from separate individual determinations of what is best to do cannot be resolved, in the sense of being made to disappear. What we *can* do is transform such disagreements, turn them from adversarial competitions into an opportunity to work toward a sound collective judgment. We can do this by recognizing that each person's effort to reach a personal judgment about a matter of public concern cannot be separated from our collective effort to arrive at a public judgment. Given each individual's limited personal experience and information, a sound individual judgment requires consideration of others' beliefs, experiences, needs, sensitivities, reactions, and so forth. By listening to the views of others, I obtain information and the benefit of different perspectives that help me work toward a sound judgment about how to resolve conflicts between the things I care about. The process by which I form a personal judgment is the same process by which, together with my fellow citizens, I work toward the formation of a public judgment. We arrive at personal judgments and a public judgment simultaneously.

This doesn't mean that when the process is complete we will have reached *consensus*. To some extent, individuals' personal judgments will (and should be expected to) differ from the public judgment we arrive at. But because the two types of judgment are arrived at simultaneously through the same process, each participant in the process will *comprehend*—that is, he or she will "understand and appreciate"—the ingredients that go into the making of the personal judgment that each of his or her fellow citizens has arrived at, even if ultimately he disagrees with that judgment. As I will explain in chapter 6, the "mutual comprehension" we require in order to deliberate together successfully enables each person to reach a unique personal judgment while at the same time assenting to a shared, public judgment that everyone will be willing to go along with.

## PUBLIC GOODS   *is it still true. community can be wrong.*

Because the things human beings consider good are various and qualitatively distinct; because conflicts between such good things have no absolute, predetermined solution; and because to know what is best requires considering the views of others, we need to engage each other in the sort of exchange that will enable us to form sound personal and public judgments. This process of coming to a public judgment and choosing—together, as a public—is the essence of democratic politics.

But there is another reason why we need to talk, think, and decide together: there are some kinds of value that can be realized only through such interaction. In chapter 1 I argued that many of the social problems that we treat as essentially individual problems are really public problems. I cited the reemergence of tuberculosis as a health menace to make the point that all of us may be endangered by the actions of individuals. In addition to problems such as these, however, some problems are public in their very nature. I offered education as an example. Because the purpose of education is to mold young people into the kind of young adults we believe they should become, educating our children requires that we as a community decide what kind of young adults we wish to create.

By myself, I can't prevent the emergence of antibiotic-resistant TB. Nor, by myself, can I ensure that my neighborhood is safe and my drinking water is clean. Without others, I can't provide adequate protection from disasters such as floods, fire, or earthquakes. But still less can I, by my own efforts alone, produce the sort of public good—a young adult—that it is the purpose of education to produce. Nor can I ensure that the rights I believe I have are respected by others. Without the cooperation of my fellow citizens, I can't achieve the sort of community life in which I can count on them to treat me civilly, respectfully, and honestly. To take another example, suppose that it's good (other things being equal) to permit a market to allocate resources. Although a market system might appear to embody the very antithesis of what is common or public, just the opposite is true. The goods that people pursue and realize within the market may be individual goods. But the market itself—the system of exchange, the activity that is governed by the rules of the free market—is a public good. Without at least the implicit consent of a substantial portion of our fellow citizens, we would be unable to establish and sustain a market. Each of these good things is an example of an inherently public good.

Questions about the public good ought to be addressed by every member of the public. They call for genuine public choices based on a sound public judgment. What sort of community shall we have? What is our vision for our future? What kinds of citizens do we wish to produce? What should our priorities be? The public problems, challenges, and opportunities we face invariably present us with political issues—questions we cannot answer satisfactorily without resolving the underlying conflicts between things people care about. To resolve such conflicts, we require a form of politics, a form of public decision making, that enables and encourages us to deliberate, judge, and choose—together.

# 3

# Alternatives to Impractical Politics

*Wisdom enough to leech us of our ill*
*Is daily spun; but there exists no loom*
*To weave it into fabric.*
　　　　　　—Edna St. Vincent Millay

## Varieties of Politics:
## "Service," "Protest," and "Communitarian"

Dissatisfaction with the consumerist version of democratic politics is not a new phenomenon. During the past thirty years or so, discontent has generated two broad forms of public activity that have challenged the preeminence of the consumerist model. Drawing on the work of Harry Boyte, I will call these forms the "service" and "protest" interpretations of democracy.[1] A somewhat more promising third approach, which has gained attention in the past few years, is "communitarianism."

　　Let me emphasize two points before I discuss these challenges to consumerist politics. First, I use the terms "service," "protest," and "communitarian" advisedly. Practitioners and supporters of these approaches might not accept the labels as accurate. Moreover, my characterizations of the three approaches are incomplete; I focus only on the implications of each for what I consider the essence of democratic politics: the formation of a public judgment and the making of a public choice. Second, I don't intend my comparison of these approaches to be invidious. The "practical politics" I recommend—characterized by inclusion, comprehension, deliberation, cooperation, and realism—is not the only legitimate form of public activity in a democracy. Nor is it the best form at all times and in all circumstances. Other approaches have strengths that make them appropriate in certain situations. For the most part, the motivations that underlie these alternatives to practical politics are unobjectionable, even commendable. I want only to suggest that none of them should predominate. Still less should any one of them become the only form of public activity in which we engage. Rather, practical politics should be our choice of first resort. Other things being equal, practical politics is most likely to help us respond effectively to the public problems, challenges, and opportunities our communities encounter. At the same time it is most likely to improve the prospects for personal growth and individual well being, justice, and the good society that are the legitimate and worthy aims of the service, protest, and communitarian alternatives to consumerist politics.

## SERVICE

"Service" is about helping others—those who are less fortunate, who have been victimized, who (it's assumed) aren't able to do for and by themselves what they need and want to do. Service means taking personal responsibility for the well-being of one's fellows. It means putting aside one's own interests and devoting some of one's own resources—time, energy, money—to the cause of helping others grow, to building human capacities, to empowering people—thereby improving their situation while strengthening one's own character. Service manifests itself most clearly in the activities of nonprofit voluntary organizations. Some service organizations tackle social problems head-on by working directly with the disadvantaged. Others, such as grant-making foundations, take a less direct route, supporting or assisting those involved in hands-on efforts. Service also finds expression in the "helping professions," many of whose members are employed by government agencies such as departments of social services. In education, service is promoted through "service-learning" programs and opportunities that combine study with experience working with and helping the disadvantaged.

Voluntary organizations have long been believed by many to be the backbone of American democracy. According to Boyte, however, most have lost their "public character." Boyte contends that the concerns of these organizations have shifted from civic matters to providing services for clients. Whatever their purpose, these organizations have in common the aim of "developing," "caring," "helping," or "empowering." For example, the Boy Scouts have de-emphasized citizenship and instituted programs centering on developing self-esteem and social skills. Other voluntary organizations stress objectives such as "self-understanding," "consciousness about one's personal values," "openness to new experiences," and the "exploration of new identities and unfamiliar roles." (Even the U.S. Army, Boyte observes, has taken on a "therapeutic" cast, as evidenced in its recruiting slogan, "Be all you can be!") The outcomes typically sought by organizations with a service orientation include "self-esteem," "learning care for others," "a sense of personal worth," and "independence."[2]

Desirable though "developing," "caring," "helping," and "empowering" are, they do not suffice as strategies for addressing the problems and issues confront-

Shitty paragraph. Tweak / point!

how are these trends linked to volunteering/service orgs?

ing our communities and society today—and they may even be counterproductive. More children and more elderly live in poverty than ever before. Educational performance has deteriorated. The incidence of violent crime in America, especially among the young, continues to exceed that in all other Western nations. Another generation of young black men is at risk, few of whom have any real hope of meaningful employment and an alarming percentage of whom may not live even to middle age. The abuse of drugs is widespread. Families continue to crumble. Children are being abused in ways and to an extent that are unprecedented. Racism and sexism have not abated nearly enough. Environmental degradation continues apace. In view of these facts, it's hard to disagree with the late Christopher Lasch when he asks, rhetorically, "is it really necessary to point out . . . that public policies based on a therapeutic [i.e., service] model . . . have failed miserably, over and over again?"[3] Where has "service" gotten us? Not, it would appear, very far.

The problem that Boyte describes as "the loss of [voluntary organizations'] public character" is closely related to their professionalization. As a society, we have abdicated responsibility for solving public problems to professionals in government and the voluntary sector. As Eugenie Gatens-Robinson observes, we have "relegated the public practices of care to the arena of expertise and have professionalized our social responses."[4] In a similar vein, Leslie Lenkowsky notes that "some groups do not even seem to want volunteers. The growing professionalization of once largely voluntary groups may also be partly to blame for the decline in membership. As paid staff members have grown in number, meaningful activities for volunteers—other than providing financial support—have become scarcer, and perhaps less important as well. What charities have gained in organizational capacity, they may have lost in their ability to involve public-spirited citizens in their work."[5]

The move toward professionalization in the voluntary sector closely parallels the development of scientific and professional expertise in the nineteenth and early twentieth centuries.[6] In a review of Ellen Lagemann's book *The Politics of Knowledge: The Carnegie Corporation, Philanthropy, and Public Policy,* Sandee Brawarsky illustrates the sea change that began to come over foundations such as the Carnegie Corporation early in this century. Citing Lagemann, Brawarsky observes that

> while Carnegie . . . was funding the [National Bureau of Economic Research, a scientific research institute made up of economists, businessmen, and labor representatives who sought to develop economic knowledge], the decision was made not to finance a competing model of social science expertise, the social settlements like Jane Addams's Hull House in Chicago. The settlements were locally based, staffed by "preprofessional" women, and rooted

in liberal values; they combined social science research with practice. In contrast, NBER was national in orientation, staffed by men, and professional in approach. . . . Its leaders studied social problems from a scientific, abstract point of view. By denying funds to the settlements, Lagemann claims, [Carnegie] aided their evolution into institutions that were seen as more important for service delivery than research. "Social work" became the central function of settlements, while "sociology" became a field of university study.[7]

This account reveals a growing split between "scientific" research and experience-based practical knowledge, and hence between a professional elite claiming to possess the former and ordinary people who were presumed to lack expertise—that is, "scientific knowledge."

The theme of professionals' loss of faith in democracy finds an echo in the writing of John McKnight, a Northwestern University professor.[8] McKnight contends that the "social map" that guides our thinking consists of an oversimplified division between "institutions," on the one hand, and "individuals," on the other. He criticizes this map for excluding the domain of "the community," which is "the social place used by . . . neighbors, neighborhood associations, clubs, civic groups, local enterprises, churches, ethnic associations, temples, local unions, local government, and local media." According to McKnight, we imagine "that our society has a problem in terms of effective human services," that is, a problem of malfunctioning institutions. But in reality "our essential problem is weak communities. . . . [W]e have reached the limits of institutional problem-solving. . . . [An institution] can deliver a service, [but] it cannot deliver care. Care is a . . . relationship characterized by consent rather than control." Institutions are concerned with control, not consent. They are built on "a vision [of a] structure where things *can be done right,* a kind of orderly perfection achieved . . . [in which] the ablest dominate." In short, McKnight contends, "many institutional leaders [*vide,* 'professionals'] . . . simply do not believe in the capacities of communities" (emphasis added).[9]

The service approach to solving public problems, then, is one in which "experts" take the lead, set the agenda, make the decisions, initiate the response. But where, in this model, is the community as a whole? What part is to be played by the public—by those ordinary citizens whose acceptance of responsibility for solving a problem and whose commitment of time, energy, and other resources are indispensable to its mitigation?

The decline of civic involvement did not begin with recent political attempts to transfer responsibility from government to the voluntary, or charitable, sector. Rather, it started with the transfer of responsibility to government. But to government from whom? From us—the public, the citizenry.

What did we do in our country before caring became institutionalized? How did we get by before we turned over the responsibility for addressing our social concerns to government and nonprofit professionals? As I noted in chapter 1, Alexis de Tocqueville, after returning to France from his visit to the United States in the 1830s, wrote of American communities that "when a private individual meditates an undertaking . . . directly connected . . . with the welfare of society, he never thinks of soliciting the cooperation of the government. . . . [He] courts the assistance of other individuals."[10] There was a time, in other words, when the citizens of our country took responsibility themselves for addressing social problems. Foundations and other nonprofits as we know them had not been invented, government was small and limited in its scope, and people did not look to professionals for solutions.

There's no going back, of course, to the days when we could rely solely on ourselves, our families, and our neighbors to deal with social problems. We can't expect individuals, acting alone, to mitigate conditions that have grown dauntingly complex and resistant to remedy. Life today is hard enough as it is. We have our hands full just trying to cope with the demands of our personal lives. We know that, in current circumstances, accepting sole responsibility for the less fortunate among us means having to care more than we can. Professional care-givers are under even greater pressure than their fellow citizens. Like the Union Army before conscription, the professional soldiers of care aren't making much headway. They may hold the line in places, even win a battle here and there, but they certainly aren't winning the war. Indeed, the need for care-inspired action seems to be growing, not diminishing. Professionals are having to work harder—to "care more"—just to keep up. Anyone familiar with the plight of many case workers employed by departments of social services knows how overburdened these professionals are.

Eugenie Gatens-Robinson has written that the pressure to "care more" arises from the same political structures and dogma that in current circumstances demand too much of parents, too much of the children of the ailing old, and too much of nurses, attendants, and teachers. "We have . . . relegated the public practices of care to the arena of expertise and have professionalized our social responses. . . . We as a people," she says, "have not taken at full reckoning what it would take to transform our educational, economic, and social institutions, our public life and its environment, in such a way that it would not require a saint to educate and care for those among us who are in need, vulnerable, or immature." Citing John McDermott, she sums up the task we must set ourselves if we are to create a genuinely "caring society": "We as a people . . . must actively come to see what is required of us . . . before really pervasive change can be made."[11] We *as a people*—we *the public*—are not making informed, conscious, collective decisions about how we should address the problems that confront us as a society.

Whether the emphasis is on personal development or on caring for others, the service interpretation of our responsibility for our communities and fellow citizens neglects the essential task of politics. The chief shortcoming of the service orientation is its failure to grasp that every problem we confront as communities and as a society involves an indeterminate conflict between things that human beings consider good, valuable, or desirable. Service is no substitute for what we really require if we're to respond effectively to our most pressing social problems and challenges. What we really require is the revitalization of our public life through a healthy practice of democratic politics in which all members of the public actively involve themselves in understanding public problems and making the hard choices that must be made if we are to move forward together toward sustainable, effective, widely supported policies.

Service may be an indispensable element in the civic maturation of citizens. But by itself it surely doesn't suffice. To become a responsible, effective member of one's society and community, a person must learn how to talk, think, and work together—as a political agent having his or her own particular beliefs, desires, and feelings—with others who are different and with whom he or she may never see eye-to-eye. Citizens need practice in dealing with others as political equals, in bringing to the table their own interests and views, and learning how to integrate and reconcile these with the often-uncongenial but nevertheless understandable interests and views of others.[12] The service orientation is inadequate because it mistakenly suggests that we can address our public concerns effectively without coming to grips with the need, both individually and collectively, to deliberate, to judge, and to choose.

## PROTEST

Like the service approach to involving oneself in the public life of one's community, "protest" is a well-intentioned but inadequate response to the dysfunction of consumerist politics. Practitioners of the "protest" strategy for responding to public problems object to a society that, in their view, has been organized to the advantage of those Americans who have long enjoyed the power to define prevailing social norms and to control its institutions. This power has been exercised at the expense of people whose skin color, ethnicity, sex, sexual orientation, and other characteristics have caused them to be treated as inferior or abnormal. Efforts to mobilize marginalized people politically have derived their impetus and outlook from the experience of oppression. As a consequence, their political focus is for the most part the struggle against intensely felt injustice.[13]

In recent years "protesters" have emphasized the political significance of personal "identity." Specifically, they are concerned about preserving and achieving recognition for the distinctive self-conceptions, values, and life experiences of groups that have been excluded from full participation in the social, economic, and political life of our nation. As Ilene Philipson has written, proponents of a politics of identity contend that individuals in a heterogeneous society such as ours have different experiences of life—and hence different conceptions of the good and the right—that are ignored (or disrespected, suppressed, stigmatized) by a white, male, Protestant ruling class. The "politics of identity," Philipson says, springs from dissatisfaction with the false homogeneity of a "diffusely defined 'American way of life'" that prevailed until the 1960s—an "ideology of sameness" that was

> profit-oriented, individualistic, . . . religious, ensconced in isolated nuclear families, rigidly segregated according to sex and race, consumerist, and politically acquiescent. . . . [Identity politics] has allowed people marginalized within larger political groupings . . . to find a political voice. . . . [It] provides a way of overriding . . . feelings of powerlessness and anomie that are, at their root, politically and socially constructed.[14]

In this view, the politically and socioeconomically dominant group in the United States—individualistic, competitive, capitalistically inclined WASP males, generally speaking—has, in William Connolly's words, "[defined] others in such a way that the latter's differences are treated as a source of evil or irrationality."[15] It has done so in order to secure its own identity (and hence its ideas about what is good and right). Because this group is blind—or indifferent—to the legitimacy of diverse experiences, values, and ways of life, the social institutions over which it exercises disproportionate control inflict serious injury on persons who do not share the dominant group's preferences. In response, racial minorities, women, gays and lesbians, the poor—people whose differences have caused them to be oppressed, discriminated against, or stigmatized—have been driven to protest American society's dominant norms, values, and institutions, and to contest the way power is exercised by those who allegedly wish to enforce conformity.

"Protesters" see themselves as waging a struggle to end the monopoly of privileges that WASP (and, by extension, middle-class) culture has succeeded in securing for its members at the expense of others. In their view, politics is at best a continuous process of subjective "judgment without criteria" and ineradicable competition between persons and groups. At its worst, politics turns into a power struggle between people bent on imposing their own conceptions on society and those who are resisting the imposition of those conceptions. In time, perhaps, we might learn to compete more sensitively and less coercively that we currently do.

But the potential for the coercive use of power will always exist and will always present a temptation. We can never achieve fully the condition of nonhierarchy, equality, and reciprocity that a genuinely democratic politics requires. Realistically, then, the central questions for politics are, How is power being used, by whom, and against whom? and How can the abuses resulting from unequal power be mitigated?

A realistic appraisal of the role of power and the way people who have it use it in their relations with those who have less is understandable and justified in view of the premium that the prevailing system of consumerist politics places on freedom and power. That said, however, there is a danger that we might become preoccupied with our differences—and with gaining political power in order to protect the personal identities we anchor in those differences—to the point where we lose our ability to use the power we have prudently and effectively. Writers such as Shelby Steele, Harry Boyte, and the late Christopher Lasch are unanimous in their belief that we have already encountered this danger and are suffering the consequences. Boyte and Lasch have called attention to the move away from protest voiced from within a shared universe of moral discourse to protest generated from "outside." Boyte's criticism of "protest" is that it approaches problems—indeed, politics itself—from the outside. The victimized and their advocates present themselves as innocents who are not implicated in, and hence not in any way responsible for, the social and political structures they find oppressive. "Protesters" condemn those in power while demanding that they take action to redress victims' grievances.

In contrast, says Lasch, the original civil rights movement succeeded not because it was less radical than subsequent efforts, but because it carried a moral authority that proved irresistible to most Americans.[16] It achieved this moral authority, moreover, without disowning the distinctive cultural heritage of African Americans or by perpetuating the mistaken idea that African Americans are white people with black skins. The civil rights movement drew inspiration from this tradition of particularism and from the ideology of black nationalism. Yet the nationalist tradition did not prevent Martin Luther King Jr. from understanding that American blacks were not only uprooted Africans but also Americans whose history was intricately intertwined with that of their oppressors. It would have been impossible to mount any kind of moral attack on segregation, Lasch argues, if King had taken the position that black people, by virtue of their special history, had developed their own special set of moral principles that whites could not appreciate, or that moral principles are a delusion anyway—just another way of advancing group interest—or that morality is whatever those in power choose to call it.

A recognition of the deep cultural differences that divide white and black Americans did not blind King to the commonality that made it possible to engage in moral debate about segregation. By rejecting a privileged status for blacks as victims of injustice, King enabled the civil rights movement to deflate the moral conceit of segregationists without expecting that an appeal to moral principles by itself would settle the issue. King understood that the issue would have to be settled by means of legal coercion. This recognition distinguished him from those people who hoped that a campaign of moral education would somehow persuade whites to give up their racial privileges willingly. The genius of the civil rights movement lay in King's insistence that a resort to pressure was compatible with an appeal to moral principles that both sides in the conflict could be made to acknowledge.

Refusing to claim exemption from shared moral standards on the grounds of victimization enabled the civil rights movement to speak from a position of overwhelming moral authority. In sharp contrast, Lasch contends, the resentment encouraged by the pursuit of black power led to the rapid collapse of this moral authority in the late 1960s. Where the civil rights movement condemned racism, black power condemned white racism, implying either that only whites were guilty of racism or that black racism could be excused on the grounds that black people had been subjected to "four centuries of oppression." Lasch's point is not that power is unnecessary or that its use is unjustifiable. Rather, his point is that reliance on power alone destroys any possibility of retaining a human connection between people that will enable them, despite their deep differences, to engage each other in productive moral and political dialogue.

The lesson of the civil rights movement's moral collapse has not prevented other movements from repeating its mistakes, as Shelby Steele has pointed out. Other groups, too, have abandoned the appeal to shared moral standards in favor of claiming that a special history of victimization entitles them to reparations or justifies the very methods they condemn when their enemies use them.[17] We should not imagine that this phenomenon is confined to "liberal" political views or to groups on "the left" of the political spectrum. Lasch maintains that political action on both the liberal and conservative ends of the spectrum has come to depend more and more heavily on the mobilization of resentment and the moral canonization of the victim. As Ilene Philipson has observed, "a politics of identity . . . has come to dominate . . . the way people of all political stripes see their place in the American political landscape and society in general."[18] According to Lasch, even middle-class white Americans now consider themselves a victimized minority.[19]

One problem, then, with the protest orientation to public problems is its preoccupation with the reality of unequal power. Protesters are convinced that they have to fight fire with fire, that power must be marshaled and used to combat the powerful institutions, groups, and ideas that currently make democratic politics impossible. We needn't deny (any more than Martin Luther King did) that power might have to be exercised to bring us closer to that ideal. Certainly, power had to be employed in the effort to end legally sanctioned and enforced racial segregation. But we should be alert to the danger of making the protest approach our strategy of first resort or making it our only strategy. Coercion is, among other things, simply not very productive. Indeed, it's often counterproductive.

For present purposes, however, the main problem with the protest outlook is that it is essentially not political. It provides no means by which, despite our differences, we can work toward making hard choices between conflicting values, and through which we might identify a general direction and a range of actions that could command general support. Like the service alternative to practical politics, the protest strategy ignores the essential political act—that of (individually and collectively) deliberating, reaching a sound judgment, and then choosing between conflicting goods. Instead, it assumes that what is good, what is best, what is right is already known, that no further deliberation or judgment is necessary, and that the only question is how to ensure that the right view prevails. The protester assumes in advance that he or she knows what is good and just. He looks upon politics as a means to predetermined ends. The protester is thus a close cousin of the practitioner of consumerist politics. For both, the question is, Who has the power to get what, from whom, when, and how?

The worldview of the protester has been institutionalized in American politics. Shelby Steele argues that "what began as an attempt to address . . . very real grievances . . . wound up creating newly sovereign fiefdoms" whose *raison d'être* is "not a matter of fairness—of justice—but of power." Ours has become a democracy in which "the power to act autonomously . . . is bestowed upon any group that is able to construct itself around a perceived grievance." Regrettably, says Steele, these "sovereign fiefdoms" have become ends in themselves: "[P]ower tends to be used now mostly to defend and extend the fiefdom." Organizations representing "grievance groups" frame issues "in territorial terms in order to maximize [their] grievance potential." For example, "framed exclusively as a woman's right, abortion becomes not a societal issue or even a family issue but a grievance issue" that is "within [the group's] territory of final authority." This gives the group moral and political power to insist on its members' entitlement to special treatment.[20]

But Steele lays much of the blame for this preoccupation with power at the doorstep of the "powers-that-be" in our country. Steele contends that they have corrupted, and thereby undermined, the movement toward a more genuinely democratic form of politics. Elites both in and out of government have found it expedient to abandon the ideal of democratic politics in favor of the consumerist version that prevails today. As Steele shrewdly discerns, professional protesters could not have made a career and created a power base for themselves through ostensible concern for the oppressed "without the cooperation of the society at large and its institutions." "Why," he asks, "did . . . public and private institutions, the corporations and foundations, end up supporting principles that had the effect of turning causes into sovereign fiefdoms?"

> The answer is that those in charge of America's institutions saw the institutionalization and bureaucratization of the protest movements as ultimately desirable, at least in the short term, and the funding of group entitlements as ultimately a less costly way to redress grievances. The leaders of the newly sovereign fiefdoms were backing off from their earlier demands that America live up to its ideals. . . . The language of entitlements is essentially the old, comforting language of power politics, and in the halls of power it went down easily enough. . . . *This satisfied the institutions because entitlements were cheaper in every way than real change* (emphasis added).[21]

By redistributing power within their own tight circle, elites inside and outside government colluded to defuse the impetus toward genuine democratic empowerment of ordinary Americans. This is just what we should have expected of persons whose model of politics is fashioned after a market, in which the point is self-interestedly to acquire and wield as much power as possible in pursuit of one's private ends. But the promise of an inclusive democracy was not the only casualty. Another was the public's readiness—and its ability—to take real responsibility for solving the country's problems by facing up to and making the hard choices that politics demands.

### COMMUNITY

In response to the deleterious effects of consumerist politics and the deficiencies of the service and protest alternatives for dealing with social ills, some people advocate a practice of democratic politics that emphasizes the idea of "community."[22] This approach holds that people can be motivated by a sense of civic duty as well as by self-interest, that they can balance their private interests against the interest all share in securing the public good. The central goal of the communitarian "movement" is a conscious, intentional effort to define and create the common good through democratic politics. The sort of politics required, however, is not one in which competing interests battle without taking responsibility for the common good, but rather one in which competing interests not only press their own demands but come forward with programs for the common good.

Communitarians reject the assumption of exclusively self-interested motivation on which the consumerist model of politics is based. They contend that, when citizens are engaged in thinking about the whole, their conceptions of their interests will broaden and their commitment to the search for a common good will deepen. To encourage this orientation to the common good, we need new forms of participation that will make citizens responsible for the whole, rather than involving them simply as interested parties who enter the public arena only when their private interests are threatened. Currently, a vigorous democratic politics is absent from our public life. A mass of claimants organized into various protest groups is not a public. Democratic government is more than the compromising of conflicting interests.

Unlike the conception of practical politics that is the subject of this book—which admittedly shares much in common with the communitarian outlook—the latter suggests that achieving a more satisfactory practice of democratic decision making requires, first, an explicit focus on and discussion of the common good, and second, a prior commitment on behalf of citizens to seek that good. We will get a healthy practice of democratic politics only after we make up our minds to supplement our concern for our private interests with a sincere commitment to pursue the common good. Although there is nothing wrong with interests, and nothing wrong with having them represented, we should enter the public arena with our eye fixed firmly on the ideal of "the good society." Good democratic politics is the result—the "reflection"—of this commitment, not the source of it. The communitarian approach suggests that before we can expect politics to become more genuinely democratic, and before we can expect it to produce the way of life we would like to prevail in our communities and in our society, we have to balance our self-interested motivation with a conscious desire to serve the public interest.

Two criticisms of the communitarian outlook bear directly on the central questions of politics (What shall we choose to do when good things conflict? and How shall we decide what to do?). One criticism is the protester's objection that we lack an agreed-upon philosophical foundation on which people in this diverse society of ours might construct universally authoritative rules for determining what is good and bad, right and wrong. In this view, there is no such thing as a common human nature, and no such thing as universal human experience. Hence there is no basis on which we might erect standards that apply to everyone. There can be no single, true version of what is good and right. For this reason, we must ask *whose* interest or conception of the good is being advanced under cover of a call to serve "the community" or to create "the good society." Diversity being a fact of life, we not only can't agree on what things we should value, what our priorities should be, how we should act and live, and so forth—we shouldn't even try. The best we can hope for is a relatively free, nondiscriminatory, noncoercive political competition.

The second relevant criticism of the communitarian approach is related to the first. Why, given the irreducible diversity of human life, should we temper our pursuit of our particular interests? Why should we cooperate? Why should we seek consensus? Why should we refrain from using the power at our disposal to counter the use that others—including those ostensibly pursuing the "common good"—inevitably will make of their own power? Why, in short, should politics be a reflection of the aspiration to contribute to the happiness of one's community? Why should *that* be our motivation? Why shouldn't we go into politics with the no-nonsense view that politics is a struggle between divergent approaches to life, a struggle in which only fools assume that we can all agree, that we can define a common good, that collectively we can fashion a single way of life that will make everyone happy?

Communitarians have persuasive replies to these objections, of course. For our immediate purposes, however, what is important is how communitarians deal with the essential task of politics: forming collective judgments about and collectively choosing between conflicting good things. Unlike the service and protest outlooks, the communitarian approach recognizes the importance of democratic politics. Unlike the consumerist conception on which our politics is currently modeled, communitarianism holds that a mass of individual claimants organized into interest groups is not a public, and that democratic government is more than the compromising of conflicting interests. Further, communitarians concede that there is nothing wrong with interests, and nothing wrong with having them represented. Although public discussion would not (and should not) eliminate interests, coalitions, or factions, it would reduce the zero-sum quality of consumerist politics by structuring a forum in which people could coherently deliberate.

Implicit in these statements (especially the last one) is the realization that we cannot create the sort of communities and society we would like to have, nor can we effectively achieve our legitimate particular goals, simply by mechanically adding up people's "top-of-the-head" opinions and desires through devices such as polls, elections, referendums, and legislative votes. The emphasis on the need for forums in which people could deliberate shows that communitarians appreciate the need to judge and choose. Compromise is not enough. Moreover, the communitarian approach exhibits an admirable practical emphasis on concrete problems and issues. Whatever agreement we achieve will arise out of agreements about concrete problems rather than agreements about theory. Finally, better relationships among citizens will emerge from public discussion about political issues. Democratic politics can and should be a process of (in Julius Kovesi's phrase) "elucidating the good" through the attempt to reach a sound collective judgment about how to resolve specific, concrete dilemmas.[23]

The communitarian approach closely resembles the idea of practical politics I recommend. However, I would like to see proponents of the communitarian outlook discuss more explicitly (as I endeavor to do in this book) how, despite our differences, we can deliberate together for the purpose of making hard choices between conflicting values. But at least, unlike the consumerist, service, and protest orientations to public life in a democracy, communitarianism does not disregard the essential political act—that of judging and choosing between conflicting goods. It does not assume that what is good, best, or right is already known, that no further choice or judgment is necessary, that the only question is how to ensure that the right view prevails. For just this reason, therefore, I believe proponents of the communitarian approach should take greater account of the fact that more than two centuries of emphasizing individual views and interests has made it difficult for us to be motivated by the common good per se. We are so accustomed to thinking in the terms of the consumerist model, which has no conception of the common good (apart from what most or a majority of individuals happen to want), that the idea of the common good makes virtually no sense. Certainly, apart from goods such as highways, a strong national defense, and the availability of disaster relief (and not always then), most of us would be hard pressed to come up with examples of common goods.

We have to begin where people are. Currently they are *not* in a society that has a readily usable concept of the common good, but in a society that at best is in a position to begin working toward such a notion. If this is so, then politics should proceed, not through an explicit search for the common good, but implicitly—through an effort to address specific, concrete problems, challenges, and opportunities that involve conflicting good things, which have to be reconciled by the political acts of deliberating, forming a judgment, choosing, and devising a way forward that everyone can go along with.

- What about large groups. ill suited for t[ ]mil. city country.

# 4

# Value, Needs, and Conflict

---

*What matters most about political ideas is the underlying emotions, the music, to which ideas are a mere libretto, often of very inferior quality.*

—Louis Namier

Before we can really understand the essential political task—that of constructing a shared, public perspective on a problem, deliberating alternative courses of action, forming a judgment about priorities, and choosing a way to proceed that everyone can go along with—we need to have a clear understanding of how and why we are motivated to act politically. The points I am about to make might not seem relevant to politics. But they are not only relevant, they are important as well.

### Action, Desires, and Reasons

Let's start with actions. An *action* is a conscious, voluntary "doing" of something. Every action that I perform I undertake in order to satisfy a *desire* that I have at the time. I might take this action either for its own sake or as a means to some end that I do desire for its own sake. This is true as much of an action that I take because I regard it as an obligation or a duty as it is of a purely self-interested action. Unless I desire to do what I ought to do, I won't be motivated to do it.

So where do desires come from? Certainly, they can stem from "noncognitive" or "affective" factors, such as emotions and biological urges. But like *attitudes* (i.e., likes and dislikes, affinities for and aversions to various situations or states of affairs), desires are always connected psychologically with *beliefs*. A belief is an intellectual conviction that something is true or real. When I act, my conduct is invariably motivated by my belief that by so acting I will obtain or realize something of *value*. (I will discuss "value" in detail below.) If a belief is a conviction that something is true or real, then a belief that motivates me to act is one that says, in effect, "If I do this, it will *in fact* lead to the realization of something valuable."

A belief that motivates my action doesn't have to be apparent to me at the time I act. I can act out of habit, for example. But every action I take rests, logically and psychologically, on a belief that provides me with an explanation of my action. As I noted above, when I act my conduct is invariably motivated by my belief that by so acting I will obtain or realize something of value. Even if I do something "because I feel like it," I do so because of my belief that "doing what I feel like (in a case such as this) is valuable for me." I may not go through this mental process before I act, but I would reconstruct the events leading to my decision along these lines. Similarly, if you write a critical letter to your city councilperson "because you are angry with him," your action is based on a belief that upbraiding the honorable gentleperson is a desirable or valuable course of action to take in response to the anger you feel.

As these examples suggest, beliefs that motivate us to act—"motivating beliefs"—require the support of *reasons*. A reason is another kind of belief—a "justifying" or "warranting" belief. A reason tells me I'm justified in holding the belief that motivates me to act. For example, suppose I hear that a new book is "good." Specifically, I hear that the author argues persuasively that there is a more effective way for communities to respond to problems than our prevailing public decision-making process. I go to the library and locate the book. I take a look at the table of contents. I read the synopsis and the quotes on the dust jacket. Now I'm faced with a choice: Do I read the book, or not? I decide to start reading the book. Why do I make the decision to take this action? I do so because I have a (motivating) belief that if I do this (read the book), it will in fact lead to the realization of something valuable. Why do I believe this? Because I have reasons to believe it. The reasons I have—the beliefs that justify or warrant my motivating belief—are considerations such as "Other people say it is good," "The table of contents and the synopsis and quotes on the dust jacket suggest it is good," and so forth.

We cite reasons both to explain and to justify what we do. Of course, the reasons I give to justify my action may not be the reasons that actually explain why I'm motivated to act. I might not even be aware of the beliefs that actually motivate me. The reasons I give for what I do often are those that I consider acceptable to others—or to myself. To complicate matters even more, the beliefs that actually motivate me aren't necessarily ones that I *have* for acting. I can act for a reason that I don't actually have. For example, I might run from the building in which I work "because it's on fire." But if the building isn't actually on fire, then "the building's on fire" isn't a reason to leave (though of course the fact that smoke is coming from under a door may be a reason for believing that the building is on fire, which would make my action reasonable). The point is, I can act on the basis of a reason that I don't in fact have. That doesn't necessarily make my action irrational or unreasonable. But it does mean *I can be mistaken* about what's really motivating me.

I can also fail to act on the basis of a reason I do have. This is another way to be "mistaken." A reason can exist for me to do something—learn to play the piano, for example—without my acknowledging it, or even without my being aware of it. So long as I would gain something of value by learning to play the piano—so long as I, myself, were I able to experience it, would recognize it as valuable for me—then I have a reason for acting, whether or not I currently have a desire to. Just because I don't currently desire something doesn't mean I don't have a reason for doing it. If I come to believe that it's valuable, then I'll desire it. The recognition of value generates the motivation—not the other way around. A reason for doing a thing can exist independently of the desire I happen to have at a given moment. It can come to motivate me through my discovering that the thing X is valuable—that is, by my recognizing that there is a reason for doing X that I previously didn't recognize.

## Value and Values

As I noted above, the belief that value will be realized or obtained gives rise to the motivation to act. It's important here not to confuse the motivating belief with the object of that belief. *A value* is the object itself—an action, experience, or state of affairs that produces some form of *satisfaction*. A value—that is, a thing that has value, that yields satisfaction—does not motivate me to act. What motivates me to act is a *belief* about that value—an intellectual conviction that the experience, condition, or state of affairs does or will yield some form of satisfaction.

In order for a motivating belief about a value to move me to act, however, I must "appreciate" the object of that belief, the thing I believe holds value for me. That is, I must feel the "pull" exerted upon me by the prospect of realizing the satisfaction I associate with the object of my belief, the value itself. Not to feel the "pull" of a value is to be unable to be motivated by it. For example, no matter how much I consciously say to myself that I value courage, if at some deeper, less intellectual level (at "gut level" or "in my heart") I do not feel pulled, or impelled, in the direction of a satisfaction I can anticipate feeling upon acting courageously, that belief will fail to move me toward action. I don't mean merely that my desire to act courageously will be *overridden* by competing desires to realize the satisfaction of other values. I mean that, even in the absence of such competing desires and values I would experience no impetus toward courageous action whatsoever. A purely intellectual conviction that a course of action or state of affairs holds value for me would not and could not—by itself, in the absence of a nonintellectual appreciation of the thing I believe holds value—motivate me to act. A purely intellectual evaluative belief—a belief unconnected to a nonintellectual appreciation of the thing believed to hold value—is like a ship's sail that has not been secured to the mast: because it is not connected to the rest of the ship, it lacks the ability to pull the vessel in any direction.

## "VALUES-WITH-A-CAPITAL-V"

In ordinary, everyday speech we often speak of what from this point forward I will call *Values,* spelled with a capital "V." For example, people sometimes say things like "our schools ought to teach values" and "traditional values are no longer respected in our country." The "values" referred to in such statements are a special subset of valuable things. I want to distinguish them from *values*—actions, experiences, or states of affairs that produce some form of satisfaction. A "Value-with-a-capital-V," so to speak, is a particular sort of value: an action, experience, or state of affairs widely believed in a community or society to be ethically or morally good, commendable, admirable, or worthy of aspiration and attainment. Many Values are embodied in social norms. They're rules or principles we are taught—for the most part not through direct experience but through inculcation—by institutions such as the family, school, or church. They're abstract in the sense that we hold them in a highly general form, without specific reference to concrete situations. "Freedom" and "equality," for example, are Values.

(Capital-V) Values may contribute to our motivation to act. But they often aren't the ultimate, rock-bottom source of our desires and actions. We frequently offer a Value as a publicly acceptable justification for what actually motivates us. Because Values are publicly acceptable, we often identify closely with them. But understanding fully a person's motivation may require that we go beyond the Value he or she offers initially as the explanation and justification for his or her desires and actions. What we need for present purposes is the ultimate explanation of why a person is disposed to act in a particular way. That is, we need (small-v) values and the motivating beliefs that attach to them. For example, "ambition"—a Value—does not explain ambitious action. Nor does "politeness" explain polite behavior. Nor do "wisdom," "equality," or "national security" explain the desires and actions with which they are associated. These are Values— "values-with-a-capital-V."

True, such Values are widely shared. But they don't really explain our political attitudes, emotions, desires, and behavior. They are merely expressions of socially sanctioned motivating beliefs. The psychologist Milton Rokeach has written that most American political attitudes turn on the relative emphasis people give to freedom and equality.[1] Conservatives more often than not emphasize the former. Liberals tend to emphasize the latter. But accurate though this observation may be, how much does it really explain? Not much. The question is, Why does someone assign priority to freedom? Why does somebody else assign priority to equality? And why in a particular situation? Consider the abortion issue. Suppose I value "life" more than "choice," and you value "choice" more than "life." Politically speaking, where does debate over such abstractions get us? Clearly, not very far. The reason, I believe, is that life and choice are not the ultimate values that provide the predominant motivation for people in this dispute. They are merely Values.

### Needs: The Ultimate Source of All Value—and Motivation

In some manner and to some degree, all of the factors that motivate a person most profoundly and persistently—that is, all the things a person values—are manifestations or expressions (often socially or culturally shaped) of *needs*. As a theory of motivation the following account is not without problems. It can be challenged conceptually and empirically. Nevertheless, it remains plausible and makes good intuitive sense. So for purposes of explaining the importance to the theory of practical politics of getting at our real motivations—our values and the motivating beliefs that arise in connection with them—it's quite serviceable.

In the theory of human needs developed by the late psychologist Abraham Maslow, a need is something (a) the absence of which tends to breed illness; (b) the presence of which prevents illness; (c) the restoration of which cures illness; (d) that in conditions of full information and freedom a person lacking it would desire; and (e) that is inactive, at a low ebb, or functionally absent in a healthy person.[2] According to Maslow, needs emerge in a rough hierarchy reflecting their relative importance for a person's well-being. When lower (i.e., relatively more fundamental or essential) needs begin to be fulfilled, higher needs begin to emerge. (Note that needs can overlap—that is, they can exist simultaneously.) This trend continues upward, with each succeeding level becoming the predominant (though never the sole) source of motivation in the person's life.

The most basic, the most powerful, and the most obvious of all human needs are those required for survival. Of these, the most important are *physiological needs:* for food, water, sleep, and oxygen. Once physiological needs are adequately addressed, so-called *safety needs* begin to appear. They include physical security, order and stability, predictability, and a certain amount of routine. When physiological and safety needs are satisfied, *connection needs*—needs for love, affection, and belongingness—begin to predominate. The second level in the hierarchy is occupied by *esteem needs,* of which there are two categories: (1) self-supplied esteem and (2) esteem supplied by others. The former category includes confidence, mastery, adequacy, and independence. The latter category includes recognition, acceptance, attention, status, reputation, and appreciation. (The survival and esteem needs together comprise what we might label "deficit" needs—"deficit" because something important for the well-being of the person is to some degree absent or lacking.) The third level encompasses what Maslow calls "growth" needs. I prefer to call these "enhancement" needs—"enhancement" because fulfilling them contributes something extra to a person's well-being but is not essential to his or her well-being in the way that the fulfillment of deficit needs is. These include the satisfactions of *personal development* and *self-actu-alization* that are realized through the pursuit of aesthetic, intellectual, and emo-tional stimulation and challenge.

Value (small-v) can be understood as the satisfaction that is realized when Maslovian survival, esteem, or growth needs are fulfilled. A value—something that has value or is valuable—is thus an action, experience, or state of affairs that produces satisfaction by fulfilling a Maslovian need. Because individuals differ in the combination and relative strengths of the needs they have, a value's moti-vational potential varies from person to person and over time.[3] As a result, two persons might assign substantially different priorities to the same values. People are often at different levels of need-fulfillment. If I'm starving and you're well fed, we're going to take rather different views of the importance of food in our re-spective lives. Although we both might love playing the piano, having the chance to do so is bound to fall a lot lower on my list of priorities than it does on yours just now. Priorities can differ as well because of past experiences, because of the way we've been socially or culturally conditioned, because of our expectations, because of the particular circumstances we find ourselves in at a given time, and so forth. Moreover, my priorities don't just differ from yours—they differ from my own at other times and in other situations. Because both your needs and my needs—and hence priorities—vary, disagreements between us can arise and per-sist even though we have the same needs. Disagreements can occur as well be-cause we seek to satisfy those needs through different means.

## Value Conflict and Political Disagreements

A *conflict* is a "collision." When we think of conflict, we usually think of conflicts between persons or groups. In this book, I'd like to use the terms "disagreement" and "dispute" to mark this sort of conflict, and reserve the term "conflict" for what happens when values or value-priorities "collide"—when, in other words, we can't have or enjoy one of the things we value without having to do without, or do with less of, some other thing we value. As I've noted in preceding chap-ters, such conflicts are an important—perhaps the most important—source of public disagreements.[4]

Public disagreements generally grow out of disagreements between persons over whether a course of action or state of affairs has value or whether it has greater or less value than alternative actions or states of affairs. Such disagreements often involve the public abstractions I've labeled "Values" (capital-V). Within communities, societies, and cultures, disagreements tend to arise over the relative priority that valuable things (including Values) should be assigned in the course of formulating public policy. Between societies and cultures (or subcultures), disagreements about whether something has value (or is a Value) are also apt to arise. Disagreements are inevitable, particularly in a society that, like ours, is large, culturally heterogeneous, and predisposed to emphasize that values are many, diverse, and incommensurable.

But dealing with public disagreements constructively is particularly difficult in American public life today. The reason has to do with the increased importance of Values as a source of political motivation, and hence with Values as a source of political disagreement. A few years ago, the syndicated columnist Robert J. Samuelson observed that "our politics are beginning to drift in a new direction. Glance at the headlines, and what you see is abortion, drugs, flag-burning, AIDS, and gun control. . . . [In contrast to the essentially economic disagreements that predominated previously, those] now pushing to the fore are different. In political lingo, they concern 'values.'"[5] The close connection between human needs (especially what Maslow calls "esteem needs") and the "values" (i.e., Values) Samuelson has in mind reveals itself in contemporary political disagreements. Disagreements that seem on the surface to be about political or economic advantage or benefit may turn out on examination to be about values that implicate personal identities ("esteem needs") and conceptions of what constitutes a meaningful and proper life ("growth" or "enhancement" needs).

Consider a dispute that occurred a few years ago between Native Americans and whites in northern Wisconsin concerning the former's treaty rights to hunt and fish, which permit Native Americans to employ methods denied by law to white citizens. On the surface, the issue appears to be essentially economic: white residents have objected, for example, to the quantity of fish taken from lakes also used by sports fishermen. But if the issue is economic, then why, when the state legislature offered the Native Americans a generous monetary compensation in return for not exercising their rights, did they refuse? Perhaps what underlay their insistence on exercising their rights is the value they attach to living a traditional way of life and to their identification, as Native Americans, with that way of life. What they might value fundamentally is the identity that living that way of life embodies. Exercising their treaty rights is valuable because it contributes to their identity, which in turn meets their basic esteem need.

Examples such as this reveal a picture of emerging political divisions that coincide with identity ("esteem-need") cleavages in our society. The coincidence of such divisions makes productive and nonthreatening political discourse increasingly difficult to achieve. There are numerous cultural subsystems in America: ethno-racial subsystems (Asian Americans, African Americans, Latinos, "white ethnics"); role-based subsystems (lawyer, auto worker, farmer, homemaker); ideological (neoconservative, feminist, environmentalist, civil libertarian); regional (southern, midwestern); class-based (blue collar, middle class); generational (baby boomers, generation X); religious (Protestant fundamentalist, Catholic, Jewish); quasi-religious (human potential movement); and so on. Each subsystem has—or at least is thought by many to have—Values, priorities, and modes of thinking that it does not hold in common with others. Appealing to common standards to resolve differences is difficult.

As Samuelson points out, "our political system works best when people focus on shared [V]alues."[6] But it is shared Values—or at least shared Value-priorities—that we appear to be losing. To be sure, over time common experiences and circumstances have grown fewer. As traditional connections—to religion, family, ethnic group, local community—have been severed, attenuated, or replaced, Values have become simultaneously more important and more specific to us as individuals. The growing importance of Values in relation to our personal identities, combined with the drift of American politics toward preoccupation with issues involving such Values, has given us troubling times. Moral and political disagreements have grown more heated and resistant to resolution precisely because of the link between Values and people's desires and actions. Samuelson was right to observe that

> if this [drift toward Value-centered disagreements] continues . . . , it may be bad for the country. We may be entering a nastier period, in which political [disagreements] escalate and workable compromises prove increasingly elusive. . . . Compromises [in Value conflicts] are difficult because the antagonists view one another so harshly. . . . People do not just disagree. They feel passionate about their disagreements. My hunch is that debate over these [V]alues issues will produce much emotion—anger, fear and hatred. . . . If [V]alues politics boldly reemerge, the experience isn't likely to be constructive or pleasant.[7]

Politics as we know it—the "consumerist" politics that closely parallels life in the economic realm—only makes matters worse, because it tries to do the impossible: resolve disagreements involving values (including Values) by invoking principles or procedures, such as majority rule, that are neutral with respect to the ultimate needs that underlie those disagreements. The perceived irrationality and unfairness that results from this attempt has already discredited politics, and has begun to undermine the authority of the republican institutions upon which we depend.

## Getting to the Value behind the Values

According to John Burton, a leading expert on dispute resolution, there are two basic dimensions to a dispute: its degree of seriousness and its deep-rootedness.[8] Seriousness has to do with how the persons directly involved in a dispute, or those in their community or society who are indirectly affected, perceive what is at stake. How do they feel about what they think they stand to lose or gain? To what degree do they feel threatened? Deep-rootedness, in contrast, has to do with both the causes and the nature of the disagreement. In a deep-rooted disagreement there are values at stake that are not negotiable. These values represent the satisfaction of needs about which compromise is completely out of the question. This doesn't mean that particular ways of satisfying these needs are necessarily nonnegotiable. Indeed, the key to resolving value conflicts, and hence to settling disagreements arising from them, is finding a way to meet or satisfy what is non-negotiable by identifying or creating political goods that are negotiable.

According to Burton, in all disagreements characterized by substantial seriousness and deep-rootedness, human beings seek to satisfy primordial and universal (Maslovian) needs such as security, identity, and recognition. They strive to gain control of their environment in order to ensure the satisfaction of their needs. This struggle cannot be curbed; it must be accepted as ineradicable. Disagreement is a universal response to the perception that one's needs are being frustrated or will be frustrated by the requirement to satisfy some other need, whether one's own or someone else's. The vast majority of human beings pursue by all means at their disposal the basic human needs that remain unmet in their lives. As Burton says, individuals are neither naturally good nor naturally bad— they are naturally needy.

Because need rather than scarcity is the source of much deep-rooted conflict, says Burton, the outcome of a disagreement arising from need-based conflict does not necessarily have to be "win/lose" or "zero-sum." The more security, identity, and esteem that one party experiences, the more opportunities there are for the satisfaction of these same needs by others. Scarcity, Burton maintains, is not a major source of deep-rooted conflict. Scarcity is relevant only to the conventional or traditional means that the parties have relied upon previously to satisfy their deep-rooted needs. It is not scarcity of identity, for example, that causes disagreements to arise, but rather scarcity of the means that people have employed in their effort to establish and sustain their identity—power, wealth, domination, and so forth.

Let me try to illustrate the importance of going beyond what the parties to a political disagreement say (and perhaps believe) is at issue to the deep, more or less persistent sources of their motivation—that is, to their needs. An issue discussion guide prepared in 1987 by the Public Agenda Foundation to assist citizens in talking about the state of U.S.-Soviet relations presented several choices for readers to consider. The first choice was informed by the importance of a country's being powerful, of "being number one." "Being powerful, being number one" is a Value. Note, however, that, as a motivation that explains people's desires, attitudes and actions, this Value is susceptible to further probing. "Being powerful, being number one" raises further questions. Why, we might ask, is it important to "be number one"? This question opens up a line of inquiry that might lead to the real source of motivation at a deeper level of value, one closer to core psychological needs.[9] A more satisfactory explanation is that people want to "be powerful, be number one" because they desire the feeling of psychological security that comes with knowing we can deter a military threat to our country. Unlike "being number one," the desire for security suffices—it explains. Further questions aren't necessary to produce a satisfactory explanation (although they might be necessary to clarify, verify, or elaborate that explanation). We understand readily the motivation (small-v value) of a person who desires to feel secure.

Consider another example: the great flag-burning debate. What needs might underlie this debate? What is the source of the anxieties and concerns that this issue evokes? Why have similar anxieties recurred in American history since the Civil War (but were unknown previously)? Are they related to the importance to people of a national identity? If so, what has threatened that identity? What do people fear? What is it they need? What underlies the Value of "patriotism" or "love of country" or "honoring America" that people invoke to explain their political attitudes and prescriptions?

Let's look now at a couple of hypothetical examples. In the first one, imagine that you're trying to find out why the person you're talking with supports a proposal to make local public school buildings into "community service centers" that would provide a wide range of assistance to families living within their attendance areas. In order to get to the bottom of his motivations—to identify what he needs, and hence what he values—you keep asking "why?" in response to the answers he offers:

> I believe our community's schools should do more to help the families of children whose home-life is not as healthy and supportive as it should be.
> *Why?*
> A growing number of children are not coming to school ready to learn. At home they're not getting the care and attention they need. Often there's just one parent in the home, and he or she may be working two jobs to make

ends meet. No one's there for them when they get back from school at the end of the day. If there are several children and some are very young, the older ones often have to look after them. Many parents don't have the time, energy, or in some cases the skills for attending to their kids' needs, especially their developmental and emotional needs. In some families children are being abused—physically, emotionally, or even sexually. In many they're simply neglected.

Teachers have difficulty teaching when children don't have the motivation or the ability to do their schoolwork. And when some children in a class aren't prepared to learn, it becomes harder for all children to learn. If other agencies in our community aren't able or willing to address the needs of these children and their families, I think it's up to the schools to do so.

*Why?*

Because if the schools don't, who will? We can't allow this situation to continue.

*Why?*

Because parents are struggling, and their children are suffering. As a community, we have a responsibility to help them.

*Why?*

Well, for a couple of reasons. One is that all of us are affected by what's going on in the lives of other people who live in our community. For example, some parents abuse alcohol or drugs. That puts them at risk of criminal behavior. More important, the neglect and abuse that the children suffer makes *them* more likely to get into trouble as they grow older. Even if the kids avoid serious trouble, they may be a disruptive influence in the classroom. And when they grow up and become parents themselves, they're likely to repeat the cycle. So we all have an interest in protecting ourselves from the behavior of people who are having a hard time managing their lives.

Another reason we have a responsibility to these families is just that they're people, they're human beings, and they're hurting—the children especially. They're innocent—they don't deserve the harsh existence they're being forced to live. And they're powerless—they can't help themselves. I can't stand the thought that right here in my own backyard there are people—especially little children—who are afraid, or lonely, or confused, or sad, or hungry. I've got to do something about it.

*Why?*

Why?! Isn't it obvious?

*Why do you feel it's your personal responsibility?*

Well, if I don't accept responsibility, I can't expect anybody else to. And I can't solve problems like this by myself. We have to work together. We all have to do our part.

*Why?*

Because if we don't, eventually life for all of us will get worse. We're all affected by the way other people live, whether they do so by choice or out of necessity. We live in a community. We're like fish who all have to swim in the same pond. What goes on in other parts of the pond will eventually affect all of us.

*But realistically, you're probably not going to be affected directly, at least not anytime soon. Is this the real reason why you feel a responsibility to less fortunate members of your community?*

Well, I suppose if you get right down to it, it's a matter of feeling sympathetic. Relatively speaking, I've had a pretty easy life. But I've had enough experience to know what it feels like to be frightened, or ignored, or unloved, or unfairly treated. I remember what it was like to be young, to be a child. I know how vulnerable a child feels, how insecure, how overwhelmed by grownups, how confused by their actions, their moods, their emotions. I know how vulnerable children are, how easily damaged and hurt. I know how needy they are, how much they need and crave love and protection. I look at my own children and think I simply couldn't stand it if they had to suffer what some other children have to suffer. I guess I can identify with them—certainly with my own children, but also with other children. I can put myself in their place. And I can't stand the thought of them hurting. When I imagine what they're going through, it's almost as if it were my own pain. It makes me feel desperate to do something.

*Why?*

Because that's the way I am. I can't change it. I wouldn't want to. I wouldn't want to be a person who doesn't feel sympathy, who doesn't care, who doesn't accept responsibility for the suffering of other people. I wouldn't want to be that kind of person. I wouldn't want to live that kind of life. Life is short. I've got to live it in a way that lets me live with myself.

Notice in this example that, with some gentle but persistent probing, it's possible for the questioner to get past the kinds of fairly broad justifications that someone might offer for the proposed policy (for example, "schools need to adapt to changed circumstances," "teachers are in the best position to help children," "this is a community need that government isn't meeting") to the values that truly motivate the person and that provide a convincing explanation for the position he takes with respect to the proposed policy. With prompting, he succeeds in bringing to the surface his sympathy and "fellow-feeling" for other people, his identification with the children, his sense of being connected to other members of his community, his feeling of personal responsibility for them, and his desire to be the kind of person and live the kind of life he considers morally worthy.

In the second example, imagine that you're trying to find out why the person you're talking with supports a call for your community's schools to get "back to basics." In order to get to the bottom of her motivations, you keep asking "why?" in response to the answers she offers.

I believe schools should emphasize basic academic skills such as reading and mathematics. They should teach other things as well, of course—science, history, music, and so forth. But their main job is to teach basic skills. That has to be their priority, and they have to do it well.

*Why?*

Schools have to foster the development of intellectual rigor and discipline that young people are going to need as adults. Trendy, "soft" subjects like "developing self-esteem," "learning to manage your feelings," and "resolving conflict" don't demand anything of students. They're a waste of time and resources.

*Why?*

Two reasons. First, that's not what good colleges are looking for. Getting into a good college and doing well is a key to career success. Second, soft subjects don't have anything to do with the real world. To succeed in a highly competitive job market and work environment, young people are going to have to have well-developed, marketable skills—especially technical skills in computers, engineering, or finance. In order to get good jobs, to keep them, and to advance in their careers, they're going to have to be good at communicating, analyzing problems, organizing people and projects, and continually learning so they can stay ahead of the curve.

*Why is that important?*

Staying ahead of the curve? It's important because the pace of economic and technological change is fast, and getting faster. If you don't stay ahead of the curve, you'll find yourself falling behind—and maybe out of work. At the same time, our economy is very competitive, and getting more so. If young people can't compete, they're not going to prosper. There aren't going to be enough good jobs that pay well for all the young people who want them. If they don't have the skills employers are looking for, they're not going to be competitive. Maybe it's a cliché, but it's true: it's a jungle out there. I want my children to be prepared to survive in it.

*Why?*

Well, who wouldn't? As adults, we know how tough it is. We know you have to work long and hard to get ahead—sometimes just to make ends meet. And it's getting worse. I can't afford to support my children financially into their adulthood. I want them to be able to support themselves and to maintain the standard of living I've been able to give them while they were growing up. I think that's important.

*Why?*

It's important for them, first of all. They're going to be disappointed, frustrated—maybe even disillusioned and angry—if they discover they can't have all the things they'd like to have or do the things they want to do. It's also important for their children—my grandchildren. Owning a nice home, going on vacation, buying clothes and cars and braces and insurance—to say nothing of college and retirement—all of these things are getting very expensive, some of them almost prohibitively expensive. To pay for them, my children are going to need financial security. And that begins with getting and keeping a good job. That's their responsibility. Mine is to make sure they get the education that'll enable them to do so.

*Why is it important to have all the things you mentioned?*

Why isn't it? Everybody wants these things. With the standard of living we've achieved, we can afford them, and we've come to expect them. Besides, a lot of the things we want—things like a college education (or these days, college plus graduate school)—aren't just good in themselves, they're means to other ends: having the money and leisure time to pursue our other interests, for example. And let's face it—the world's getting to be a tougher place to live. If you don't want to live in a high-crime area; if you don't want to have to see the air you breathe or taste the water you drink; if you want the best medical treatment if you get cancer or have a heart attack or develop Alzheimer's Disease, you've got to be prepared to pay for these things. People who're in good financial shape are in a better position to ensure that they'll have a safe, enjoyable, and probably longer life.

As in the first example, persistent probing gets us past the "publicly acceptable" justifications (the Values) someone might offer in support of the proposed policy (for example, "schools are educational institutions, not social service agencies," "teachers should do what they do best—teach," "it's up to parents—not the schools or the community—to provide the support and help their children need to do well in school," "even if we had the money to provide services to families, which we don't, it would be a misuse of taxpayers' dollars"). It enables us to arrive at the needs and values that actually motivate the person and thereby explain her position with respect to the proposed policy. She cites the desirability of personal security in a competitive, "dog-eat-dog" world and the need for financial security to achieve it. She talks about independence and not having to rely on others for what one needs in life. She reveals her feelings about taking responsibility for oneself and one's children.

In both of these examples, the values that are brought to the surface by questioning are the actual sources—or at least very close to the actual sources—of the person's motivations. We know this because we can see that further probing, even if the person were able and willing to continue responding, would not yield a deeper level of understanding. In terms of the person's motivation, there are no more "layers of the onion" to peel back. It is at this level of motivation that we can comprehend—that is, understand and appreciate—why others believe, feel, or act as they do. At this level we can see that a person's motivations are genuine, and hence both comprehensible and "not unreasonable."

If ultimately what is at issue in a political disagreement is a conflict between human values (and the needs they reflect), the motivations involved are ones that each of us, whatever our experiences and priorities, can understand and appreciate. If we can specify the values in conflict and identify the needs that underlie them, we might transform our political disagreements into discussions about things that each of us can recognize as a comprehensible source of human motivation. Getting to such motivations requires that people talk with each other. As we will see in chapter 6, however, not just any sort of talk will do. Only talk that enables and encourages people to identify the actual sources of their motivation, and to explain these to one another in a way that permits them to be understood and appreciated, will promote the resolution of conflict (especially deep-rooted conflict) and hence the settling of disagreements that result from such conflict. If our political discourse remains stuck at the level of debate over opinions, preferences, or positions—or even (especially) Values—discussion is likely to prove inconclusive, with the result that people will become even more frustrated, angry, and inflexible.

# 5

# First Principle: Inclusion

*The whole purpose of democracy is that we may hold counsel with one another, so as not to depend upon the understanding of one man.*
—Woodrow Wilson

**First Principle: Inclusion.** Strive to include every member of your community in the process of making decisions and taking action. Don't expect people who are left out to lend their support. And remember that many heads are better than a few: if you don't include everyone, you're just depriving your community of important information, valuable experience, good ideas, and much-needed resources.

Who is the public? As the term is used today, "the public" can mean several things. Sometimes it means a majority or plurality of people, as inferred, for example, from the results of an opinion poll. Other times it means those folks who make their views known to elected officials with respect to a particular matter of concern. "The public" might also mean the representatives and spokespersons for the various groups and interests that constitute a community. Or it might mean "ordinary folks," those members of the "silent majority," who usually don't involve themselves in public affairs.

Practical politics understands "the public" as meaning *all* citizens. An effective community decision-making process has to make room for meaningful participation by all citizens for two kinds of reasons, one moral and one practical.

## The Moral Argument for Inclusion

Democracy rests, both historically and theoretically, on respect for the equal moral worth of all persons. We might think of democracy as the political expression of the Golden Rule: I should do unto you (in my actions having consequences for you) as I would like you to do unto me. In other words, I'm morally obliged to show the same concern and respect for you that I want you to show for me. In theory, therefore, each person ought to be able to withhold his or her consent from public decisions he sincerely believes to be contrary to his or her interests.

Why is unanimous consent required in theory? Because the value that you and I place on our respective individual lives raises the question of the legitimacy of *any* form of collective decision making. How can we justify subordinating your interests (and hence freedom) to mine? The principle of democracy derives from the value to each person of his or her individual life and the consequent desire of each person to live free of interference with his efforts to secure the things he wants and needs. As Aristotle observed, "the basis of a democratic state is liberty." Abraham Lincoln also saw the connection between freedom and democracy: "As I would not be a slave," he said, "so I would not be a master. This expresses my idea of democracy. Whatever differs from this . . . is no democracy." In principle, then, the policies we decide upon ought to be approved by each of us. Decisions should be unanimous. This is so because my moral worth and the value of my ends are neither more nor less valuable (to me) than yours are (to you). In principle, there can be no justification for my forcing you to acquiesce to my wishes if you do not share them. We value democracy because we believe that "what touches all must be approved by all." Hence the importance of *inclusion* as the first principle of practical politics.

In practice, of course, democratic decision-making institutions rarely require unanimous consent. Sometimes they require a majority of two-thirds or even three-quarters. But typically, only a simple majority is needed. We should recognize the principle of majority rule for what it is, however: a compromise, a concession to the fact that unanimity is unworkable. Both fairness and self-interest recommend that, if as communities and a society we want to get anything done, we as individuals must drop our insistence on the personal authority to veto collective decisions we dislike.

As I pointed out in chapter 1, however, majoritarian decision making has its drawbacks. As a principle of democratic decision making it is more workable than unanimous consent. But that doesn't mean it's satisfactory. Nor does it mean it can't be improved upon. The argument of this book is that "practical politics"— a practice of democratic decision making built around the principles of inclusion, comprehension, deliberation, cooperation, and realism—represents an improvement upon the strategy of making decisions by mechanically aggregating ("adding up") the preferences, desires, or opinions of the individual citizens we (mistakenly) regard as "the public." I believe that the approach embodied in the five principles fulfills democracy's requirement of equal concern and respect for all citizens more fully than do alternative approaches. But it, too, must come to terms with the fact that unanimous consent is, for all practical purposes, unworkable. As I note below, it is not imperative even in practical politics that every individual be actively involved with respect to every matter of public concern. What is imperative is that, as we undertake the tasks of forming a public perspective, reaching a public judgment, and making a public choice, we demonstrate equal concern and respect for all citizens by ensuring that they have a meaningful opportunity to participate in this process and to have their needs, concerns, and interests understood and appreciated by their fellows. Democracy makes inclusion a moral requirement. If it is democratic decision making we wish to engage in, and not some other kind of politics, then we have a duty to include everyone in the decision-making process.

## Practical Arguments for Inclusion

A practice of democratic decision making built on the principle of inclusion is — in the long-run and all things considered—the best way to ensure that we respond effectively to the problems, challenges, and opportunities our communities will face. Failing to honor the first principle of practical politics—*inclusion*—undercuts a community's efforts to devise effective responses. It does so in three ways: by making the decision-making process unproductive or even counterproductive; by discouraging people from taking personal responsibility for the community's well-being; and by impeding our efforts to ascertain what is good (valuable, desirable) for us, both as individuals and as communities.

### EXCLUSION IS UNPRODUCTIVE

Today, few communities can expect to respond effectively to the problems, challenges, and opportunities they face by relying on a few experts, professionals, managers, or specialists to devise and implement effective policies. The fact is, if we want policies that enjoy strong, widespread support, and that as a result stand a chance of remaining in place long enough to work, ordinary people must be involved, and involved in a meaningful way, from the very outset of the decision-making process.

Why? One reason is that few things are as simple and straightforward as they were in earlier times. The roots of problems such as underemployment, functional illiteracy, poverty, crime, air pollution, urban congestion, and other contemporary ills lie in a tangle of multiple contributing factors. We need everyone's perspective in order to understand them adequately. Think about the fable of the blind men and the elephant. The experience of the blind man who touches the animal's trunk needs to be complemented by the perspective of (among others) the blind man who encounters the creature's left hind leg. None of us can know the whole of the elephant. By myself I can't see the whole picture. My vantage point, like yours and everyone else's, is partial. The challenge is to preserve the distinctiveness of each perspective as we complement each by taking in every other perspective. This isn't to say that all views are "equal," that any view is as valid or true as any other. Some views *are* better than others. But by itself, a single view is incomplete—it captures only part of reality.

In a public disagreement over, say, criminal violence, the contention that poverty causes such violence is not false, any more than is the contention that violent behavior is caused by child abuse, or the absence of a strong father figure, or the character of a permissive society, or the persistence of racism, or the need for "respect" (i.e., self-esteem), or the decline of religion, or the failure to punish offenders surely and severely. No single viewpoint can capture reality in its full complexity. Each has something to contribute to our understanding; by itself, none is complete. If we don't include every perspective in our community, we deprive ourselves of valuable experience, insights, and information, which we need if we're going to arrive at a thorough, comprehensive understanding of the problem, challenge, or opportunity before us.

A related reason why communities can't work effectively without the meaningful participation of ordinary people is that the complexity and deep-rootedness of the problems and challenges we encounter require not only the experience and insight of a large number and diversity of people, but also their ideas, their creativity, and their energies. Official representatives of organizations and institutions tend to be too wedded to particular solutions. Consumerist politics both entices and forces these folks to defend the positions they have staked out. Their power and their jobs depend on meeting the inflexible demands of their constituencies. For genuinely effective policies to be devised, the decision-making process requires the liberating and moderating influence of people who are able to bring creativity and new energy to bear on the effort to respond to it.

## EXCLUSION IS COUNTERPRODUCTIVE

Current social, economic, and technological changes are dispersing power and authority more widely than ever before. If it seems that no one's in control anymore, it's because today a great many people have enough influence to demand that their views be taken into account. In itself this isn't a bad thing; on the contrary, a wider distribution of power and authority is more egalitarian, more democratic. But it also poses a challenge: unless people who can exert political influence are included in the decision-making process, they can prevent decisive action from being taken. Sometimes they can block it outright, other times they can delay it or water it down to the point where it has no impact.

A few years ago, for example, a rural area in Appalachia was suffering from serious unemployment and underdevelopment.[1] Public officials considered and pursued several policies designed to bring jobs and money into their area, but without success. Eventually, a proposal was developed to create a landfill for out-of-state solid waste. Public officials studied the proposal carefully. They talked with members of the public about the proposal. They publicized it in the newspaper, on the radio, and on the street. They held public meetings. Everything they heard was positive. Only a handful of people had questions about the project.

Yet at the last minute, just as the contract was about to be signed, opposition to the project materialized. The first stirrings of dissent came from a local teacher. He didn't know officials hadn't yet signed the deal, but he felt he had to act quickly to stop it. He organized a group called DIE-PROP: Dump It Elsewhere—People against Ruining Our Paradise. The group stirred up fears that toxic waste would be brought from out of state into their pristine valley.

For months a political battle raged. Pro-landfill officials ran ads calling their opponents "environmental radicals." Employers received anonymous phone calls informing them which of their workers had attended DIE-PROP meetings. People taunted each other in the street. Officials began to press for a referendum on the landfill. But DIE-PROP, which initially had called for such a vote, was feeling its political oats and now opposed a referendum. DIE-PROP wasn't willing to risk losing on a popular vote. The group's members realized they had a better chance of appealing directly to the governor, who was up for reelection in the fall and in no mood to enrage a well-organized citizens' group. DIE-PROP turned on the heat. Carloads of landfill opponents streamed into the state capital for a week's worth of rallying and lobbying lawmakers. They were followed by a band of unemployed folks, who were bused in to fight for what they saw as their best shot for a decent job.

The governor eventually agreed to a bill limiting the size of the state's landfills to thirty thousand tons a month. His compromise solution amounted to a *de facto* ban, however, because even at fifty thousand tons a landfill that meets EPA standards can't make the kind of money the waste-hauling industry has come to expect. In the end, four years after it was proposed, the project had to be abandoned, and the county is now back to square one.

This story illustrates one of the flaws in the consumerist version of democratic politics that I discussed in chapter 1: people who feel left out of the process by which political decisions are made tend to gravitate toward forms of political behavior that are essentially coercive. The point here is not that the opponents of the proposed landfill were wrong to oppose it. Rather, it is that, when people are excluded (intentionally or unintentionally), or feel excluded, from the policy-making process, the outcome is apt to prove costly to all concerned.

Although, like initiatives and referendums used to take decisions out of the hands of policy makers, popular efforts to veto or block governmental decisions do put the public back into politics, they do so at a huge cost to the civic fabric of our communities.

Every community has groups and individuals with considerable power to influence what the community as a whole can do. Some of these folks have found in the past that they can get their way by pressuring others. Some take perverse pleasure in antagonizing their opponents. Others simply can't see that there's an alternative to adversarial competition. Many, however, feel frustrated by their inability to make their real concerns known and their influence felt. They sincerely believe that their real interests cannot be represented, at least in current circumstances, by anyone but themselves—including persons who claim to speak for or on behalf of "the public."

But whatever the explanation for people's disinclination to work together in a pragmatic effort to solve a problem, meet a challenge, or seize an opportunity, the fact remains that we should not expect people who do not participate in the decision-making process to support the decision we eventually reach. Purely as a practical political matter, therefore, achieving effective, widely supported public policies requires the attempt to include all stakeholders in the decision-making process.[2] The process must permit everyone who is affected by the problem, who will be affected by any attempt to solve it, or who believes he or she will be affected, to have a real say in the formation of the community's response.[3]

## EXCLUSION DISCOURAGES THE TAKING OF RESPONSIBILITY

In chapter 1 I argued that consumerist politics undermines personal responsibility for resolving conflicts that originate within the public. Here, I want to argue specifically that failing to respect the first principle of practical politics by excluding members of a community from the public decision-making process discourages people from taking personal responsibility for the well-being of their community.

There's a saying in philosophy: "ought implies can." It's pointless to insist that a person has a duty or an obligation to act in a certain way if he or she is unable to take that action. For example, it wouldn't make sense for me to expect my son to pick up his sister after her soccer practice if he hasn't yet obtained his driver's license or even learned to drive. "Ought implies can" has a psychological correlate: if a person lacks the authority or power to carry out an alleged duty or obligation, he is unlikely to accept that he has such a duty or obligation and hence will not be disposed to act in the desired way. If I were to tell my son that it's his responsibility to pick up his sister, he would be justified in asking how this can be so when he's clearly unable to do what I've told him he should do. After a couple of such reminders, he would undoubtedly begin to feel rather annoyed, and understandably so—who wouldn't be irritated by being told he must do what he obviously can't do? A proper response would be, "It's not my responsibility because there's nothing I can do about it—so do it yourself or leave me alone!"

If people believe they lack the political authority or power to act in response to a matter of public concern, they will not take personal responsibility for responding to it. If they feel there is little or nothing they can contribute to the discussion, or if they believe they have no real choice, or if they believe they will have little or no influence in the decision-making process, they will not accept responsibility for working with their fellow citizens to address it. Their motto might be, "Don't expect me to take responsibility if there's nothing I can do about it anyway." Indeed, we shouldn't be surprised if people act "irresponsibly," that is, in a way that undermines or obstructs the good-faith efforts of others. Who can blame them? Even at the best of times it's frustrating, demoralizing, and alienating to feel we're powerless to act.

This is why excluding people from the public decision-making process is so harmful to the cause of generating effective responses to the problems, challenges, and opportunities confronting our communities. All of us need to feel we have a measure of control over our lives. The less control we feel we have over events in the larger world we live in, the more we will want to exert some control over the public life of the communities where we live. If I'm not included in the decision-making process in a manner and to a degree that lets me feel I can make a contribution and can influence the decisions that affect me, I will conclude—understandably even if not justifiably—that the work of my community is someone else's responsibility, not mine. And if I believe the work of my community *should* be my responsibility but I'm prevented from assuming that responsibility, I may use what influence I do enjoy to disrupt or nullify the process from which I feel excluded. Because we want to believe—and for the most part do believe—that our communities are democracies, disillusionment sets in quickly when the public decision-making process comes to seem democratic in name only. The irony of lacking political authority and power in a system in which citizens are supposed to be the ultimate source of such authority and power is not lost on any of us. When it grows too strong and persists too long, that irony breeds frustration, estrangement, cynicism, and eventually apathy, despair, or anger.

The remedy for this political malady must include reengagement by ordinary citizens with the public decision-making process and restoration of their confidence in its ability to produce decisions that have demonstrably effective results. Meaningful inclusion in the decision-making process—enabling all citizens to make their concerns known, to have their needs and interests acknowledged and addressed, to be treated seriously, fairly, and respectfully, and to be accorded influence appropriate to their standing as citizens—is a precondition for the acceptance of personal responsibility for a community's well-being.

## EXCLUSION IMPEDES THE PUBLIC PROCESS OF ASCERTAINING THE GOOD

In chapter 2 I argued that conflicts between good things are indeterminate. When valuable or desirable things conflict, I cannot know, in advance of deliberation with my fellow citizens, what is best or right to do. All I can do is strive to reach a sound judgment. But to make the best judgment I'm capable of, I need to test and supplement what I believe by exposing my views to sources of information other than my existing beliefs and desires. Because my own experience, information, and abilities are limited, I need to consult other people. Including in the decision-making process persons whose views differ from mine provides me with an opportunity to clarify and reevaluate my initial position. Excluding any members of my community from the decision-making process deprives me of information, experience, and insights I need in order to reach the soundest *personal* judgment of which I'm capable.

If indeterminacy makes it difficult for an individual to decide which of several good things he or she ought to give priority, it makes the achievement of a sound collective judgment a far more daunting challenge. By definition, the question of what is good, best, or right for a community as a whole cannot be answered without taking account of what the community's constituent members—individual citizens—believe is good, best, or right, both for themselves as individuals and for the community of which they are a part. Excluding any member of a community from its deliberations thus renders the ultimate decision maker—the community as a whole—incomplete. And because it does so, excluding anyone from the decision-making process deprives the community of the information—experiences, sensitivities, perceptions, concerns, needs, interests, Values, principles, and priorities—that it requires in order to make the soundest *collective* judgment of which it is capable. We cannot know what is good, best, or right for our community as a whole unless everyone who has information relevant to that determination is present and able to offer it for our consideration.

## Politics Face-to-Face

Other things being equal, discussing matters of public concern face-to-face is more likely to prove productive than discussion that is mediated by institutions such as government and newspapers. As Daniel Kemmis points out,[4] when people in political disagreement address each other indirectly—whether through letters to the editor, comments at public hearings, or phone calls to their city councilors—they rarely engage in genuine exchange. They listen not to understand, but to win a debate. They hear what they are predisposed to hear: statements that confirm their fears and suspicions. This is what they hear because it's what they expect and what they have prepared themselves for. As a consequence, they tend to see those who disagree with them as caricatures—as oversimplified, unsympathetic representatives of beliefs, attitudes, and positions they reflexively dislike.

Face-to-face interaction makes it difficult to sustain caricatures and stereotypes. Literally to see the other person is to begin to put a human face on our disagreement. The antagonist in our presence has a name, and with that name comes an identity, a personal history, and a humanity. To be sure, face-to-face exchange by no means guarantees constructive, productive political discourse. (If it did, television public affairs shows would be paragons of civic—and civil—discourse.) But it is important enough to justify going to great lengths to secure it. When one has to look the other person in the eye, it is much less easy to engage in the kind of behavior—be it dogmatic, close minded, indifferent, contemptuous, condescending, combative, or angry—that inhibits the resolution or moderation of disagreement. Misunderstanding is less likely as well, for the simple reason that we communicate so much nonverbally, through tone of voice, posture, and gestures.

For those of us (and that's still the vast majority of us, thankfully) who are neither pathological liars nor seasoned practitioners of the arts of negotiation, public relations, poker, and other forms of socially sanctioned dissembling, more of our common humanity comes through when we speak face-to-face. This is significant because, as I will make clear in chapters 6 and 8, the key to the success of practical politics is the rehumanization of our civic relationships. Because so many issues of public policy turn on value conflicts—conflicts between courses of action or states of affairs each of which embodies something of understandable human aspiration—it is important to bring those conflicts to life. Turning the values in conflict from abstractions into good things having concrete importance for real, flesh-and-blood human beings is imperative for the achievement of the "mutual comprehension," the reciprocal understanding and appreciation that is essential to the formation of an integrated public perspective. When we see and hear our fellow citizens identify the things they value and explain why they're concerned about protecting them, the hard choice we face as a community is rendered vivid, immediate, and comprehensible. Face-to-face exchange enables us to develop a more complex, more realistic—more human—picture of those with whom we disagree. We begin to see that our fellows are human beings too, with comprehensible needs and motivations. Face-to-face discussion helps us respect the moral standing of those with whom we have to live even though we disagree. Precisely for this reason, it encourages us to live up to the commitments we make in the course of reaching a collective decision. It makes us more accountable to each other, and so makes us more reliable partners.

## The Practicality of Inclusion

### THE PROBLEM OF NUMBERS

America is a nation of more than a quarter of a billion people, the great majority of whom live in urban areas with populations in the tens or hundreds of thousands. In our country today, even at the local level of government it is not possible to include literally everyone simultaneously in a single forum for public discussion. A community of even a few thousand cannot fit everyone into the town hall or the high school gym to discuss decisions that have to be made. It's simply not possible for literally every citizen to participate all the time, especially if we place a premium on face-to-face interaction.[5]

While conceding this difficulty, we can, however, insist that everyone have a genuine opportunity to participate. What is important is that everyone feel entitled to participate, welcome to join in, and able to influence the decision. If individuals choose not to take part, they should nevertheless feel assured that others who share their perspective will articulate their concerns. Each person should feel that his or her experiences, beliefs, interests, fears, and needs will be understood, appreciated, and acknowledged.

The concession we make to the reality of numbers—relaxing the requirement that literally every citizen must be included in the public decision-making process and substituting the requirement of a genuine opportunity to participate—only mitigates the challenge, however; it doesn't eliminate it. As will become clear in what follows, we still face a substantial obstacle to achieving a satisfactory level of inclusion. In the next section we will look at a tool—the community conference—as a potentially useful mechanism for involving a large and representative number of citizens in the public decision-making process.

### THE COMMUNITY CONFERENCE

The greater the number of citizens who involve themselves in discussing a matter of public concern, and the more constructive the setting in which they do so, the better able they will be to move together toward a response that will enjoy sufficiently deep and widespread support to have the desired effect. In our communities today, we lack readily usable public forums where citizens can meet each other (and policy makers can meet with them), not to complain, criticize, and assign blame, but to deliberate together. An effective decision-making process must therefore enable a large number of people to carry on a sustained, informed discussion. It must also create a truly public, neutral space where all citizens will feel welcome, safe, respected, and hence inclined to talk, think, and work together.

How might a community initiate and sustain such a discussion among a large group of people? Broadly speaking, there are two ways to go about this. One I call, somewhat whimsically, the "contagious" approach, the other the "concerted" approach. By the former I mean simply informally convening groups of citizens to discuss a matter of public concern, and then encouraging participants to convene additional groups. The "contagious" approach might be likened to a chain letter or "pyramid" scheme: every person who participates in a forum organized by one of his or her fellow citizens is encouraged to organize one of his own, to which he will invite a new group of persons who haven't participated previously. The process expands, spontaneously, as far as people are willing to take it.

The advantage of this approach lies in the low degree of coordination it requires. The downside is that it doesn't provide for connections between the outcome of any particular group's discussions and those of other groups. More important, there is no direct link to the governmental policy-making process. "Free-standing" forums may not generate a clear "community voice" that will give impetus to and authorize the adoption of a widely supported, durable, effective policy. For this reason, I recommend consideration of a more highly coordinated, "concerted" approach to involving the public: the *community conference*.[6]

A community conference might take any one of several forms (see table 1 and figure 3). The version I am going to discuss here combines open participation with a random representative sample of a community's residents.[7] As I noted above, even in small towns and cities it isn't feasible to assemble thousands of people in one place at one time for the purpose of deliberating the community's options and reaching a public judgment about what to do. As a practical matter, the next best thing is to combine multiple opportunities for active participation in small open forums with a "conference proper" that includes a randomly selected group of citizens who reflect the diversity of the community. (See versions

*Compare Jury duty...*

*Table 1.* Some Possible Forms of a Community Conference

| First Round | Conference Proper |
|---|---|
| 1. Community forums open to all citizens | Conference proper open to all citizens |
| 2. Community forums open to all citizens | Delegates from the open community forums |
| 3. Community forums open to all citizens | A random sample of participants from the open community forums |
| 4. Community forums open to all citizens | A random sample of the community |
| 5. Community forums open to all citizens | Delegates from the open community forums, *plus* a random sample of nonparticipating members of the community |
| 6. Community forums open to all citizens | A random sample of participants from the open community forums, *plus* a random sample of nonparticipating members of the community |
| 7. Public information-and-study period; no community forums | A random sample of the community |

Version 2: Community forums
open to all citizens.

Delegates from the open community
forums attend the conference proper.

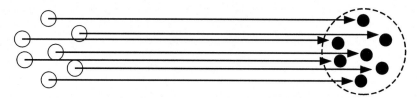

Version 3: Community forums
open to all citizens.

Randomly selected participants from
the open community forums attend
the conference proper.

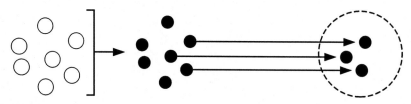

Version 4: Community forums
open to all citizens.

Randomly selected community members
attend the conference proper.

*Figure 3.* Three Varieties of Community Conference

3, 4, 5, and 6 in table 1.)[8] This combination reflects the importance of trying to honor two competing goods: the *opportunity* for anyone who wishes to do so to participate, and the *representativeness* of those who participate.[9]

The opportunity to participate is afforded by a number of small forums held in various locations over the course of several weeks. Each is open to anyone to attend. Sites should be "citizen-friendly"—they should be close by and convenient to reach, familiar, and socially, culturally, and politically "safe." At the conclusion of each forum, participants select one or more persons from their number to represent the forum's perspective in succeeding rounds of the community-wide discussion.[10] Small, open forums maximize the opportunity for citizens to participate actively and to engage each other in face-to-face discussion in a comfortable setting. Small forums allow ordinary people's concerns, needs, fears, and aspirations to be articulated and transmitted to the culminating event—the conference proper.

Undoubtedly, the most challenging component of a community conference is the task of organizing and conducting a potentially large number of small, open public forums. Let's consider three examples, one a small community of 5,000, the second a medium-sized city of 50,000, the third a large city of 500,000. Assuming an average household is made up of four persons—two adults and two children—then the first community has about 1,250 households, the second about 12,500, and the third about 125,000.

Suppose folks in these three communities want to hold a public discussion, and they want as many households as possible to participate. But they also want everyone to have a chance to express his or her views and to discuss them thoroughly with others. How big should each forum be? Between 15 and 25 participants is optimal. Assuming one person from each household, and assuming a participation rate of only 30 percent (which is bound to be on the high side and might take years to achieve), how many forums would the first community have to conduct? In the small community, 30 percent of 5,000 households divided by, let's say, 25 participants per forum is 15—a manageable number of forums. For the second community, the number of 150—an unwieldy number of forums, though less so than the 1,500 forums the third community would have to organize.

Because of the difficulty of offering enough forums for citizens to talk with each other in groups small enough to permit substantial exchanges, medium-sized and large communities might opt to select conference participants by making use of random samples (see versions 3, 4, and 6 in table 1).[11] These variations call for a workable number of open forums to be held at different locations throughout the community. The number might range from a handful—say, a half-dozen—to a substantial number (perhaps twenty to thirty). Delegates to the conference proper would be selected from a random sample of those who participate in the open forums. These delegates would be joined at the conference by another randomly selected sample of citizens who attend one of the open forums (version 3), the public as a whole (version 4), or a combination of the two (version 6).[12]

The conference should use the same formulation of the matter to be discussed and the same deliberative format employed in the open forums. (For more on formulating a subject for public discussion and deliberating, see chapter 6.) It should be considerably lengthier, however—six to twelve hours over one or two days, rather than just two or three hours on a single evening or Saturday morning—in order to give the larger composite group a chance to deliberate thoroughly together.

Between the last of the small, open public forums and the conference proper, it is important to report back to the community (e.g., through newspaper stories, an interim written report to be made available at various public locations, or interviews and speaking engagements). People deserve to know what general, tentative conclusions have emerged from the discussion up to this point. The chief purpose of feedback is to assure participants that their views have been heard and will find expression in the upcoming conference. A second purpose is to enhance the sense of community-wide deliberation—to foster the feeling of a community in dialogue—by calling attention to both similarities and differences in the perspectives articulated in each of the small forums. Finally, a third purpose is to help people understand the hard choice that the community faces, to call attention to the consequences of different options, to convey that tradeoffs will have to be made, and to stimulate people to begin thinking about a direction for action that might win general assent.

Someone will have to take the initiative to organize the conference process.[13] The best place for an inclusive public discussion to originate is with citizens whose desire for a particular substantive outcome does not overwhelm their loyalty to the principle of inclusive, deliberative community decision making. What is needed at the outset is a workably small group of citizens who are—and whose fellow citizens will view them as—committed to the principles of inclusion, comprehension, deliberation, cooperation, and realism. Care must be taken, however, when enlisting the aid of persons and organizations whose resources, standing, reputation, or prominence seem to make them the logical or obvious organizers of such an undertaking. It's precisely these assets that can render them suspect in the eyes of people who must not be left out of the conversation. Don't reject them out of hand, but be wary of good people who are accustomed to using their power and influence to "get things done." They sometimes confuse what's good for the community with their own goals and agendas.

Bearing this caveat in mind, it should be possible nevertheless to identify potentially valuable allies in the cause of getting a conference underway: the public library, a community college, the League of Women Voters, a community foundation, the town newspaper, the local citizens' league, a public TV or radio station, a religious interfaith council, or a service organization (for example, Kiwanis or Rotary). Depending on the matter of public concern you want to take up, other organizations may be willing to help organize the process. (For example, a hospital or health maintenance organization might serve as a cosponsor of a discussion of rising health care costs. Again, exercise caution in cases where a willing sponsor might have a strong interest in advancing a particular viewpoint or solution.) Organizations such as leadership groups, chambers of commerce, neighborhood associations, and professional associations can be approached, though it's important to keep in mind that enlisting the aid of one kind of organization might necessitate balancing your small band of organizers with people who take a different view initially of the matter to be discussed. If you want to take up race relations, for example, your organizing group obviously shouldn't be composed of people of just one race. If you want to discuss your community's economic development, you ought to have someone from an anti- or slow-growth organization as well as from the chamber of commerce and the realtors' association.

In general, it's desirable for your organizing group to be widely perceived as nonpartisan, diversely constituted, and civic minded. If you can't guarantee that it will be regarded as such, at least make sure you include persons who represent the range of perspectives, interests, and attitudes in your community. And don't forget about people who might seem indifferent. They might care a great deal but in the past just haven't been involved much.

Perhaps the biggest challenge that conference participants will face is how to connect afterward with their fellow citizens and public officials who did not participate in person. Although there will always be a danger that some participants in the conference process will treat their conclusions as something that they have to "sell" to others,[14] the greater danger by far is that people who do not participate will regard those conclusions as the conclusions of a particular group, not those that the community as a whole would reach. This is why participation must be as widespread and as representative of the community's diversity as possible. The more broadly representative the participant group is of the community as a whole, the more disposed everyone will be to treat the judgment arrived at by the conference as the judgment of the community.

Even in the best circumstances, however, there will be persons who, because they chose not to participate or because they disagree with the conclusions reached by the conference, will question the representativeness of the delegates and the legitimacy of the process. (This is especially likely in the case of persons who have narrow agendas or who do not wish, for whatever reason, to take into account the concerns and interests of their fellow citizens.) The challenge for conference delegates, then, is to determine how best to proceed. How should they approach their nonparticipating fellow citizens? What should they say and do? How might they move the judgment they've reached and the general direction they've arrived at outside of their group into the larger community? Conference participants have a number of options, which we will consider in chapter 9.

It's important to help the local news media capture the essence of the conference and to distinguish it from politics-as-usual. The real story of public discussion in a community conference is not the "score," the tally for and against different options, people's comments taken out of context, or the conclusions that individuals have reached. The real story is the give-and-take, the listening as well as speaking, the sharing and comparing of personal experiences, the reflection, the grappling with a problem, the weighing of consequences, the facing up to hard choices by the group as a whole. The conference should be reported not as a referendum but as a conversation among citizens that requires interpretation. To use an analogy from sports, the "story" is not the score at the end of the game, or the statistics that have been compiled, but rather the "dynamic drama" of the event: What was the real struggle and why did it go one way rather than another? What were the turning points? What dilemmas did people face? What concerns did they have? How did they resolve conflicts? Were they able to understand, appreciate, and acknowledge each other's viewpoints even if they disagreed with them? What common ground were they able to forge? Did they settle on a direction for action that everyone could live with? In short, what collective "voice" did they articulate for their community?[15]

## OTHER AIDS TO PUBLIC PARTICIPATION: THE COUNCIL OF NEIGHBORHOODS

Few communities enjoy a civic structure that allows citizens to participate routinely in conversations about matters of public concern. An example of such a structure is the *council of neighborhoods*. A council of neighborhoods parallels and complements the governmental structure of a community. It creates a public "space" where citizens can talk with each other.

An analogy might make this idea clearer. In many public school districts each school has a parent-teacher organization (PTO, or PTA). Parents, teachers, and (sometimes) community representatives meet regularly to discuss school affairs. The president or chairperson of each PTO represents his or her organization on a district "council of PTOs." The council provides a forum where PTOs can communicate with each other. The PTO system is in effect a "civic" structure that parallels the official governing structure of the school district: the school board (see figure 4). Analogously, a council of neighborhoods would parallel and complement a community's municipal government in the same way that the PTO structure parallels and complements the government of the school district (see figure 5).

The importance of the council of neighborhoods lies in its ability to facilitate "lateral" or "horizontal" community discussion. It creates a public "space" where citizens can communicate with each other. In the absence of a civic structure such as the council of neighborhoods, communication by and large remains confined to "vertical" channels connecting citizens with government through city council sessions, hearings, and other formal venues. The council of neighborhoods is a vehicle by which neighbors and neighborhoods might communicate with each other—a precondition for the public deliberation that must occur before people can reach a judgment and make a choice together, as a community. goal.

Here are two anecdotes that illustrate why a civic structure such as the council of neighborhoods is desirable. When Joe and Judy moved into their neighborhood there was no existing neighborhood association. Joe created a loose, unofficial association by preparing a two-page newsletter and sending it to their neighbors. Those who indicated they would like to receive the newsletter (about a third of the households in the immediate area) went onto his mailing list, which constituted the association "membership." At one point Joe asked folks whether they would like to ask the city to design a logo for their neighborhood and affix it to street signs, as it had done for three other neighborhoods. The response was favorable (in fact, no one objected), and they chose a red fox.

Shortly after the new signs went up—to general acclaim—an irate resident,

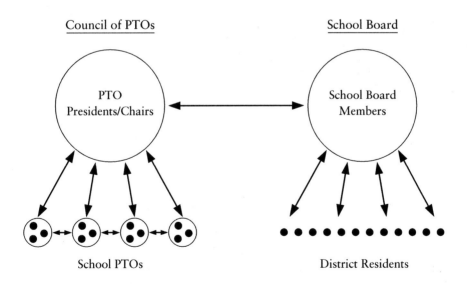

*Figure 4.* Parallel Educational Structures:
Relation between Council of PTOs and School Board

Council of Neighborhoods    City Council

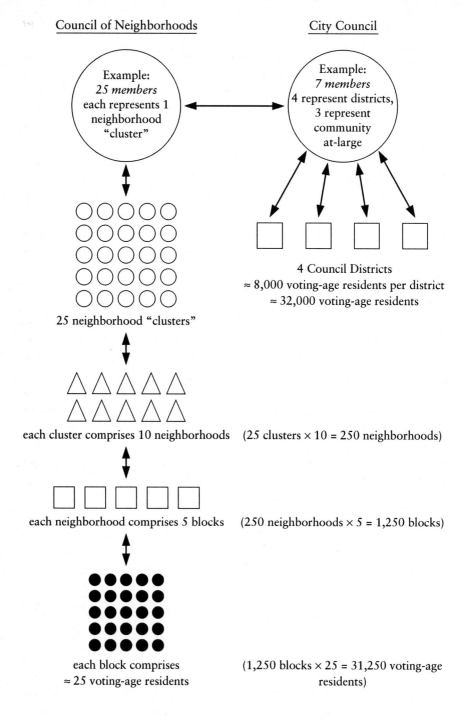

*Figure 5*. Parallel Civic Structures:
Relation between Council of Neighborhoods and City Council

who was not a member of the neighborhood association, called the city's public services director and berated him for not having informed people of the city's action. (He had no specific objection to the new signs. He simply thought the city should not have "wasted money" on them.) The public services director explained that the city had acted in response to a request from the neighborhood association. The resident ranted about not believing in neighborhood associations and not wanting to belong to one. The public services director's response was that belonging to the association (which has no covenant, no rules, no officers, no membership fee) and receiving its newsletter would have given him the chance to express his views to his neighbors, and thereby to influence their decision. But he thought he should be able to speak directly to the city and demand that it conform to his wishes. In essence, he wanted to be able to exercise a personal veto. He did not want to have to put up with the potentially conflicting views of his neighbors, even though, ironically, he probably would have had greater influence had he worked with them through the association.

The second anecdote involves a matter of common concern in the neighborhood: the volume and speed of traffic passing through to and from the high school in the area. Residents on one of the streets that are most affected have on many occasions urged measures such as installing "photo-cop" cameras, building sharply angled speed bumps, closing off the street completely, placing a gate across it, extending other streets near the school that currently are dead-ends (thereby creating alternative routes allowing access to the school), and closing the high school to private vehicles. Needless to say, there is little agreement among street residents about which measure should be adopted. Moreover, those who favor particular solutions are adamant that theirs is the only acceptable one. Few are happy with the city's proposal to install "traffic-calming" devices such as islands and traffic circles. No one has expressed appreciation for the unprecedented and creative collaboration between the city and the school district to jointly fund a police officer who has been assigned full-time to the area around the high school. Despite at least three opportunities for residents to meet with their neighbors and city officials to work out a response to the problem, most remain unwilling to budge from their favorite remedy and prefer to express their views directly and in private to city officials.

Moreover—and this is the chief point of this second anecdote—residents of Joe and Judy's neighborhood have no way to communicate with residents in other neighborhoods affected by traffic to and from the school. In particular, they have no way to communicate with the residents of the neighborhoods that currently have no problem with traffic because their streets are dead-ends and do not go through to the school. It is these neighborhoods that residents in Joe and Judy's neighborhood would like to see accept some of the burden by opening their streets to the school. Naturally, residents of these neighborhoods oppose opening the streets. Everyone prefers to speak directly to the city instead of to each other. This is a classic example of "displacement"—conflict that originates within the public is transferred into the institutional decision-making arena, where public officials are subjected to pressure from all sides and are presented with a dilemma that is zero-sum, and that politically is a "no-win" situation. A civic structure that parallels and complements the governmental structure would at least provide citizens with an opportunity to accept responsibility for addressing shared problems. In time, it might encourage people to work together instead of simply making inflexible demands on public officials who, no matter what they do, will leave some people feeling frustrated and angry.

The council of neighborhoods is built on a geographical basis.[16] Its basic unit should be the *block*. The block would consist of residents from a small number of households, people who literally live next door to each other. Suppose your community has 50,000 people, of which, say, 30,000 are of voting age. If we assume that each neighborhood consists of about 5 blocks of homes, and that there are roughly 25 residents of voting age on each block, then there are approximately 1,200 blocks in your community (30,000 ÷ 25 = 1,200), or 240 neighborhoods (1,200 ÷ 5 = 240). If we assume that a workable size for the council is 25 persons, then each member of the council will have to represent roughly 10 neighborhoods (240 ÷ 25 ≈ 10). You might divide your community, then, into "clusters" of about 10 neighborhoods. (Each *cluster* of 10 neighborhoods would thus consist of 50 blocks [because 1 neighborhood = 5 blocks] or 1,250 residents [because 1 block = 25 residents]; see figure 5.)

Your council of neighborhoods thus has four levels: the *block*, the *neighborhood*, the *cluster*, and the *council*. Each block needs to designate a person to represent it within the neighborhood, each neighborhood needs to designate a person to represent it within the cluster, and each cluster needs to designate a person to represent it on the council. The block would meet from time to time (say, every three months and other times as needed) in an informal setting: a room in an elementary school, or a church basement, or someone's living room. Each block would then select one person to meet with representatives of other blocks in their neighborhood. In turn, each neighborhood would select one person to meet with representatives of the other neighborhoods in their cluster. Each cluster would choose someone to represent their ten neighborhoods on the council of neighborhoods, which (like the other levels in the structure) would meet as often as its members deem feasible and desirable. Finally, the council would designate a liaison to communicate with city council.

## Including Government

No matter how well organized citizens are, they can't do everything themselves. Government action of some kind is often necessary or highly desirable. Lamentably, though, it's when the public and government need each other most that officials and citizens often have the greatest trouble communicating with each other. As I noted in the introduction, citizens feel shut out of the policy-making process. They believe public decision making is controlled by organized interests and that they have been abandoned by public officials, who act in their own self-interest and are out of touch with citizens' concerns. People see no way to participate meaningfully in decisions that affect them. For their part, public officials often are as frustrated with the public as the public is with them.[17] They find it nearly impossible to have productive discussions with the public. They see too many people who are impatient, emotional, intolerant of ambiguity and complexity, ill-informed, concerned only with their narrow, immediate interests, and unwilling to face up to and accept unavoidable costs and tradeoffs.

*[margin annotation: power inequality]*

The common assumption that politicians don't care about the public except as voters during an election campaign is an oversimplification. The truth is, neither understands the other very well. Government is fragmented, just as the public itself is. Citizens are insensitive to the jurisdictional problems between departments and between different levels of government. They seldom even know about, let alone sympathize with, the struggle of officials to deal with intra- and intergovernmental conflict and differing (sometimes overlapping) areas of responsibility and authority. Unlike citizens, government officials put a premium on standardized solutions, ones that apply everywhere, with no exceptions for special cases, and that fall clearly within what is legally permitted. Moreover, citizens don't appreciate that the amount of effort needed to turn around government once it has embarked upon a particular course is draining and often demoralizing.

It's important for citizens to understand as well that we are living at a time when the rules for and expectations we have of our public officials are changing. Some policy makers feel caught between the traditional way of conducting a community's business and the demands of an electorate that knows it doesn't like the old way but doesn't know what to put in its place. Most public officials continue to reach out to the public through town meetings, open hearings, visits to organizations, taking polls and making surveys, and listening carefully to what people tell them. But they assume that there are only two options for governing the community. One is to listen to the public's concerns, exercise their own best judgment about what to do, and then devise and implement the best policy. The alternative is to let the community make decisions directly through initiatives or referendums. They see no middle ground between these two extremes—they see no way of governing *with* the public. This polarized way of seeing the relationship between the public and policy makers grows out of the latter's self-conception as leaders and decision makers. In these roles, officials believe they bear sole responsibility for coming up with and implementing solutions. Governing means persuading people to accept solutions that officials have developed.

It's encouraging, therefore, to see that public officials are beginning to recognize that we need a new partnership between government and the community. In *Connecting Citizens and Their Government,* a report issued in 1996, the National League of Cities (NLC) recognized that "the broad divide that separates citizens and government . . . stands in the way of our ability to work together, as communities and as a nation, to solve common problems."[18] According to Mark Schwartz, an Oklahoma City Council member and NLC first vice-president, "A major challenge as we approach the new millennium is connecting citizens and government in a democratic framework of civility and responsibility. . . . To the extent that people don't trust government or just don't care, that has a real impact on what we as elected officials can accomplish."

The authors of *Connecting Citizens and Their Government* go on to observe that "strengthening democracy at the local level is more than a 'feel good' exercise. . . . What is at stake for local officials in working to rekindle a spirit of civility and responsibility among citizens can be summed up in one word: effectiveness." Anthony Capizzi, chair of the NLC advisory council and a Dayton, Ohio, city commissioner, notes, "With public involvement comes public support for solutions to the problems facing our communities." For local elected officials, better involvement by citizens in community decision making carries a number of benefits:

—Citizens develop a better understanding of the complexity of the
   problems and challenges facing government.
—People who have a stake in the outcome of decisions and who will
   be affected by government action are more likely to accept personal
   responsibility for making and implementing those decisions.
—Information and ideas are elicited from a broader audience.
—The entire community, not just government, becomes accountable
   for results.

The challenge is for elected officials to recognize that success in local politics today often requires new approaches to community problem-solving, and therefore to begin redefining their role in the community. According to Carol Ratto of Turlock, California, "this takes us beyond looking at structured city programs to looking at what we can do to help create an environment that encourages people to self-initiate things. It's about creating opportunities for people willingly to become civic-minded and to take responsibility, creating a situation where civility exists without government having to impose it."

Leadership by elected public officials is essential. The authors of *Connecting Citizens and Their Government* list four things officials can do to begin connecting citizens and government.

1. *Serve as a model.* Officials can set the tone for productive problem-solving by maintaining a spirit of civility and cooperation in their relations with each other, with citizens, and with other government officials. According to Frank Benest, city manager of Brea, California, "local government leaders need to take the high road and model positive attitudes and behaviors, especially when dealing with controversial or divisive issues." Taking the high road means focusing on civility and constructive consensus-building. In turn, that means mastering skills quite different from the conventional decision making skills of the traditional politician. Bruce Adams, a former elected official from Montgomery County, Maryland, says that "in order to break political gridlock and solve problems, elected officials . . . must learn the skills of convening, listening, and facilitating."

2. *Serve as a messenger.* Municipal leaders must make it clear to citizens that every member of the community bears responsibility for building a stronger public life. Everyone needs to do his or her part. By bringing people and organizations together, elected officials can plant the seeds for sustained community-wide collaboration.

3. *Create and sustain processes for connecting citizens and government.* Elected officials can devise various means by which citizens might participate in community decision-making. These include visioning processes, citizen advisory panels that represent individual neighborhoods, leadership development programs, and workshops or "charettes" for neighborhood-level planning.

4. *Lead.* Elected officials are in a better position than other members of their community to change the way we make public decisions. Officials need to use their positions to facilitate constructive, productive public discussion. Government in the United States has evolved into a large-scale provider of services, and thus plays an important role in meeting people's needs. But while an emphasis on "customer service" is a healthy antidote to bureaucratic unresponsiveness, there is a danger that it will reinforce the tendency for citizens to see government as bearing sole responsibility for solving problems. Fostering a "customer" mentality among citizens is a recipe for frustration and dissatisfaction, because government acting alone cannot solve the problems that cause a community the greatest concern.

While providing basic services efficiently is what we should expect of good government, the authors of *Connecting Citizens and Their Government* understand that it is time for officials to consider whether a "barn raising" model of governance might be preferable to the service-oriented "vending machine" model. According to Frank Benest, the vending machine approach leads citizens to expect a direct benefit in services for every dollar they pay in taxes or fees. This narrow conception of government's purpose creates the mistaken impression that government is just one service provider among many, no different (in principle) from businesses in the private sector. Citizens start seeing themselves only as individual customers—they have no interest in the needs of others, or in the needs of the community as a whole. "Barn raising," in contrast, asks people to focus on what the community can achieve together. Just as Americans used to come together to raise a neighbor's barn, the members of a community can work together to achieve results they cannot and would not achieve by acting alone.

### FORWARD, TOGETHER

In an interview published in 1997, Gene Feldman, a four-term alderman on the city council of Evanston, Illinois, explained his dawning realization that, despite its best efforts, his community's municipal government was "for all intents and purposes impotent" with respect to many problems facing the community:

> As program after program failed, it became clear that these [matters] were far beyond our ability to deal with and, as I learned from . . . discussions with elected officials all over the country, . . . beyond the ability of most governments. . . . I came into office believing that it was my responsibility to solve the problems facing [my] community. . . . After repeated failures, I began to question . . . whether anyone holding this office could have succeeded where I had failed. [I came to] understand that nowhere was it written that we, as elected officials, had to know and be able to do everything, or be expected to solve every problem . . . , that the responsibility for the solution of major societal problems was shared by our society, our communities, our neighbors.
>
> This understanding is incompatible with the traditional view of a "leader." In the past, officeholders as well as citizens thought of leaders in unrealistic terms—as a solitary figure, the head of an army riding in on a white horse, or as a Solomon, always ready with the wisest decision. . . . The problems of today will not be solved by the lonely figure on a white horse. Present-day problems require a partnership with communities. . . . The future must include a real collaboration between government and community. If there is to be a strong and independent community, there have to be institutions of government that not only allow, but support it. . . . And that means that elected officials must find their way to the insight that allows them to say to themselves, "I want to work with citizens, with an engaged community. I need these people. We need these people. We can't solve our problems with-

out them." . . . All of us must change our perception of citizens as consumers of government services or clients needing government programs, to an understanding of people as responsible, as involved, as effective, and certainly as necessary within the community as any officeholder.[19]

Alderman Feldman is right: citizens and public officials need to establish a new partnership.[20] In this partnership, neither the public nor policy makers should dominate. Each should take responsibility for carrying out those tasks that it is best suited to perform or that only it can do. Public officials ought to concentrate their energies on crafting specific, detailed solutions, not on trying to make the fundamental judgment and choice that only the public can make.

In order to focus on this task, however, the public must set a clear direction for policy makers to follow, one that will indicate the factors they should take into account and the range of responses the public will consider acceptable. Government needs the public; it does not possess the moral and political authority to make the basic judgments and choices that, in a democracy, by definition only the citizenry is entitled to make. A government cannot define a community's purposes (e.g., what do we want to educate our children *for?*) or the standards by which what it does will be evaluated. (For example, a government can't determine what level of risk people ought to be willing to assume. Nor can it determine the point at which a problem becomes "significant" or "intolerable.") A government cannot legitimately determine the basic direction that the community should follow. In conflicts between beliefs about what is good and bad, right and wrong, only we, the public, can decide authoritatively how to resolve such conflicts. We cannot delegate that responsibility to anyone else.[21]

# 6

# Second Principle: Comprehension

---

*To sit silently face to face with a stranger [is] one of the most direct ways I know to persuade oneself that there is no such thing as an individual, that each of us is a multitude.*

—Joel Agee

---

**Second Principle: Comprehension.** Understand the people you disagree with. Beneath their attitudes and positions you will find needs, desires, and feelings you can understand and appreciate. Work to help them understand you better. Mutual comprehension is the key to creating common ground and to avoiding the trap of thinking that there have to be winners and losers.

---

The usual way of conducting the political business of our communities—proposing solutions, debating them, and then voting—results in "solution wars" that, more often than not, fail to produce an effective collective response to the problem, challenge, or opportunity we are facing. Nobody wins solution wars. Nobody wins them because they're inherently unwinnable. They're inherently unwinnable because they grow out of conflicts between human goods that we cannot choose between without loss. No matter which we decide to give priority, we must forego something of value, value that would be realized if we were to choose otherwise. Reconciling conflicts between things we value—that is, deciding what, on balance and all things considered, it would be best to do—requires that we reach a judgment. But solution wars don't advance the task of working toward and reaching a judgment—they impede it. The only way out of the dead-end of solution wars is for us to work together toward a shared, integrated perspective that will serve as the foundation—as the common ground—upon which a widely supported public judgment can be built.

The good news is that, if a conflict between human goods lies at the heart of a political issue, then those goods are ones that all members of the public have the capacity to understand and appreciate. The key to arriving at a sound and widely supported public judgment, as opposed to a mechanically obtained political result, is for all members of the public to "comprehend"—to understand and appreciate—the goods in conflict and the human values and needs they reflect. Reciprocal understanding and appreciation, or "mutual comprehension," makes it possible to recast a political issue as a question of how jointly to prioritize goods that everyone can acknowledge as legitimate sources of political motivation. Mutual comprehension allows us to reformulate a political disagreement as a difficult choice—a shared, collective choice—that bids us deliberate together for the purpose of arriving at a sound judgment about how to resolve the underlying conflict. Mutual comprehension creates common ground—a shared understanding and appreciation of goods in conflict—that otherwise would not exist. In doing so it gives people the chance to back off the positions they have staked out and that give rise to the perception of a "zero-sum" dispute. Mutual comprehension helps dispel the perception that one party's gain is necessarily another party's loss.[1] It does so by encouraging them to think and work together at the level of the underlying, "*non*-zero-sum" sources of their differences. The ability and willingness of people to comprehend other people's motivations is the key to rendering politically inert the malign effects of perceived zero-sumness. The second requirement of practical politics—its second principle—must therefore be (mutual) *comprehension.*

## Motivation and Public Perspective

In chapter 4 I argued that the belief that value will be realized or obtained gives rise to the motivation to act. *A value* is the object of such a motivating belief: an experience, action, or state of affairs that produces some form of satisfaction. "Small-v" values—that is, things that have value, things that yield satisfaction—do not motivate me to act. What motivates me to act is a *belief,* an intellectual conviction that an experience, action, or state of affairs does or will yield some form of satisfaction for me.

In order for a belief to motivate me to act, however, I must "appreciate" its object, the thing I believe holds value for me. That is, I must feel the "pull" of the prospect of realizing the satisfaction I associate with the object. For example, no matter how much I consciously say to myself that I value courage, if at some deeper, less intellectual level I do not feel drawn in the direction of a satisfaction I can anticipate feeling upon acting courageously, that belief will fail to move me toward action. It's not merely that my desire to act courageously will be overridden by competing desires to realize the satisfaction of other values. Rather, I would experience no impetus toward courageous action whatsoever. A purely intellectual conviction that a course of action or state of affairs holds value for me would not and could not—by itself, in the absence of a nonintellectual appreciation of the thing I believe holds value—motivate me to act.

If I am to reach a personal decision about how to resolve a conflict between competing values, I have to weigh the value likely to be realized by pursuing one course of action against the value likely to be realized by pursuing alternative courses. To be able genuinely to weigh these values, I must "appreciate" each of them—I must feel the "pull" that each exerts upon me. Recognizing this, we can see why *inter*personal disagreements involving conflicting goods are so difficult to resolve. Unlike internal conflicts experienced by a person facing such a choice, disagreements between persons are often marked by the inability or unwillingness of one person fully to appreciate—to feel the "pull" of—the goods that motivate the other. For example, we shouldn't expect to resolve a disagreement over what our public schools should teach and how they should teach it if the parties to the disagreement fail to understand and appreciate the deep-level motivations that underlie their respective positions on the matter. Agreement might continue to elude them, of course; mutual comprehension is not a sufficient condition for the achievement of agreement. But it is a necessary condition; without it, agreement in cases of deeply felt value-based conflict almost always proves unattainable.

In order for two or more persons collectively to deliberate and reach a shared judgment about which of several conflicting goods to assign priority, they must approximate the situation of the individual who realizes that he or she is faced with a choice. We can't act together until first we become *able* to act together. If we fail to comprehend each other, we will be no more able to think and act coherently and effectively than would a person with multiple personalities if all of those "selves" were present simultaneously and were clamoring for the authority to determine the person's action.

Mutual comprehension does not require that I give up or subordinate the deep motivations that underlie my own outlook and disposition. Rather, it requires that, in addition to holding the motivations I hold, I understand and appreciate your motivations so that they become quasi-real for me. Suppose you and I initially are inclined to take different positions with respect to some issue. You take position 1, and I take position 2. Figure 6 shows that, although we have the same motivations, you give priority to motivation $M_1$ (which is third on my list) and I assign priority to $M_3$ (which is third on your list).[2] The different orderings we give our respective motivations—specifically, the conflict between $M_1$ and $M_3$—stand in the way of a shared judgment about which to give priority. If, however, I comprehend your motivations as if they were my own, and you comprehend my motivations as if they were your own, our ability to form a judgment together, and to reach a decision together about what to do, will improve considerably. Mutual comprehension permits us to "reconcile" our conflicting motivations without giving up or subordinating our own.[3] Our mutually comprehended motivational sets might be depicted as in figure 7. Having comprehended each other's motivations, you and I have "reconciled" our conflicting priorities. We are now in a position to make a decision *as if* we were a single decision maker. We are in a position to work toward forming a judgment—together—about which motivation *we* should assign priority.

It is crucial to grasp that mutual comprehension does not require us to abandon our respective individual perceptions and dispositions. Quite the contrary. Each of us has a distinctive perspective on life and the world around us. We are, after all, individuals. Our experiences, our circumstances—even our basic constitutions—vary, giving each of us a unique set of perceptions and dispositions as well as sensitivities, aversions, and receptivities to the states of affairs that can motivate human beings to act. In the United States, we tend to think of ourselves first and foremost—indeed, almost solely—as individuals. Not surprisingly, we conceive of "the public" as a mere aggregate of individual persons or, more recently, as members of narrowly defined groups.[4] Because we're accustomed to taking our sameness for granted and emphasizing instead our individuality, it's

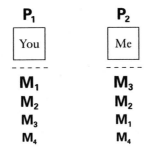

$P_1$ $\quad$ $P_2$

| You | Me |

$M_1$ $\qquad$ $M_3$
$M_2$ $\qquad$ $M_2$
$M_3$ $\qquad$ $M_1$
$M_4$ $\qquad$ $M_4$

*Figure 6.* Differing Motivational Sets

| You | Me |

$M_1\,(M_3)$ $\qquad$ $M_3\,(M_1)$

*Figure 7.* Mutual Comprehension of Motivations

often hard to imagine, let alone adopt, a shared perspective that might encompass each of our individual outlooks. It's difficult to view matters of public concern from a genuinely public perspective. But a genuinely shared perspective is precisely what we require if we're to devise effective, widely supported responses to the problems, challenges, and opportunities that face our communities today.

When I say we have to combine our individual perspectives into a single, integrated, composite perspective that all of us can share, I do not mean that we have to see eye-to-eye. We don't have to reach a thorough-going consensus. Still less do we have to stop desiring or valuing or feeling what we did before engaging each other in the effort to form a shared perspective. Practical politics does not require that people renounce what is fundamentally important to them, whether it be a need, a conviction, a perception, or an identity. It does not ask them to make sacrifices simply for the sake of agreement, to give in simply for the sake of "peace in the family," to compromise simply for the sake of getting along.

What it does ask of us is that we join our individual perspectives in such a way that we lose nothing of the distinctiveness and worth of each individual perspective, while at the same time we enhance each through exposing it to the others. Integration does not entail assimilation. Recall the blind men and the elephant. Their individual perspectives are neither true nor untrue. The point has to do, rather, with completeness. No matter how substantial or significant it is, a single view remains incomplete—it captures only part of reality.

On the other hand, the fact that each individual's perspective is limited and incomplete doesn't mean that all views are "equal," that one view is as good as another. A given view may contain more information, or information that is more accurate, more relevant, more useful, or more important, than that of other views. Some views *are* better than others. Yet, as George Watson has written, "the best view of the Taj Mahal is only one view among many. . . . The best [reading] of *Hamlet* still leaves things out."[5] Every person's perspective has something important to contribute to our understanding. Ignoring it, failing to give it its due, merely deprives us of potentially crucial information. The challenge is to preserve the unique contribution of each perspective while complementing it with the (partial) reality or truth of every other perspective. It is the second principle of practical politics—*comprehension*—that enables us to meet this challenge.

## What Does It Mean to "Comprehend"?

The term "comprehend" has the useful connotation of "encompassing" or "taking in," of "getting our arms around" a thing. To comprehend is to understand and appreciate how some other person, in his or her circumstances, with his or her experiences, needs, sensitivities, dispositions, and priorities, could be motivated as he or she is. In comprehending you, I try to "see" and to feel those motivational factors as if they were my own. Comprehension requires more of me than just understanding you—more than intellectual empathy. It also requires that I experience, albeit vicariously, the motivational power that your perspective carries for you. As the veteran diplomat and international negotiator Harold Saunders has observed, "learning people's real interests requires probing the deep-rooted fears, hopes, wounds, perceptions, and values that form people's sense of what is threatening and what is vital to protect their identity. What do they 'care about'? . . . Real interests—exactly what we fear or want and how much—are not easy to know. . . . Probing may reveal premises more *visceral* than analytical—and perhaps politically more significant. As we learn the other's identity we may uncover the roots of interests in . . . human *feelings*" (emphasis added).[6]

Because the ultimate sources of human motivation are emotional in character—need, fear, pain, sensitivity, pleasure, longing, and so forth (mediated, of course, by cognitive and quasi-cognitive perceptions, interpretations, and beliefs)—I can't comprehend with my intellect alone. I have to imagine what it's like to *feel* the way you do. As Maurice Friedman observes, the comprehension required is not mere empathy, which is an intellectual understanding, but "a bold swinging into the other that demands the most intense action of one's being in order to make the other present in his whole uniqueness."[7] Only by imagining what it's like to feel the way you do can I understand and appreciate why you are moved as you are. When I comprehend you, your motivations become real for me. I feel the pull they exert on you. I may continue to disagree with you (indeed, I might become even more convinced that you're mistaken), but at least I'll see that you're motivated by considerations that could motivate me (or anyone else). At the same time, my own motivations lose none of their validity or force. Indeed, they will always be more real and more powerful, more immediate and potent for me than yours can be, no matter how sympathetic I am.

Comprehension requires me, not to put myself in your position, but to imagine what it's like to be *you* in your position. I must try to avoid projecting my own motivations onto you. If I put *myself* in your position, then what I understand is what I would feel in that situation, not what you feel. To comprehend, therefore, I have to use my imagination. I have to use my imagination because I don't have precisely the same experiences, perceptions, concerns, sensitivities, and dispositions that you have. To comprehend you I must be able to relate what you feel to a motivation (rooted, as we shall see, in a universal human need) that could produce such a feeling in any human being, myself included. This means that the greater the difference between us, the deeper I must probe in order to locate the motivational level at which we are "the same." If I fail to locate this level, our differences may overwhelm us, and we'll be unable to understand and appreciate each other's motivation.

Comprehension doesn't require that you like the objects of my motivating beliefs. It doesn't mean you have to like the way I fulfill or express my motivation. If you and I both value feeling energetic and physically robust, for example, we don't have to agree that running five miles a day is superior to yoga for this purpose. To comprehend my preference for yoga, you don't have to go in for it yourself. You only have to appreciate how, given similar circumstances and experience, any person—yourself included—could find yoga a satisfying way to achieve relaxation. We'll comprehend each other if we realize that your preference for running and mine for disciplined contortion are both expressions of the underlying need for, and hence value of, physical vigor. Of course, we might still disagree strenuously about the relative merits of these different ways of achieving it. People can remain locked in a disagreement despite having the same ultimate needs and values. The point is, we often exaggerate the differences between us, and this impedes our ability to work together. Realizing that we have something in common, being able to recognize something of ourselves in each other, is crucial to achieving the mutual respect on which practical politics depends.

## Is Mutual Comprehension Necessary?

If we were incapable of comprehending each other at all, it would be impossible to form a genuinely shared perspective. And if that were impossible, we would have no hope of constructing a practice of democratic politics that, because it authorizes actions consistent with a shared public judgment about how to reconcile conflicting goods, works better than the "mechanical" methods of consumerist politics. Effective democratic politics depends on our ability to deliberate, judge, and choose together, as a public.

Reluctance to concede that at some level we are "all the same" causes many persons to balk at the suggestion that we need to comprehend each other's perspective. They maintain that a workable, productive democratic politics requires only mutual *respect*. In their view, politics is more successful if citizens simply work together on a problem despite their differences, instead of attempting to resolve, overcome, or even just understand those differences. In contrast to private life, where we associate with people who share similar outlooks and values, in public life we meet people from backgrounds unlike our own. Our guiding principle should not be "we're all the same," but rather the presumption that we're all different. This should lead us to a recognition of the moral ambiguity of politics, to the awareness that we cannot expect simply to impose our values. The only commonality we must acknowledge is the fact that we have to live together despite our differences.

Clearly, in many instances of political disagreement people possess enough respect for each other to work together despite their differences. Unfortunately, many people today not only presume dissimilarity, they can't see anything but dissimilarity. Difference becomes so great (or comes to seem so great) that people lose sight of each other's humanity. In extreme cases—war, murder, terrorism, sociopathic violence—people dehumanize others to the point where they are no longer subjects, but mere objects to be acted upon without consideration for what they feel. We should not presume, therefore, that dissimilar people recognize enough commonality even to grant each other a hearing. Based on their demonstrated ability to live next door to each other as neighbors and fellow citizens of Yugoslavia, one would have expected Bosnian Serbs, Croats, and Muslims to possess sufficient respect for one another to go on doing so after the breakup of their country. Clearly, they didn't. Equally, many young men in our society today "respect" each other to the point of being willing to kill and be killed. Such "respect" is in reality a prudent fear of another's power, resolve, toughness, or ruthlessness. Such "respect" leads to the very antithesis of democratic politics.

Sometimes, paradoxically, the more similar people are (or appear to be), the more intense are their disagreements. Consider, for example, the tensions that exist between African Americans as different as Louis Farrakhan and Thomas Sowell, between women as different as Camille Paglia and Andrea Dworkin, between Jews as different as Elie Wiesel and the late Meyer Kahane. Anyone who has witnessed the actions of the most extreme animal liberationists, earth-firsters, straight-edgers, white supremacists, paramilitary survivalists, and anti-abortion militants (to say nothing of the fratricidal disagreements among the Palestinians and Northern Irish, and in virtually every sub-Saharan nation-state in Africa—most notoriously in Uganda and Rwanda) must admit that there is a fine line that separates politics as we usually think of it from war. Less-extreme political disputes—over segregation and the Vietnam War during the sixties, over abortion today—reveal that our public relationships can be, and often are, stretched to the breaking point.

Respect understood in the "thin sense" that I've attributed to persons who might contest the necessity of mutual comprehension thus can be negative as well as positive, based on fear and loathing as well as on genuine regard or esteem. (If you doubt this, ask any young member of a gang why he carries a gun—to get respect.) As the foregoing observations suggest, respect in the thin sense is not a sufficient condition of effective democratic decision making. To be sure, the respect needed for practical politics doesn't require that you and I like each other, nor does it require that you and I like, value, prize, or desire what the other seeks. But even if we grant this, respect does seem to imply our acceptance of the "not unreasonableness" of each other's motivations. How can you respect me without believing that my interests are rooted in needs that themselves are "not unreasonable"? How can you respect me without recognizing that I am moved by considerations that in the right circumstances might motivate anyone, yourself included?

Respect requires that I recognize that what motivates you can be valued by— that is, "value-*able*" for—any human being. If I don't understand and appreciate your motivation, I won't see how you can value the object of your desire. I will regard *you* as incomprehensible, and hence at best I am likely to remain indifferent to you. Worse, I may attribute to you motivations I find threatening. Unnerved by uncertainty, I might project my worst fears onto you. In either case I won't develop the kind of respect for you that I require in order to work with you politically. If respect is to lead to practical politics, it must be based on something other than the emotional hunger, fear, anger, and hatred that lead people to "objectify" others rather than work with them. It is these emotional factors that must be mutually comprehended if people who are deeply divided and estranged are to respond effectively to the problems and challenges that confront our communities today.

Respect isn't automatic, and it doesn't arise in response solely to the recognition of different interests. As Amy Gutmann and Dennis Thompson have written, genuine respect requires "a favorable attitude toward . . . the person with whom one disagrees." One must recognize that an "opponent's position is based on . . . principles about which reasonable people can disagree."[8] One's opponent must appear to be motivated by considerations that are comprehensible and that therefore might influence any human being. Respect of the sort required for practical politics arises in response to the recognition of comprehensible—that is, understandable, "appreciate-able"—motivations. It cannot be assumed as a precondition of effective democratic decision making.

Granted, in some political disputes our awareness of commonality is overwhelmed, and we must try to interact politically in the absence of the respect we need in order to deliberate, judge, choose, and act together. But this is precisely why the effort to achieve mutual comprehension is imperative. If we can't assume that people are able and willing to comprehend each other, then politics must enable and encourage them to do so. As Andrew Sullivan has written in a review of the motion picture *Philadelphia,* "the present is a foreign country for many of us now. Increasingly, we need correspondents. . . . [*Philadelphia*] is a work of translation. . . . To those who simply don't want to know, it's an irritation. . . . But translation has to start somewhere; and it is infinitely preferable to a silent separatism."[9]

## Is Mutual Comprehension Possible?

It might be objected that, although we ought to show respect for persons whose perspectives differ from one's own, it's often not possible genuinely to understand

and appreciate these perspectives. We simply have to learn to tolerate and respect others despite—or preferably, because of—their differences. The experiences human beings have can be so disparate—and those experiences so heavily influenced by the ideas, history, language, relationships of power, social norms, and habits that define the way we think and live—that we can't truly appreciate perspectives different from our own. For example, although I'm not convinced that the slogan "It's a black thing, you wouldn't understand" is meant to be taken literally, on its face it does suggest that at least some folks think that differences between African Americans and European Americans render us genuinely incomprehensible to each other.

Whether we would understand is one thing; whether we *could* understand is another. Fortunately, we're capable of understanding and appreciating each other's motivations. To say we're capable, of course, doesn't mean we're able and willing. It's difficult in the best of circumstances to understand and appreciate the motivations of others, and we shouldn't underestimate the obstacles to doing so. Nonetheless, there is no insuperable barrier to comprehending different perspectives. We can grant that each partial perspective is constructed out of the ideas people are exposed to and the experiences they have. But however much these may vary, they are still *human* ideas and experiences. If this is so, then they can be grasped by human beings. In principle, at least, a shared, public perspective can be constructed—albeit with effort—if there is a will to do so. As Richard Bernstein has remarked, if we can't communicate with each other, it is not primarily an intellectual or linguistic failing, but a moral one.[10]

Admittedly, mutual comprehension is maximally achievable only by persons occupying points along (or at least close to) the spectrum of "normal" human intelligence and mental health.[11] In time and with effort, we may be able to "push the envelope" of our ability to enter imaginatively into the worlds occupied by those who, although we cannot communicate with them, are affected by the public problems confronting us and by the way we choose to respond to those problems. For purposes of establishing and sustaining a practice of practical politics, however, we need not be able to comprehend everyone and everything. Most political issues arise between persons who can comprehend others and who can be comprehended by them. We should make the effort to comprehend others to the best of our ability, even if we can do so only imperfectly.

A public perspective is possible because we share a human nature that, despite the endless variety of ways of thinking, acting, and living that people find satisfying and meaningful, is built around a limited and universal set of human needs. I have cited the late psychologist Abraham Maslow's belief that human beings are motivated by evaluative considerations growing out of needs that, however much they may vary in manifestation or expression, are unchanging and common to all human beings. When human ends are studied cross-culturally, Maslow argued, such needs prove to be far more universal than the methods taken to achieve them. While beliefs about what has value vary greatly among cultures and societies, even from individual to individual, the ultimate sources of those beliefs—the needs that underlie them—seem to be identical.

The philosopher Robert McShea has made the same point. McShea argues that people who deny a common human nature confuse the question of what determines the way we act with the question of why we act: "Because humans have no instincts and since our genetically determinative reflexes are not of primary interest to theorists of human value and society, the nature-nurture discussion about *behavior* is at once settled in favor of the nurturists. The question is whether human *motivation* is determined by human nature or by culture."[12] McShea contends that a universal human nature—dynamic, incompletely realized, and difficult to characterize though it might be—supplies all our motivations. We shouldn't suppose that, because what we believe, feel, desire, and do is greatly influenced by social factors, the ultimate motivational sources of our action must be as well. According to McShea, our common membership in a determinate biological species, *homo sapiens,*

> determines that [the emotions we experience] will be aroused in specific ways by experiences in situations that have been common and important in the very long history of our species. We have evolved to have particular emotions in certain sorts of situations. . . . [Our development in the past few hundred thousand years] has complicated but not essentially altered the fundamental character of our species's emotional profile. Emotional dispositions, such as the tendency to desire health, are the source of all motivation for all human beings. Species-typical feelings are, for humans and for the higher animals, the only possible motivating force.[13]

Thus, while human beliefs, desires, attitudes, and actions may be socially constructed, our ultimate motivations are not. As McShea argues, "society calls upon innate human motivations. It does not create them and it cannot operate in disregard of them."[14] Note that this claim is compatible with the constructedness of people's beliefs about what is good and bad, right and wrong. As Martha Nussbaum has written in regard to admittedly constructed sexual categories and norms, "there is no reason in principle why someone who recognizes and stresses the great variety with which societies have constructed [such] categories and norms might not also believe that beneath this variety lie certain 'natural' regularities. These regularities might even be invoked to explain why, in each concrete set of circumstances, the specific cultural manifestations take the form they do."[15] Human behavior, in all its manifest diversity, may, as Nussbaum suggests, simply represent the influence of highly various circumstances upon a relatively few universal human dispositions. This view of human nature explains how we can explain ourselves to each other despite our obvious and substantial differences. A human being possesses certain attributes that, although they may find expression in a multitude of values, norms, and practices, can be understood and appreciated by any other human being.[16]

## A Place for Emotion

If mutual comprehension of our motivations is an indispensable element in an effective practice of democratic politics, then human emotions cannot be banned from the forums where we engage each other politically. Motivations are "emotional"—they have to do with needs and the feelings, inclinations, sensitivities, and desires that relate to those needs.

It is not sufficient in politics for people to "express themselves," to "get things off their chest." That path leads nowhere. But whether emotional expression is necessary is another question. For some people it can be, particularly in the early stages of discussion. Granting that we must guard against expression of feeling simply as catharsis, to what extent and in what ways must we allow—even encourage—people to convey the nature and strength of the motivations that are really at the bottom of their perspectives?

Michael Lerner, a clinical psychologist and founder of the Institute for Labor and Mental Health, believes that emotional pain is so prevalent in American society that people must "work through" their feelings before their energies can be directed productively into political action.[17] In his work with blue-collar workers, Lerner discovered that even those workers who appeared to be most emotionally healthy were experiencing a great deal of inner pain about their jobs and their lives. They were upset primarily with "the daily denials of their self-worth." Each day they were confronted with the fact that the work world assumed that they were less capable and less intelligent than they could be or wanted to be. As their lives went on, they began to feel a deep and pervasive self-blame. This self-blame explained in part why they didn't try to engage in collective action to change their workplace.

Lerner believes there is a direct link between a person's psychological state and his or her readiness to take political action. Even though for most people psychological states are induced by external conditions, when they are internalized they can become an (internal) obstacle to healthy political action. Lerner's workers didn't even feel like talking about their situation. They felt it was pointless or self-destructive to reveal to others what a "mess" they had made of their own lives. They saw no connection between the emotional pain and discouragement they felt and what had been happening to them.

Lerner understood that what some critics might denigrate as an individual "therapeutic effect" is often a necessary precondition for political action. His response was to organize stress-reduction and support groups, which were run for "healthy workers" facing "normal stress," and which were construed as training rather than therapy. This enabled participants to learn from one another's experiences. When they listened to one another's stories, they could see that the other group members were unfairly blaming themselves. It was that recognition that eventually made it possible for them to see how they were doing the same thing in their own case.[18] Once the dynamic of self-blame was uncovered, participants were much more in touch with their anger (a therapeutic effect), but that anger was directed more at the larger social system than at themselves or the people they had contact with on a daily basis. They exhibited a greater interest in joining their fellow workers to try to change things in their work world.

Moreover, participants developed a deep sense of compassion, first for themselves (another therapeutic effect), but ultimately as well for everyone else around them. They were able to identify with (i.e., "comprehend") others more easily, including people who had previously seemed unattractive or even offensive. Once again, however, the result was not just therapeutic. Turning away from self-blame did not lead to an attitude of irresponsibility or passivity. On the contrary, the less people felt inclined to blame themselves, the more empowered they felt to take responsibility for the areas in their lives where they could exercise control. The energy freed up in this process went into cooperative work for social change.

Although Lerner links psychological change with the prerequisites for political action, he distinguishes the psychological, which necessarily has an individual locus, from the private, which lacks a social dimension. Change must occur within and for the individual, but not by and for the individual alone. As Lerner points out, this is very different from the "medical model," in which the sickness is inside each person, and each can be cured through some therapy that happens to that person alone. Mental health for any given individual requires mental health for much larger numbers of people. The healing and repair of one person requires healing and repair on the community level as well. Political action is necessary to secure the psychological state that in turn is essential for empowerment, and hence for action. The two are interrelated; each requires the other.

If self-blame and anger are so deeply implicated in unhealthy political behavior, it is imperative that practical politics promote the "therapeutic effects" that will make healthy democratic political action possible for all Americans—from disempowered, marginalized persons to the angry-but-impotent majority to sublimating intellectual elites. It's in everyone's interest to try to comprehend his or her fellow citizens. By revealing honestly and unashamedly our desires for what we genuinely need, by trying to understand, appreciate, and acknowledge each other's motivations, we can begin to build respect and hence productive working relationships. Politics cannot dispense altogether with the effort to recognize the common humanity of the people who practice it. That is what mutual comprehension is all about.

## Comprehension and "Confirmation"

When we find ourselves in disagreement with others, it is not enough simply to understand and appreciate their motivations. In addition, we must openly *acknowledge* our comprehension. Explicitly acknowledging that we comprehend others helps achieve what Maurice Friedman, following Martin Buber, calls *confirmation.*[19]

In general, to "confirm" a thing is to approve it, chiefly in the sense of attesting to its truth or vouching for its genuineness. In the context of political dialogue, confirmation means that we attest to the validity, to the "truth," of the needs, the beliefs about value, and the desires that motivate one another. Confirmation—comprehension plus acknowledgment—serves what is perhaps the most important need we have when we're engaged in a political disagreement with others: our need for reassurance that we are individual human beings who have needs, beliefs about value, feelings, and desires that are essential to our unique identities. By calling attention to our (equal) status as human beings and as citizens, confirmation helps break down the isolation and anxiety we feel when we find ourselves in political disagreement. It thereby opens the door to mutually supportive, and hence productive, working relationships. Note in this connection that, because what we seek is confirmation as *individuals,* we need to be comprehended and confirmed by people who differ from us. Our sense of uniqueness depends on being comprehended and confirmed by those whose experiences, beliefs, and dispositions contrast with our own. Such confirmation is more powerful than confirmation by people who are like us. Of course, seeking confirmation from those who differ from us is also more frightening—it carries with it the risk that we will fail to obtain the confirmation we want.

Confirming another person—acknowledging that we have comprehended him or her—can be as simple as saying something like this: "So, the security of your family is important to you." Typically, the other person will respond, "Yes, that's exactly what I mean." The latter feels understood, and hence less beleaguered. She is also clearer about her own motivations. But the acknowledging party often experiences just as great a shift in his outlook and attitude. When we comprehend another person's motivation, she no longer seems irrational, selfish, or malevolent. Once we understand and appreciate her motivation, her attitudes and actions seem "not unreasonable." We realize that she, too, is motivated by considerations that could motivate us. This realization permits us to move to a level of communication at which we can begin talking productively with each other. We may disagree strongly about each other's perceptions, beliefs, attitudes, and actions. But mutual comprehension affords us enough mutual respect to begin working together.

Consider the example of a mediator who was trying to resolve a neighborhood dispute between a young man of European descent and an older Hispanic woman. According to the woman, the young man's father had directed ethnic slurs toward her. She wanted the son to condemn his father, which he refused to do. After some conversation, however, she understood that the young man refused to condemn his father because he loved and respected him despite his flaws, not because he thought his father was right. When she realized this, she no longer felt it necessary for him to criticize his father. She even discovered something about the young man that she also valued. As a consequence, the two of them were able to begin talking with each other about how to solve the problem, rather than "talking at" each other in an effort to assign blame, establish innocence, and win concessions from each other.

Confirmation is especially important today because of the state of our public relationships. I have cited Maslow's and McShea's contention that all human beings have needs, such as the need for a sense of belongingness, for recognition and acceptance by others, for status, appreciation, and respect. Milton Rokeach points to the same needs when he observes that there is a class of beliefs that are even more important for a human being than what he or she values: namely, the beliefs that collectively form his conception of himself, that tell him who he is. These include conscious and unconscious physical, moral, and intellectual images; national, regional, ethnic, racial, and religious identities; and sexual, generational, occupational, marital, and parental roles.[20] In our country today we're seeing the emergence of "identity cleavages"—divisions based on distinctions between us of the sort Rokeach describes.[21] "Identity" and the need for recognition (confirmation) of one's identity may be growing in importance precisely because the connections that once tied us to family, community, church, religion, our ethnic origins, and other traditional sources of identity have weakened to the point where we've become unsure exactly who we are. The writings of scholars such as Robert Bellah and his colleagues reveal a society populated by persons whose tendency to conceive of themselves almost exclusively as individuals—abstracted from any defining social context—has left them with little to fall back on in the effort to define themselves. For this reason, our values (and our Values) have taken on huge importance. We rely on them to tell us not only what is important in life, but also who we are.

Because what we care about is tied so closely to our self-conceptions, having what we value confirmed is tantamount to being confirmed as persons. For this reason, we become anxious that what we care about not be challenged, undermined, or shaken. But inevitably this is precisely what occurs (indeed, it's what should occur) when political issues arise. Involving as they do conflicts between things we value, such issues are likely to implicate our self-conceptions. Because we crave the agreement and approval of others, we become defensive, intolerant, or hostile when what we care about isn't confirmed. How can I feel good about myself if I can't get others to confirm the feelings that are the touchstones of my worth as a person? As psychologists such as Maslow, Rokeach, and Daryl Bem have pointed out, of all a person's psychological needs, the need to maintain an acceptable self-conception is the most important. Hence any threatening belief or action that is tied closely to a person's self-conception (the way "choice" threatens "life" for someone who is "pro-life," and vice versa) will likely be rejected. As a matter of psychological necessity, if what I care about conflicts with what you care about, I will resolve the conflict in favor of my self-conception.

Practical politics makes a virtue of the need for confirmation from those who are not like us. The uncertainty we experience concerning what we value, and the psychological insecurity that accompanies it, naturally incline us to care what others think. If those others stand ready to comprehend us, then political engagement can provide us with the recognition—the confirmation—that we need. We might not get the agreement that initially we want and think we must have. But we can get something even better: understanding, appreciation, and acknowledgment from persons who differ from us and who differ with us. Think about it. By whom would you find it more satisfying to have your deepest motivations understood, appreciated and acknowledged—someone just like you, who already thinks and feels as you do? Or someone very different from you—someone who initially not only disagrees with you but who can't even see that you are motivated by genuine human needs, someone who after talking with you concedes in all sincerity that, though he might still disagree, he recognizes and acknowledges that your motivations are not unreasonable? If you're honest, I believe you'll say the latter. And that is what makes the mutual comprehension and acknowledgment that is required and encouraged by practical politics—with its emphasis on transforming interpersonal disputes into intrapersonal conflicts between good things—so valuable in our efforts to resolve the political issues that divide us.

## Comprehension: When and How Much?

The more dissimilar you and I are, the deeper will be the level at which comprehension must occur in order for us to recognize our common humanity. The more dissimilar we are, the less we share experiences, perceptions, circumstances, priorities, sensitivities, dispositions, and so forth. Only at the most basic levels of human motivation—at the level of universal human needs—will we be reliably able to find the commonality that will enable us to comprehend each other. Conversely, the more similar you and I are, the easier it will be (other things being equal) for us to comprehend one another. The more we share or hold in common—Values, beliefs, experiences, cultural background, personality characteristics, habits, personal circumstances, and so on—the less we'll have to struggle to understand and appreciate each other's motivations. Within a friendship, relationship, a family, or even a community, mutual comprehension might be more or less automatic. But as difference grows—across personality types; value systems; cultures; socioeconomic classes; religions; gender, ethnic, or racial experiences; ideologies—the more difficult it becomes to comprehend, and the more it becomes imperative to do so.[22]

Like practical politics itself, mutual comprehension is an ideal to be pursued. No doubt we can never completely comprehend another person, because we can never *be* another person. But we shouldn't underestimate our capacity for comprehension. I will never experience precisely what you feel. But we mustn't infer from this fact that sympathy is either impossible or undesirable. Insofar as an experience is a human experience, I almost certainly will have experienced something like it. If it doesn't take much probing on my part to understand and appreciate your perspective, so much the better. Yet even when I do have to get well beneath the surface to comprehend your motivations, that undertaking requires only that I be able to relate imaginatively to motivations that any human being could have.

### Comprehension: Some Examples

Here is a hypothetical dialogue between two middle-school boys, both fourteen, who have gotten into a fight. Jamal is black, James is white. A school counselor is trying to understand what happened and why. As you read it, ask yourself, what is the issue between James and Jamal? Is it the only issue? The fundamental issue? Can we understand and appreciate why Jamal has acted in this way? What are the real reasons for his behavior?

> Counselor: I understand you two have been fighting. You want to tell me
>     what happened?
> James: He started it.
> Counselor: Jamal?
> Jamal: (says nothing)
> Counselor (to James): Started it how?

James: He shoved me. Tore a button off my shirt.

Jamal: He dissed me. No honky homeboy is gonna do that and get away with it.

James: Diss him!? All I did was look at him.

Counselor: Did you say anything to him, make any rude gestures—anything like that?

James: No. I just looked at him—like, "Why don't you just leave us alone?"

Counselor: Jamal, is that so?

Jamal: He didn't have to say nothin'. I know what he was thinkin'.

Counselor: And what was that?

Jamal: Like I don't belong here, I ain't good enough, I'm just some nigger who don't know his place.

James (rolling his eyes and shaking his head): Yeah, right.

Jamal: Yeah, that's right.

Counselor: Jamal, how do you know that's what James was thinking?

Jamal: 'Cuz I seen that look before. White people are always lookin' at black folks that way.

Counselor: Were there many white people in your old neighborhood, Jamal?

Jamal: A couple. That old priest and some nuns over at St. Aloysius.

Counselor: What about at your old school?

Jamal: A few. Mostly teachers.

Counselor: Did they look at you that way?

Jamal: No. 'Least, not the wrong way.

Counselor: What about your classmates?

Jamal: Maybe they did—one time. But I straightened 'em out real fast. Let 'em know nobody messes with Jamal.

Counselor: How'd you do that?

Jamal: Got in their face. If they didn't get right with me, I whupped their ass.

Counselor: Just for looking at you?

Jamal: That's it. You gotta have juice.

James: Juice?

Jamal: Respect.

Counselor: When somebody looks at you, they're not showing you respect?

Jamal: Maybe, maybe not. But you can't take a chance. Probably they be movin' on you, tryin' to get more juice for theirselves.

Counselor: So if somebody tries to get more juice by moving on you, you've got to fight back?

Jamal: That's right. When somebody tries you, you gotta show nerve. "Do or be done to"—that's the only way to make sure you're treated right.

Counselor: James, did you mean to disrespect Jamal by looking at him?

James: No, I just wanted him to lighten up, let us play the game. [To Jamal:] That's word, man.

Counselor: Jamal, can you accept that?

Jamal: Maybe. I guess.

Counselor: Could I get you guys to trade apologies? I know James didn't mean any disrespect. Right, James?

James: Yeah. Sorry, Jamal, no disrespect intended.

Counselor: Jamal?

Jamal: Okay. Maybe I was just a little jumpy. Sorry about your shirt, man.

Counselor: Good. Jamal, just remember: You don't have to be on the defensive around here. Folks aren't going to be trying you or messing with you like where you used to live. They don't mean to disrespect you. So give 'em a chance, will you? You might even make some new friends.

As you might have guessed, Jamal has recently moved to a new area from an inner-city neighborhood. In many of these neighborhoods, what Elijah Anderson calls "the code of the streets" governs people's behavior.[23] At the heart of the code, Anderson says, is the matter of "respect," or being "treated right." The basic requirement of the code is showing that a person is able and willing to engage in violence in order to enhance and hold onto his respect, both in his own eyes and in the eyes of others. Respect is seen as a "zero-sum game." If one person increases his respect, somebody else's decreases. There's a general sense that there's very little respect to be had, it's in short supply, so you have to compete for your share.

Because there are always other people looking for a fight to increase their share of respect, it's important to deter aggression. The ways others talk to you and behave around you are serious indications of their intentions toward you. So you become very sensitive to slights. This is especially true among young people, whose self-esteem is more vulnerable than that of adults. Even maintaining eye contact too long can be interpreted as an act of "dissing" (disrespecting). A person has to have the right look—facial expression, posture, clothing, and so forth. If you don't look like you're a person who is "respected"—who everybody knows can take care of himself—someone will "move on" you or "try" you. If you've got the respect of others, you can avoid "being bothered." You won't be "dissed." But to deter being tried or moved on, you've got to communicate that you're ready to resort to violence to maintain your respect. The lesson Jamal has learned is that readiness to fight is both a virtue and a necessity for self-defense.

Wisely, the counselor doesn't try to assign blame. He tries to get the boys, particularly Jamal, to articulate what they were feeling, and why. He keeps asking gentle, matter-of-fact questions, probing for the deep concerns that motivate them. As the discussion moves to the level of ultimate motivation, the two boys begin to see that they have something in common: a need that motivates them both but that resulted in different judgments about what constituted rational behavior in their situation. Despite their differences, both boys have a common motivation, or "value": the contribution of respect from others to their self-esteem. Jamal has brought to his new environment his assumption that he's vulnerable to losing respect to anybody at any time. His sensitivity quickly creates a situation in which James also feels threatened. The problem for both is how to avoid making each other feel disrespected, how to reassure one another that they're no threat to the other's self-esteem. With the counselor's help, they begin to understand and appreciate—that is, to comprehend—each other's perspective. Their mutually comprehended value of self-esteem and respect provides them with common ground from which to begin constructing a healthier relationship.

Here is another hypothetical dialogue. This one takes place between two women who hold conflicting views about abortion. As you read it, ask yourself whether the issue over which Maria and Roberta are divided initially is the only issue. Is it the fundamental issue?[24] How do the Values of "life" and "choice" relate to their identities—their self-conceptions, how they define themselves? How does the issue of abortion affect these values?

Maria (pro-life): I think abortions should be illegal. Life is the most precious value we have. Women have got to stop treating life so callously just for the sake of their own convenience.

Roberta (pro-choice): But what about the *woman's* life? Doesn't it have value too, and not just for reproducing? Women should have the chance to choose when and whether to have children. And what about cases like that of the twelve-year-old girl—a baby herself— who is a victim of incest? Or what about the woman whose life is endangered by continued pregnancies?

Maria: But by permitting abortion society sanctions a cavalier attitude toward life. I know a woman who has had six abortions in the last two years! She's using it as birth control. She doesn't respect life, or her potential for motherhood—or herself!

Roberta: I understand, Maria, but I'm not like the person who has had six abortions. In fact, I disapprove of her behavior. But preventing me from taking personal responsibility for what I do with my life isn't the answer.

Facilitator: Maria, you said something about abortion being a "convenience." If I hear Roberta correctly, that's not why she favors choice in this matter. But why do you think convenience is not a justification?

Maria: Young women—especially immature ones, like teenagers—think they can sleep with somebody, risk getting pregnant, and then get out of paying the consequences if they do. Also, abortion means young men can get away with having sex and not taking responsibility for their actions. The result is that we're encouraging promiscuity and in the process destroying the importance of strong, permanent bonds between men and women, which we need for a healthy family life.

Roberta: I don't disagree with you, Maria. But for me, the issue isn't convenience. I don't want to be discriminated against just because biologically I'm capable of becoming pregnant. Choice is essential for genuine human equality. Women have an equal contribution to make to society. We should have equal freedom and independence to make our contribution in whatever way we feel it best to use our individual talents. If your talents lie in raising a family, that's a very valuable contribution. But if I choose not to have a family, or do something in addition to having a family, that shouldn't make me feel any less valuable.

Facilitator: Why do you think you would feel less valuable, Roberta?

Roberta: Because motherhood is something I should be free to choose, not something I should just have to accept. In fact, I want to be a mother some day. But I know I wouldn't want to endure what my own mother did. She was a very intelligent woman, but she couldn't use her intellectual ability because she had to raise six kids. I'm sure she didn't resent having any of us, but I know she was disappointed not to be able to do more. That affected me. I decided I wouldn't let myself get tied down the way she did. I value family, but I also want to contribute to society—as an individual, and as a woman.

Facilitator: So, you're saying that motherhood is an identity a woman should be able to choose, but shouldn't be forced to accept.

Roberta: That's right.

Facilitator: It sounds like, for you, abortion isn't the real issue. The real issue is how people think of you—as a potential wife and mother, or as a person for whom raising children is just one of several things you might do with your life.

Roberta: Exactly.

Facilitator: Let me ask Maria about these things. Maria, Roberta has talked about the importance to her of contributing according to her individual talents as a person and as a woman. Does being a mother have a similar sort of importance for you?

Maria: Yes, very much. As a wife and mother, I feel I have an important role at the center of the family. It makes me feel valuable because it's something only a woman can do, and I'm above all a woman. Raising my children is the most important contribution I can make in my life.

When I was little, my best friend's mother had a job. She didn't have to work, but she insisted on it. She left my friend with strangers all day

SECOND PRINCIPLE · **119**

until her father could pick her up. I know when I was young I really needed my mom, and she was there for me, unlike my friend's mother. I swore that when I had kids of my own, I'd always be there to give them the attention they should have, especially when they're small.

You see, abortion tells me that being a mother just isn't that important. It says to me I shouldn't be content to be a mother, that I'm not really making an important contribution by doing so. And that bothers me.

Facilitator: Roberta, can you understand Maria's feelings?

Roberta: Yes, I can. Maria, I do understand why it's important to you to feel you're a good mother. I need to feel I'm doing something important, too. But you and I are different. We have different needs, different strengths and talents. The same things don't give us the feeling of importance we want for ourselves.

Facilitator: Let me ask you each a question. Maria, how would you feel if circumstances prevented you from devoting your time and energy to being a mother—say, if you had to work two jobs just to make ends meet?

Maria: Well, I think I would find that very distressing. I'd be worried about not being there for my children. Being a mother is what I do best. It's who I am. Having to work so much would mean I'd be neglecting my biggest responsibility.

Facilitator: And how would you feel, Roberta, if you weren't free to work outside the home?

Roberta: That's hard to imagine. For one thing, I think I'd feel dependent, and that would make me feel powerless. But I'd also feel my life didn't really have any direction. You see—for me, to a large extent, I *am* what I do. So if I didn't have anything to do, who would I be?

Maria: You know, that's kind of the way I feel, too. I am what I do. If I couldn't be a devoted mother, who would I be? So I can see how you feel that way. But you know, I still can't help feeling that the freedom to have an abortion means having children isn't a serious responsibility.

Roberta: Maria, I agree with you that having children is an important and serious responsibility. But if for some reason I don't become a mother, or if I do become one and I still decide to have a career that takes a lot of my time and energy, I want you—and other women and men—to respect the contribution I make. Being a good mother is important. It's just not the only thing that's important. I want to be recognized and respected for the other things I can do. And I don't get that respect if I don't have the freedom to choose when to become a mother, or whether to become one. I need to be free to choose *not* to be a mother. And that means I need to be free, if necessary, to have an abortion. When I insist on the right to choose, I don't mean to disrespect your role, or anyone's role, as a mother. It's just that being free to choose is a precondition for the respect I think I'm entitled to as an individual human being.

Facilitator: Maria and Roberta, it seems to me that you at least see things a bit better from each other's perspective. Do you feel like you've got anything in common?

Maria: Yes, I think so. I'm still against abortion, but I can also see that Roberta needs to feel valued and respected, as a person. And I can see that feeling that way depends on what she does with her life. The same thing is true for me. We're both trying to feel valued and respected for what we do.

Roberta: I have to say that, before having this conversation, I wouldn't have guessed that the right to choose could be threatening to a woman. I wouldn't have thought it would cause feelings like those I get when somebody goes on about the right to life. I still believe a woman should have the right to choose, but I do understand where you're coming from, Maria. I just wish that what we have in common could become at least as important as what we disagree about. Maybe then we could find a way to take some of the heat out of our differences over abortion.

Notice that the discussion moves from arguments about the positions each woman has adopted to revelation of her deeper concerns—to her motivating beliefs and what she values. For Maria, it is a woman's role to exhibit and uphold the values that sustain family life. She identifies closely with this role. For Roberta, in contrast, a person might choose to be a wife and mother, but she also might define herself in other ways. It's important to Roberta that she be free to choose how best to use her individual talents and interests. As the discussion moves deeper, the two women begin to see that they have a need that motivates them both but that results in different conclusions and inclinations. Despite their differences, both women have a need for an identity or self-conception they can feel good about. They've begun to understand and appreciate—to comprehend—each other's viewpoint. They've begun to see that they share the value of having an identity or self-conception they can feel is worthy. This mutually comprehended value provides them with "common ground" that can serve as the basis for establishing a good working relationship, which in time may enable them to find a political way forward that both can live with.

### Promoting Mutual Comprehension

The effort to achieve mutual comprehension of a public concern can be aided greatly by analyzing and presenting it in a way that facilitates understanding and appreciation of the different perspectives that people hold with respect to it. Usually, this will require that we recast the matter—organize it in a new and fresh way, one that takes into account the deep motivating needs, desires, fears, and hopes that influence the different views of the matter that different people hold. What we need is a new formulation, or "framing," that will help us achieve a more constructive, more productive discussion.

## 1. COLLECTING STATEMENTS

The first step in reformulating a matter of concern for public discussion is to find out how other people in your community view the matter you're considering.[25] Begin by identifying the different categories of folks whose views need to be encompassed—for example, senior citizens, people in ethnic groups, people whose income falls below the official poverty line, unemployed persons, small business owners, people in the professions, politically conservative and politically liberal persons, people who rarely involve themselves in public activities. (The categories that are relevant will vary from community to community, from topic to topic, and over time.) Then, find out what people in these different categories think about your proposed topic. A fairly reliable and efficient way to do this is to conduct a couple of "focus groups." These are really just free-flowing discussions among ten to fifteen people you get together for a couple of hours on an evening or a Saturday morning. You can gather much of the information you need by talking one-on-one with a couple dozen people who represent the diversity of your community. But the interaction between people in a focus group will usually yield much richer information in a short period of time than will individual interviews.

You want from your focus groups a comprehensive list of the statements people in your community might make about the matter you're considering for discussion. Suppose the matter of public concern is "the use of abortion as a response to unwanted pregnancies."[26] Here are a few of the things people might say:

> Opponents of abortion are trying to impose their traditional, rigid, religiously biased morality on people like me who don't share it.

> Abortion advocates are killing innocent lives with no justification whatsoever. Not even life itself is sacred anymore. People like this think they should be able to do anything they want. I think they're just plain immoral.

> Opponents of abortion are invading my right to privacy in matters of sex and procreation. It's none of their business what I do with another consenting adult.

> People who favor abortion are "playing God." They arrogantly violate clear moral rules, which as fallible human beings they have no right and no authority to do.

Opponents of abortion are afraid of accepting personal responsibility for making difficult moral judgments in hard cases where our general moral principles don't provide clear answers, or where the consequences of following those principles would produce unjustifiable suffering.

## 2. IDENTIFYING MOTIVATIONS

The next step is to ask your focus group to help you identify the deep concerns that shape their beliefs, attitudes, and positions. Ask them to help you underline or highlight those words or phrases that point to or hint at the existence of an underlying motivation.[27] For example:

Opponents of abortion are trying to *impose* their traditional, rigid, *religiously biased morality* on people like me who don't share it.

Abortion advocates are *killing innocent lives with no justification* whatsoever. Not even *life* itself is *sacred* anymore. People like this think they should be able to *do anything they want.* I think they're just plain *immoral.*

Opponents of abortion are *invading* my *right to privacy* in matters of sex and procreation. It's none of their business what I do with another consenting adult.

People who favor abortion are *"playing God."* They arrogantly *violate clear moral rules,* which as *fallible human beings* they have *no right* and *no authority* to do.

Opponents of abortion are *afraid of accepting* personal *responsibility* for making *difficult moral judgments* in hard cases where our general moral principles don't provide clear answers, or where the consequences of following those principles would produce *unjustifiable suffering.*

Now "translate" the words you've underlined or highlighted into a list of the motivations that underlie people's views. For example, the following items might be fundamentally important to people:

—being (and thinking of oneself as) a virtuous, morally good person
—respecting, even revering, human life
—recognizing and accepting human fallibility
—recognizing and accepting the existence of moral truths, of absolute moral rules
—freedom, independence, and control over one's life
—being treated the same as others
—acknowledging and accepting moral complexity
—personal moral responsibility for one's decisions
—the desire for tolerance, mutual respect, and forbearance

### 3. "CLUSTERING" MOTIVATIONS INTO VIEWPOINTS

Because of the limited time you have available for discussion in your focus groups, you may wish to perform this task after concluding your discussions. Using your judgment about which statements belong together, group the statements into three or four viewpoints.[28] Here's a (much-simplified) example of how you might develop two of the (several) views people might hold with regard to abortion:

> *Viewpoint 1:* Dealing with unwanted pregnancy by taking innocent lives is irresponsible and morally intolerable. If such life is not sacred, nothing is. It means there are no moral absolutes, everything is relative, right and wrong are just a matter of personal preference. Anything goes. But there *are* clear moral rules, which we as fallible human beings have no right and no authority to violate, change, or apply at our discretion. What's right and wrong isn't up to us.

> *Viewpoint 2:* Dealing with pregnancy by terminating it before the fetus is viable outside the mother's body is a right that derives from the right of any person to exercise full control over his or her physical self, to be free of interference with and intrusion into this most personal and sacrosanct area of human life. There are no moral absolutes, not even with respect to life. Ultimately, right and wrong are a matter of "personal choice." We have to accept that there are conflicting moral views that can't be resolved. We must not be afraid to take personal responsibility for making difficult moral judgments.

### 4. CLARIFYING THE ISSUES

You should detect a "tension" between the motivations you've identified and the viewpoints you've constructed around them. It should appear difficult—at least on initial examination—to reconcile them. It should seem unlikely that we can fully satisfy, advance, safeguard, or promote what people care about from one point of view without sacrificing, compromising, slighting, or disserving what people care about from other viewpoints. The viewpoints should be "incompatible" in that the conflict between them can't be resolved without assigning one priority over the other.

What you're doing here is making explicit the underlying *issues* that must be addressed and resolved in order to respond effectively to a public concern. Issues are disagreements over the relative importance we attach to different ultimate motivations—the things we need and value that influence our actions, attitudes, and even our beliefs. The abortion example contains several issues. Here is one (of several):

> At issue is *whether there are objective rules of right and wrong* that govern questions such as abortion. Are moral beliefs ultimately subjective, matters

of personal preference or choice? How do we decide what's right and wrong? By appealing to moral authority? (If so, which one?) By taking a vote? By letting each person decide for himself or herself? By "reasoning together" toward a common judgment?

A related point of contention is *whether* (assuming there are moral rules that everyone must live by) *such rules indicate clearly what we should do* in every situation we might encounter. Is every case "open and shut," or are there "gray areas" where we can't be certain what's right and what's wrong?

## 5. RESTATING DIFFERENT DEFINITIONS OF THE PROBLEM

From each viewpoint you've constructed, how would the matter of concern—in this case, the practice of abortion—best be characterized? What is the "real" problem? What, at bottom, is the issue "really" about? For example:

*Definition 1:* The problem is people's dangerous and repugnant belief that right and wrong is a matter of personal preference and that people have the moral authority to decide for themselves what is right and wrong.

*Definition 2:* The problem is people's insistence that there are objective moral standards, when in fact these beliefs are subjective at best and superstitious at worst. We can't escape responsibility for having to exercise our judgment about what's right and wrong.

## 6. REFORMULATING THE MATTER FOR PUBLIC DISCUSSION

Now you need to find some way to capture the new viewpoints you've developed in a single description of the matter that is cause for public concern. How might you put the matter into words so that everyone, no matter which new point of view he or she might feel most comfortable with, can "relate" to it?[29] What is the concern, generally speaking—from the point of view of *the community as a whole?*

For example, about abortion you might say, "The matter that is cause for concern is the fact that we are deeply torn about what values we should honor and give priority, what ethical and moral rules we should live by and how we should determine them, and what political rules we should follow and abide by in dealing with these conflicts that divide us. The dispute over abortion, important though it is, is just the tip of the iceberg. It's a symptom of—it grows out of—much more fundamental differences over how to answer these basic psychological, ethical, and political questions."[30]

Now you have a reformulation of the abortion issue that has the potential to generate a more constructive, productive public discussion than would be possible otherwise. In the next chapter we will examine the task of deliberating together to arrive at a public judgment about how to respond to this matter of concern.

## Conclusion

If a conflict between human goods lies at the heart of a political issue, then those goods are ones that all members of the public have the capacity to understand and appreciate. Arriving at a sound and widely supported public judgment, as opposed to a mechanically obtained political result, requires that we "comprehend"—that is, understand and appreciate—the goods in conflict and the human values and needs they reflect. Reciprocal understanding and appreciation, or "mutual comprehension," makes it possible to recast a political issue as a question of how jointly to prioritize goods that everyone can acknowledge as legitimate sources of political motivation. It allows us to reformulate a political disagreement as a difficult choice—a shared, collective choice—that both enables and encourages us to deliberate together to reach a sound judgment about how to resolve the underlying conflict. Mutual comprehension creates common ground—a shared understanding and appreciation of goods in conflict. It helps dispel the perception that one party's gain is necessarily another party's loss. It does so by encouraging them to think and work together at the level of the underlying, "*non-zero-sum*" sources of their differences. The ability and willingness of people to comprehend other people's motivations is the key to countering the malign influence of perceived zero-sumness. The second requirement of practical politics—its second principle—must therefore be (mutual) *comprehension*.

**7**

# Third Principle: Deliberation

---

*If a man will begin with certainties, he shall end in doubts; but if he will be content to begin with doubts, he shall end in certainties.... [Therefore,] read not to contradict and confute; Nor to believe and take for granted; Nor to find talk and discourse; But to weight and consider.*

—Francis Bacon

---

**Third Principle: Deliberation.** Carefully weigh the considerations— the motivating beliefs, supporting reasons, and values—that underlie the different views that people hold with respect to the matter of public concern you are discussing. Recognize that whatever you decide to do, there will be an "up side" and a "down side." The question of what to do has no single correct answer. The best we can aspire to is a well-founded "on-balance" judgment.

---

In this chapter we turn to the third principle of practical politics: the transformation of (individual) opinions into a shared (public) judgment through (collective) deliberation.

### Opinion, Judgment, and Deliberation

If a belief is a conviction that something is true or real, then a belief that motivates me to act is one that prompts me to say, in effect, "If I do this, it will in fact lead to the realization of something valuable."[1] But such beliefs call for justification. If there is no warrant or ground for accepting that a motivating belief is true, it has no claim on us. We should feel justified in ignoring it. To warrant attention and respect, a motivating belief requires the support of *reasons*. A reason consists of information that increases (or decreases—there can be reasons for not holding a belief) the probability that the belief is true.

For example, suppose I believe that children learn better when they're actively engaged in solving a problem or performing a task. This belief might motivate me to enroll my child in a school that emphasizes experiential learning. One reason for holding this belief might be that the results of a study of children who move from traditional schools to those that feature experiential learning indicate significant improvement in standardized test scores. Another reason might be my neighbor's observation that her child is doing much better after having transferred to a school with an experiential approach. A third reason might be that, after reflecting on my own experience in school and my subsequent learning, I believe that my child would do better in such a school.

Of course, as I argued in chapter 4, my motivating beliefs can be mistaken; I can act on the basis of a belief that is not true. It might be that, "if I do this, it will not lead to the realization of something I consider valuable." It might be, for example, that if I enroll my child in a school with an experiential philosophy, he will not do better academically. The possibility that a motivating belief of mine could be untrue raises the question whether I will realize the value that my belief tells me I will. The greater this possibility, the more prudent it will be to ask myself whether acting on the basis of my belief is warranted. In other words, the greater the possibility that my motivating belief is untrue, the more I ought to reexamine my reasons for holding it. If evidence suggests that improvement in test scores is only temporary, it will be prudent to reconsider whether my belief in the benefits of experiential education is justified.

A motivating belief (or a set of such beliefs) that I bring initially to a situation can be called an *opinion*. That term suggests that my belief is provisional and tentative. It hasn't yet (or recently) been "tested" in the particular circumstances I now face. It hasn't been confirmed or disconfirmed as a result of my reexamining it in light of reasons that could be given for not holding it. We also need a name for the motivating belief I hold after I've assessed and weighed my reasons for holding it against those that count in favor of not holding it. The revised (or strengthened) belief that results from this reexamination can be termed a *conviction*. A conviction, then, is a motivating belief that has been carefully and thoroughly reexamined and reevaluated in light of all the relevant reasons that are available. This doesn't mean that convictions are "final." A conviction will be stronger and firmer than the opinion it supersedes, but it's not permanent. It remains a conviction only until new information appears or until circumstances change substantially. Then it becomes another opinion, and I have to start the process over again. Of course, over time some convictions may gain a measure of stability. But it's always possible—indeed, given the constant flux of life, it's almost certain—that eventually they will be unsettled by a new situation.

As I said in chapter 2, a number of courses will be open in virtually every situation in which action is possible. Even in a situation where I seem to have only one option, I have to choose between doing X and not doing X. ("Not to choose is to choose.") Each of my *options*—the courses of action actually open to me—will have consequences, good or bad, and usually some of both.[2] Every situation in which action is possible poses a conflict between things that are good (valuable) either in themselves or as a means to some end that is intrinsically good. When valuable outcomes conflict, I have to choose which valuable outcome to pursue. In order to make this decision, I must conclude that one of these potential outcomes should take precedence over the others. I have to decide that one of the valuable things is relatively more important, at least in the circumstances, than the other good things I might pursue. This means that the relative ordering of my motivating beliefs must change. I can't continue to want two or more desirable outcomes equally. In order for me to decide, to choose, and to act, one of them will have to win out.

If in order to decide and to act my motivation must change, I must come up with reasons that will tip the balance in favor of one outcome rather than others. Obviously, the reasons that currently support my motivating beliefs won't suffice, because (we're assuming) they've already produced a standoff. When a new situation introduces some uncertainty about what I should do, I need reasons—new ones, better ones, or more of them—that will incline me more strongly toward one course of action than toward others. *Deliberation* is the process of identifying, assessing, and weighing different motivating beliefs and the reasons that support them in order to rank those beliefs.[3] It is the process of reconciling conflicting opinions (i.e., my initial motivating beliefs) in order to decide which of the valuable outcomes should determine what I should do.[4]

A value conflict is a situation in which there will be both desirable and undesirable consequences of choosing any of the courses open to me. Therefore, the question of what I should do invariably must be answered with an *on-balance* assessment. Which of the various outcomes that will result from the options open to me do I desire, *all things considered?* "All things considered" means taking into account all information that might have a bearing on my motivation. Such information might come from deep within me. Or it might come from the reasons, opinions, experiences, values, and desires that other people have. In either case, as I noted in chapter 2, the question of how to resolve a conflict between good things is one I can't answer definitively by myself. There is no predetermined right answer, no logically deducible or empirically discoverable correct solution to a conflict of values. Because of this, the most I can aspire to is a sound *judgment* about what, on balance and all things considered, it would be best to do. To reach such a judgment, I need others to deliberate with me.

### Transforming Political Disagreement

In chapter 2 I said that the need to choose—both individually and collectively—between good things in conflict lies at the heart of politics. But how, as a community or society, should we go about making decisions that will enable us, collectively, to choose? How do we resolve political disagreements between persons who have different individual opinions? The answer I gave was: We don't. (It was a trick question.) Disagreements that arise from individual determinations of what is best to do cannot be "resolved" in the sense of being made to disappear. What we can do is transform such disagreements, turn them from adversarial competitions into a joint effort to reach a sound shared judgment.

The sort of discourse we usually engage in when trying to resolve political issues—*debate*—can be characterized as the process of proposing actions based on our opinions and supported by our reasons for holding those opinions. Debate is unlikely to produce real closure. (Recall my discussion of the "solution wars" to which consumerist politics is prone.) If debate does not settle the question of what we should do, and if we wish to avoid the kinds of unhappy results that mechanical "decision-making" devices such as majority rule often lead to, the alternative is for us to deliberate: to jointly identify, assess, and weigh the motivating beliefs (about what holds value for us) and the reasons that support those beliefs (which together constitute our respective opinions) in order to decide which of our conflicting motivating beliefs we should give priority.

In chapter 6 I said that, in order for two or more persons collectively to deliberate and to reach a shared judgment, they must approximate the situation of the individual who realizes that he or she is faced with a choice. In order to approximate individual rationality in our collective decision making, we must combine our individual perspectives into a single, composite perspective on what is best (most valuable) for *us*. And for that to occur, each of us must understand and appreciate the other person's motivation. I must feel the "pull" of the value you believe inheres in the good that motivates you, and you must feel the "pull" of the value I believe inheres in the good that motivates me.[5]

Consider, once again, the disagreement over abortion. If initially I'm of the opinion that the Value of "life" is paramount, then if I'm to experience the conflict between the Value of "life" and the Value of "choice" as real (more precisely, quasi-real) for me, I will have to acquire a substantial appreciation for the motivating beliefs and reasons that underlie the Value of "choice." I don't have to want

*What about solutions that are mutually exclusive.*

choice for myself. I don't have to give it the same priority that others might. But I do have to appreciate how it "not unreasonably" might hold substantial value for others. Merely assessing and weighing the consequences of different options or proposed solutions in terms of a (capital-V) Value such as choice will not generate the mutual comprehension we require in order to create the common ground that will enable us to work together on resolving this issue.

Indeed, the evidence from the abortion debate suggests that considering consequences in terms of the abstract Values life and choice is likely to produce very little appreciation for whichever Value is assigned lower priority. Suppose I'm a proponent of life. No matter how much I might value choice in the abstract, when it comes to choice with respect to abortion I care very little for it. It's something I place little value on relative to life. So I honestly don't see choosing it as reasonable. Hence I don't see *you* as reasonable. So the divide between us narrows not at all. Moreover, if I don't feel the pull of choice almost as strongly as I do the pull of life, then why would I turn to you for the benefit of your perspective in helping me decide what to do? I won't see that it's relevant. I'll feel so convinced of the value of life relative to choice that I won't see the usefulness to me of trying to appreciate your view. Consequently, I'll continue to feel I'm "on my own" instead of feeling that we share an experience of a dilemma that will lead us to think in terms of "we," not just "I."

The basic point is this: deliberating per se—simply assessing and weighing our motivating beliefs and our reasons for holding them—doesn't by itself move us "from I to we." It doesn't transform our interpersonal dispute into a shared, quasi-intrapersonal dilemma in which I experience conflict as if it were internal to me. For this transformation to occur, mutual comprehension is a prerequisite—and mutual comprehension, moreover, not only of the good things themselves (for example, "life," or "choice"), but also of the ultimate human needs and associated emotions that render us comprehensible to each other, that reveal to us the "not unreasonableness" of our respective beliefs, attitudes, and desires.[6]

When together we grapple honestly and in good faith with a conflict between things that we can recognize and accept as valuable, we share an experience. This shared experience has three salutary effects. First, each of us can now see the other not as an alien being but as a fellow human being.[7] As a result, we experience a new sense of "we-ness." We are not pitted against one another but joined against the conflict to be resolved. Second, having realized that each of us is sincerely unsure about what to do, we can see the benefit and wisdom of sharing our experiences, our insights, and our feelings—of using what we can learn from each other to help weigh the good things in conflict and to reach a sound judgment about what to do. Although in the end we might not agree, at least we will comprehend each other's perspective, which is the precondition for mutual respect.

In turn, mutual comprehension and mutual respect will help nurture the relationship that begins to grow up between us when we first realize that each of us is pursuing something of comprehensible value, something that acquires its value from the comprehensible needs that underlie our motivations. Finally, the energies that previously went into fear, anger, and disputation will be freed up for the task of creatively and collaboratively responding to the issue in ways that otherwise we would not have imagined and would not have explored.

To summarize: Actions I take, or am disposed to take, are invariably motivated by beliefs that by so acting I will obtain something of value—something that will yield a satisfaction of a particular quality, intensity, and duration. My motivating beliefs are buttressed by reasons—considerations I can offer as justifications for accepting that those beliefs are true. My motivating beliefs have their roots ultimately in the (nonrational) needs I have as a human being. Therefore, a purely intellectual conviction that a course of action will lead to the realization of value won't motivate me to act. I have to feel the "pull" exerted upon me by the prospect of realizing the satisfaction it will yield. In order to reach a personal decision about how to resolve a conflict between things I consider good, I have to identify, assess, and weigh the value (the prospective feeling of satisfaction) likely to be realized by pursuing one course of action against the value likely to be realized by pursuing alternative courses.

## From the General to the Specific

On some occasions that require us to make a moral or political choice, the circumstances will be straightforward, ordinary, and familiar enough that we can simply apply our beliefs about what's good and bad, right and wrong. But frequently the situation is such that two or more good (or bad) things conflict. In such a situation, deciding what to do on the basis of our beliefs—making a decision by relying on our opinions—won't get us far. This is because our opinions give us conflicting advice. We have to deliberate—weigh the goods in conflict against each other—in order to reach a judgment about what's best, all things considered, to do.

The beliefs about what is good and bad, right and wrong that we bring to situations of conflict—our opinions—are invariably *generalizations*. They embody responses to countless situations that have occurred over time, not only in our own individual lives, but in the lives of our community, our society, our culture, our civilization—even our species as a whole. These beliefs are preserved in social norms, Values, habits, laws, ethical principles, folk wisdom, institutional rules, cultural practices, and the conclusions we've reached through our own experience. Yet no matter how firmly we believe something, no matter how many times a belief has been reinforced, no matter how obviously and absolutely without exception it might seem, it remains a generalization. It cannot and will not ever cover every situation that could or will arise. Every one of my convictions about what's good or valuable is based on a large, but limited, number of experiences that I or other human beings have already had—not on ones I might or will have. There might always be a situation or circumstance, not yet encountered, that would throw my conviction into doubt.[8]

We should therefore treat our evaluative opinions as *presumptions* (sometimes, of course, justifiably strong). By treating our opinions as presumptions, we acknowledge that they're valid only in general. They are not tailored to specific situations, each of which is in some respect unique. Life is too changeable, too variable and unpredictable, too open-ended for me to say with certainty that an opinion I hold is a timeless truth, without exception. There always could be—and eventually probably will be—a situation that forces me to reconsider whether to maintain my belief or to modify it so that, in the case at hand, I will choose to do what will produce the best outcome, all things considered.

If I wish to persist in arguing that an opinion of mine is true, at the very least I must be prepared to specify exactly when, how, and to what extent it is so. The inadequacy of generalizations for deciding what to do in particular cases, especially complex or novel ones, has long been recognized by our common law tradition. General principles, the legal wisdom goes, don't decide specific cases. Nor should they. No two cases are identical. Whether a legal case should be decided by applying an existing legal principle, by modifying an existing one (e.g., by creating an exception), or by creating a new rule entirely requires judgment. But before a judgment is possible, the case has to be understood in its particularity, in its uniqueness.

And so it is with our opinions about what is good and bad, right and wrong—especially when we have to devise a policy in response to a matter of public concern. Public policies are nothing more than general public opinions put into the form of legally binding rules. Mechanically applying them would in many cases prove ineffective or harmful (which is why we make them subject to review by the courts). No general rule will fit every situation that could or will come up. For example, most of us are of the opinion—indeed, most of us hold it as a conviction—that killing another human being is wrong. But whether we hold a killer responsible and morally and legally accountable depends on the circumstances. We long ago created exceptions (killing in combat), justifications (self-defense), and excuses (insanity) to preserve the validity of the general prohibition against killing while preventing it from being applied mechanically, and hence unfairly. Today, new situations are forcing us to think even harder about when killing is wrong. Abortion, assisted suicide, capital cases involving minors, and sexual activity by persons who know they have AIDS often involve situations in which our existing general principles don't yield a definitive answer about what to do. It is not logic or the application of moral rules to such cases that enables us to deal with the new situations we encounter, but rather our experience and our considered judgment.

As we deliberate together, then, for the purpose of reaching a shared judgment about what to do, we must examine and analyze the cases—the specific factual circumstances—that confront us and that require decision and choice. In order to identify the beliefs and reasons that will serve as the ground for our decision, we must compare and contrast the case (or cases) in question with those that are prototypical or "paradigmatic"—cases that we have encountered previously and to which our existing beliefs apply clearly, straightforwardly, and uncontroversially. To use the common law analogy, we have to examine the "precedent" we've established and consider whether the case in question differs—and, if so, whether it differs significantly—from those out of which the precedent emerged. Can we simply apply the "precedent"—the opinion we bring to the situation—or do we have to create a new precedent by specifying which beliefs and reasons among several conflicting ones will decide the case? What are the facts? What consequences likely will result from deciding one way rather than another?

We might consider, for example, our conviction that killing another human being is wrong. Currently in our country we're debating how to resolve issues that have arisen concerning the termination of pregnancies and assisting terminally ill persons who wish to end their lives. Although many people who have strong opinions in these matters insist that we can and must decide what to do by applying the relevant beliefs absolutely and without exception, probably most of us sense that this is an unsatisfactory way of dealing with a wide variety of situations, many of which involve conflicts we cannot resolve readily because it's not at all clear what would be best to do.

We can again take the issue of abortion as an example. We can easily imagine a case (and probably could document an actual one) in which most reasonable people would be reluctant simply to apply their beliefs unreflectively. Let's say the pregnant person is a child of twelve who was raped repeatedly by her mentally defective and abusive father. The girl is motherless and has no other family. Already pushed to the brink of psychosis by her emotional and physical trauma, she also has a serious heart defect that virtually guarantees that she could not survive childbirth. Tests show that her sixteen-week-old fetus suffers from a congenital disease that in all known cases has brought death within a year of birth, and that the infant would endure inconceivable pain during its short life. In such circumstances, is it clear that applying a policy of strict prohibition of choice would be the right thing to do? In such a case is there not room for reasonable doubt about the wisdom of proscribing abortion? Conversely, we could imagine a situation in which a well-educated, happy, and healthy thirty-year-old professional woman wishes to begin a family with her husband. Five months into the pregnancy the couple learns that the child will be a boy. Both prospective parents prefer a girl. So they want to terminate the pregnancy. In such circumstances, is it clear beyond any reasonable doubt that applying a policy of unconstrained choice would be the right thing to do? In such a case is there not room for reasonable doubt about the wisdom of permitting abortion at will?

Although it might be reasonably evident that we shouldn't uncritically and unreflectively invoke our existing beliefs as we endeavor to answer the question of what to do in extreme cases such as the foregoing hypothetical ones, it might be just as unfair or harmful to try to apply them in much "grayer" situations. On balance and all things considered, the best thing to do might not be indicated by *any* of the (general) beliefs that we invoke in our effort to reach a decision. We may have to struggle with those beliefs to figure out what specific formulations of, exceptions to, or combination of our beliefs would yield the best, fairest, least harmful result. It should be obvious that the further we move away from extreme situations, the more difficult it becomes to judge what to do. General principles that work well in prototypical or "paradigmatic" cases provide little guidance in the host of specific situations that exist in the gray area between the extremes.[9] At best they give us a starting point for our thinking. Beyond that, we must think together in an effort to "specify" the belief or principle that we want to guide our decision *in the particular case before us.*

## The Facts of the Matter

When people disagree over how to respond to a matter of public concern, differences of opinion about "the facts" often feature prominently in the discussion. It would be a mistake to conclude, however, that disagreement stems solely, or even chiefly, from such differences. Most of the factual assertions that become points of contention in political disagreements are statements that, on their face at least, are susceptible to more than one interpretation—as anyone familiar with the uses and abuses of statistics can attest. The "wiggle room" in a typical factual statement having political implications is more than adequate to the needs of someone who is strongly disposed to accept or reject it. Most intractable political disagreements can be traced ultimately to a conflict of values or value-priorities. Because the parties to such disagreements typically are strongly committed or attached to one of the values or priorities in conflict, they are apt to experience a powerful desire to preserve that commitment or attachment, sometimes at any cost (for example, when their core identity is threatened).[10] When facts get in the way of something we intensely want or need to believe, the facts will be the first casualty. We will try to interpret them in a way that leaves our evaluative commitments and attachments undisturbed. Failing that, we will reject the facts outright, even if it means living with inconsistencies in our belief structure.[11]

Nevertheless, facts are important. We can't give up trying to determine what is factually true and what isn't. If we're psychologically secure enough to approach political disagreements with an open mind, inquiring into the facts will go a long way toward helping us resolve those disagreements. Even if we're not, being compelled to deal with assertions of fact remains a valuable constraint on our inclinations and behavior, which if unchecked by such considerations might otherwise lead us into serious trouble. Unfortunately, much of the time we resist the mental effort that's required to ascertain and verify the facts that would help us understand the difficult cases that present the greatest challenge to forming a sound public judgment. For this reason I now want to digress somewhat to discuss work done by D. N. Perkins, Richard Allen, and James Hafner, researchers at the Harvard Graduate School of Education.[12]

If I understand Perkins and his colleagues correctly, the sort of "rationality" or "logic" that's appropriate for practical judgments of the sort we have to make in politics is not the deductive or inductive logic that constitutes the subject matter of textbooks on critical thinking.[13] Rather, it's a much less formal system we've developed to help us "make sense" of a situation. Yet even though the relevant standards aren't those having the precision and rigor of formal logic, practical rationality does set *some* standards, standards that people can and do fail to live up to. As Perkins et al. remark, "people aren't very good at ['everyday' reasoning]." They encounter a number of difficulties in building up an adequate and coherent model of the situation they're trying to assess.

According to Perkins, Allen, and Hafner, the sort of practical rationality appropriate for political discussion consists of (largely implicit) guidelines for "plausible conjectures that hang together well enough to be worth believing in." The mechanism that drives the process is the effort to devise sound premises, which are tested through "a series of objections to the argument [as it's developed] so far. . . . Each objection amounts to a challenge of some premise lying behind the previous statement." The authors give an example of people discussing whether to establish a policy of encouraging consumers to recycle bottles and cans: "To the proposition that people will return bottles and cans for five cents, the objection is that five cents will not persuade people to bother. The objection could be rephrased, 'The law assumes that five cents is sufficient to motivate people to return bottles. But five cents isn't enough.'" Note that in the example the discussants aren't sure whether recycling can be achieved through the positive incentive of a cash refund. Their reasoning begins with the assertion that people will recycle if they're promised a five-cent refund. To this assertion someone "objects"—that is, offers a counterassertion—that the prediction is false. The objection in effect says, "We're assuming that this is true, but we can't make that assumption because in fact it's not true."

The authors make four noteworthy points about this sort of practical reasoning. First, the premises (i.e., the assertions, whether explicit or implicit) change and accumulate as reasoning proceeds. They have to be generated by the discussants—they aren't "given." Second, even when objections are raised, reasoning is constructive. It has the effect of increasing understanding. Third, the premises "are very context specific. . . . [The issue] cannot be decided by any . . . sweeping general principle." We have to state very precisely the circumstances we're talking about if we're going to be able to judge whether a general proposition holds in this instance, and, if it should, how its application is to be specified. Finally, people don't necessarily hold tightly to their assertions. When a better (more satisfactory) one comes along, they're able to substitute it for the old one.

What sorts of objections help move the process of practical reasoning along? What challenges to our beliefs help us improve our understanding of the situation we're examining? Perkins et al. found that 80 percent of the helpful objections raised in their study fell into eight categories. Here, roughly in the order of frequency, are the eight (constructive) "troublemakers":

—*Contrary Consequent.* "That's not what'll happen."
—*Contrary Antecedent.* "That might happen, but that doesn't mean it'll happen for the reason you say it will. If it does, it'll be because . . ."
—*External Factor.* "In general that might be true, but it isn't so in *this* case, because . . ."
—*Disconnection.* "The point you've made doesn't justify your conclusion. It doesn't follow. The assertion you made in support of your conclusion might be valid, but your conclusion is still not warranted."
—*Scalar Insufficiency.* "Yes, that's so, but it doesn't hold strongly enough. It's not true to a sufficient degree."
—*Neglected Critical Distinction.* "There's an important distinction that you're overlooking. What you say might be true generally, but it doesn't apply in certain types of cases, and this is one of those."
—*Counterexample.* "But what about this [example]? It suggests that just the opposite is true."[14]
—*Alternative Argument.* "OK, you've got a point. Your objection's valid. But my conclusion's still justified because . . ."

Raising such objections in the course of political discussion is useful and desirable, and hence ought to be encouraged. Unlike many objections cited in textbooks as examples of fallacious reasoning, the objections cited by Perkins et al. are essentially constructive—they promote collaborative inquiry rather than competitive debate. Unfortunately, as the authors note, people aren't very good at raising and responding to these objections. They don't take advantage of the opportunity to use such objections to construct a perspective on the situation that both makes sense to them and holds up in the face of most serious objections. People seem unable—or unwilling—to undertake the kind of mental effort that's needed in situations that call for the exercise of judgment. Why?

Perkins et al. contend that skilled practical reasoning requires a number of things. First, the reasoner needs a "large knowledge repertoire"—for example, plenty of facts and an understanding of causation. Second, he or she needs "efficient knowledge evocation"—the ability to recognize patterns, envision probable consequences, construct plausible scenarios, rule out unlikely explanations, and so forth. Third, and perhaps most important, skill in practical reasoning depends on the person's ability and willingness to "interrogate [his or her] knowledge-base in order to construct arguments pro and con." What separates the more-skilled from the less-skilled practical reasoner is the former's ability and readiness to criticize and revise his own assertions, assumptions, arguments, and conclusions. In short, he remains open minded and self-critical; he holds his view tentatively and provisionally; he rethinks what he believes in response to new information and new situations.

In contrast, less-skilled reasoners are always too ready to be satisfied. They "act as though the test of truth is that a proposition makes intuitive sense"—it "sounds right," it "rings true. . . . They see no need to criticize or revise accounts that do make sense. [For them,] the intuitive feel of it suffices." For example, to a less-skilled reasoner it might "make sense" to assume that people who act in a reprehensible manner have reprehensible motivations. Or it might "make sense" to assume that people will return their glass bottles if promised a five-cent refund. Equally, it might appear to "make sense" that AIDS is a just penalty for sexual behavior that shouldn't be engaged in by anyone in any circumstances. Or it might "make sense" that holes in the earth's ozone layer and global warming are the result of burning fossil fuels. For the less-skilled reasoner, that's the end of the matter. Why is it the end of the matter? Perkins et al. suggest that the "makes-sense" reasoner seeks "to minimize cognitive load." Complicated cognitive activity "is shunned in favor of the simplest, most straightforward interpretation that seems to fit" because that's the least demanding—or least unsettling—way of dealing with situations. In short, psychological needs may dispose people to resist rethinking what they have come to believe.

As the authors duly note, approaching most situations with a "makes-sense" attitude works fairly well. The problem is that it's not suitable for circumstances that are novel or where certainty is elusive. Of course, it is precisely in these kinds of situations that conflicts between values occur. In such situations, we can't straightforwardly and unproblematically apply our beliefs about what's good and bad, right and wrong, true and false. We need to exercise our judgment. The "makes-sense" strategy is not very helpful in these situations. Indeed, it's actually an impediment to reaching a sound judgment.

For this reason, we need to be on guard against the danger of failing to raise and respond adequately to the sorts of objections Perkins et al. have described. We should try to develop strategies and methods for ensuring that these objections are raised routinely and dealt with properly. This effort might include structuring the deliberative process in such a way that objections are more likely to arise. It might also include cultivating the skills of practical reasoning, either as a preface to deliberation or as a "learn-as-you-go" aspect of deliberating itself. For example, Perkins recommends that we frequently ask ourselves, Why might this *not* be the case? Why might this *not* be the explanation? As he observes, "asking 'Why *not?*' runs . . . contrary to the makes-sense [way of thinking], because it refuses to accept at face value what seems to be an adequate account. Instead of settling for the first decent fit, the 'Why not?' tactic expects that a dialectical process of argument and counter-argument will gradually evolve a more differentiated model."

Happily for those of us who recommend practical politics, deliberating together with our fellow citizens (especially if the community is represented in its full diversity) offers some built-in protection against the failure to consider and respond to objections that will move us beyond an inadequate "makes-sense" understanding toward a judgment in which we can have confidence. As Perkins et al. rightly observe, "the soundness of an objection . . . can[not] be defined in any more rigorous way than through the evaluation of other human judges." When it comes to the sort of practical reasoning required for political deliberation, the final authority about what count as standards for sound judgment, and hence what counts as a sound judgment, is the public itself. This is why the group that is discussing a problem or issue must be as inclusive as possible, representing all the various perspectives—including reasoning styles—that people might bring to the situation.

## Deliberation in Practice

In chapter 6 I showed how the debate over abortion might be reformulated (at least in part). I offered that there are several basic value conflicts in the debate that constitute underlying *issues*. One of those issues might be whether there are objective rules of right and wrong that govern such questions and whether such rules apply in every situation we might encounter. There are several responses that people might give to this issue:

> Issue: Are there objective rules of right and wrong? If so, do they indicate clearly what we should do?
>
> View A: Yes, there are objective rules. If people with good intentions think carefully about this question, they will know what's right and what they should do.
>
> View B: Whether or not there are objective rules, we still need to engage each other in constructive dialogue. If we try, we can arrive at a common-sense conclusion that most reasonable people will accept.
>
> View C: There aren't objective rules. We could never reach agreement about what's right. So we should let majority opinion decide.
>
> View D: There aren't objective rules. We could never reach agreement about what's right. So we should leave it up to the individual to decide.

At this point we could take the foregoing views and develop policy options based on them. However, I believe it's better not to do so. The policy options that would emerge would probably resemble too closely the ones familiar to us in the long-standing debate over abortion. A discussion that begins by asking participants to consider such options probably would lead them down the well-worn path to deadlock. It would invite people to make the same arguments they usually make, and to make them in the same way. It is more productive to ask participants to examine the different *viewpoints* that have been developed through the process (explained in chapter 6) of (1) collecting statements, (2) identifying motivations, (3) clustering motivations into viewpoints, (4) clarifying the issues, and (5) reformulating the matter for public discussion. The question of what we (as a community) should do—what policy we should adopt, what action we should take—should be put off as long as possible.

The person or persons who take responsibility for facilitating a public discussion have three tasks to perform.[15] First, they must help participants to *comprehend* (understand and appreciate) the motivating beliefs, reasons, and values underlying each viewpoint and to *confirm* (acknowledge) the "understandability," the "not unreasonableness," of those motivating beliefs, reasons, and values. Second, they must help participants *deliberate*—to assess and weigh the motivating beliefs, reasons, and values that influence the different views that people hold. Third, they must help participants reach a *judgment*—a prioritized order among the various motivating beliefs participants hold—about what to do.

We need to add one more ingredient to our deliberative stew, however:

*cases*—specific, concrete situations that will enable and encourage (indeed, compel) participants to struggle with the task of applying their initial general prescriptions to a variety of factual circumstances. To start this process, it is helpful to begin with examples that represent opposite extremes: one a situation in which the vast majority of people would likely agree (in our example) that abortion is not a morally acceptable response (and therefore should probably, though not necessarily, be prohibited), the other a situation in which the vast majority of people would likely agree that abortion is a morally acceptable response (and therefore should probably, though not necessarily, be permitted). The facilitator would start with one of the cases and ask participants to consider their views in light of the circumstances specified by the case. He or she would ask them whether they would still hold their view unchanged "*in a case like this,*" or whether they would modify it, and if so, how.

The facilitator should take every opportunity to ask participants to (1) explain why they believe their view is justified, probing gently but firmly until it appears that the speaker is unable or unwilling to say anything further that might shed light on his or her motivation; (2) weigh the different motivating beliefs, reasons, and values that have surfaced within the group; and (3) explain why he or she gives priority to one of these over others. For example, this dialogue might take place:

> Facilitator: Let's consider a hypothetical case. What if the person who might be a candidate for abortion is a child of twelve, now two months pregnant, who was raped repeatedly by her mentally defective and abusive father. The girl's mother died several years ago, and she has no other family. Already pushed to the brink of psychosis by her emotional and physical trauma, she also has a serious heart defect that virtually guarantees that she could not survive childbirth. As if that weren't enough, tests on the sixteen-week-old fetus reveal that it suffers from a congenital disease that in all known cases has brought death before the child's first birthday, and that tortures the infant with inconceivable pain during its brief existence.
>
> Let's look now at the four viewpoints that have been prepared to help us begin working toward a sound policy that would deal satisfactorily with a case like this. How does the view that comes closest to your own "fit" a case like this? Would you continue to hold your view unchanged? Or do you think the hypothetical case would prompt you to modify your view somewhat?
>
> Participant 1: Well, my own view is pretty much the same as View A. I don't think this case makes me want to modify my view, although I'm not entirely sure. *If* it's factually true that we can't save both the girl and the child, and *if* as a matter of fact the child wouldn't survive long

and would be in great pain the entire time, then there might be room for an exception. Maybe, in a case like this, we need a provision that permits abortion if the mother's life can be saved only by sacrificing the child. But even if I were to change my view for this particular case, that wouldn't affect my view in the great majority of cases.

Participant 2: My view is definitely the same as View A. I couldn't approve of an exception even in circumstances such as the ones we're considering. Doing so would permit a terrible wrong to occur. I can think of at least two reasons why I would oppose abortion even in this case. First, we're assuming that the facts as presented are true. The problem is, in the real world we couldn't be that certain. We couldn't know for sure that the girl would die in childbirth. And we couldn't know that the child wouldn't survive—especially if a new treatment for the baby's condition were suddenly to appear during her first year of life. And that could happen. Second, even if we knew for sure that the facts of the case are true, as far as I'm concerned making a decision about which life to save amounts to "playing God." I don't think it's up to me to make that decision.

Facilitator: Let me see if I understand what you're saying, and then ask you a couple of questions. You don't think we can ever be certain about the facts in actual cases, correct?

Participant 2: Right.

Facilitator: And if we can't be 100 percent certain about the facts, then we can't make the decision—anything less than 100 percent isn't enough. Is that right?

Participant 2: Yes.

Facilitator: So even if we could be sure in ninety-nine cases out of a hundred, that's still not enough certainty?

Participant 2: To my way of thinking, it's not. This could be the one case in a hundred.

Facilitator: Okay. Let me ask you a question, though, just to be sure I understand you. Suppose your spouse were diagnosed with a rare but extremely virulent form of cancer, one that ninety-nine times out of a hundred proves fatal. There's a treatment, but it works in only one case in every hundred, and even then it only extends life by about a year. Would you want your spouse to have that treatment?

Participant 2: Well, I don't know some of the facts I'd need to take into account, such as the side effects the treatment would have, but I'm pretty sure I'd want him to have it, yes.

Facilitator: So, one percent certainty is enough certainty for you?

Participant 2: Yes. But it's a much different matter. If I take the one chance in a hundred and we're fortunate, my spouse lives, even if it's only for a year. That's a life *saved*. In the hypothetical example we're considering, the decision I make will take a life.

Facilitator: Would it be accurate to say that your concern isn't really how certain you can be, but whether you're willing to take responsibility for a decision that could result in a life being taken?

Participant 2: You're right about my attitude toward taking responsibility. But I still think certainty matters. If by my decision I could save the life of the pregnant girl without having to take responsibility for the death of her child, I wouldn't hesitate to make that decision, even if the odds were ninety-nine to one against me. But taking a life is serious business. I'm not going to accept responsibility for that, even if I'm 99 percent sure I could save another life by doing so. God in his infinite wisdom could make that choice, but I can't. I don't have his authority, and I don't have his wisdom.

Facilitator: It sounds to me as if you wouldn't be willing to accept responsibility for such a decision even if you were 100 percent certain that the girl would live. So if I may I'd like to ask you to try for a minute—try to imagine, as a kind of thought experiment—that you really could be 100 percent certain that by deciding to let the girl have an abortion you would save her life. Would you still refuse to make the decision?

Participant 2: (after thinking hard for a few seconds) Okay. *If* I were *absolutely* certain . . . No, I still don't think I could make that decision. It's something I just have to leave up to God. If he chooses to spare her life, wonderful. But if he chooses to take it, he has his reasons. It's not for me to decide.

Facilitator: Let me ask one last question before we move on. Do you think it's true that "not to choose is to choose"? Would you agree that, by not deciding, you're still deciding? So your decision not to do anything to save the girl's life is still a decision that has consequences—specifically, the highly probable consequence that she will lose her life.

Participant 2: I agree that by deciding against a policy that would permit the girl to have an abortion I would in effect take an action that would increase the risk that she'll die. But I don't believe that's the kind of action that's morally objectionable. For one thing, whatever consequences it might have would be unintentional. I wouldn't be doing it to hurt someone. Another thing is, I don't think I have a moral duty to act in a way that reduces the risk of the girl dying. As tragic and heartbreaking as her situation is, she's at risk in the first place through no action, or inaction, on my part. Hers is just one of countless misfortunes in the world that, realistically speaking, I can't even begin to remedy. I have to believe there's a reason for this, and only God knows what it is.

In my opinion, I should be morally responsible only for situations in which I possess enough wisdom at least to do no harm, and maybe do some good. For example, I'm not a Christian Scientist. If I can save my child's life by getting him medical treatment I'm going to do it. His well-being is my responsibility, and I think God expects me to accept that responsibility. But in that kind of situation I don't need the wisdom of Solomon, or God, to make the right decision. The right thing to do is clear. In the case we've been discussing, it's not clear. I don't think I have, or anybody else has, the infallible judgment that's required to know whether it's justifiable to sacrifice one life to save another. What I *do* have is the ability to decide whether or not to intentionally take a life. And that's what I would be permitting if I sanctioned a policy that would have the effect of saving the girl's life at the expense of her unborn child. It's my moral responsibility to not take a life. It's not my responsibility to decide which of two lives is to be saved. I believe we have to leave that to God. And that's what we accomplish by adopting a policy that flat out prohibits the taking of life.

Participant 3: Could I ask you a question about your position?

Participant 2: Sure.

Participant 3: Thanks. My question has to do with what you said about the consequences of your action being unintentional. I think you said that, by supporting a policy that strictly prohibits abortion, you wouldn't be setting out to deliberately hurt someone. Is that right?

Participant 2: Yes.

Participant 3: Well, it seems to me that we often have moral objections to actions that are unintentional. I'm no legal expert, but I know that in law there are well-established principles that assign blame to people who cause harm even if they didn't intend to do so. Probably the most familiar one is negligence. We can be held legally accountable for harm we cause if we're careless or inattentive. Another principle is the tort law doctrine of "last clear chance." We can be at fault in a traffic accident if we had the last clear chance to avoid the accident and we didn't take it, even though we didn't create the dangerous situation in the first place. And then there's the principle of felony homicide, which holds that you're guilty of murder if you kill someone in the course of committing a felony, even if you didn't intend to do so. My point is, it seems to me you're on shaky ground if you try to excuse your decision by saying you didn't intend to cause any harm.

Participant 2: Maybe I misspoke. Maybe it would be more accurate to say that any harm that the girl in this hypothetical case suffers is an unfortunate but unavoidable side effect of the greater moral duty I have to preserve the life of her unborn child. When I described her predicament just a minute ago as "tragic," I meant it in the familiar sense of the word. But it occurs to me now that her situation is tragic in the narrower sense that harm is an unavoidable consequence of doing the right thing. I think we have a prior moral duty to protect the life of the unborn child. If carrying out that duty causes harm, that's terrible, and it's sad. But there's nothing we can do about it. The situation is just such that harm can't be avoided. That's what I meant to get at by saying the harm would be unintentional.

Participant 3: All right. That makes more sense to me.

Participant 4: I'd like to ask you about your attitude toward personal responsibility. You say you can't accept responsibility for making a decision about which life to save—only God can make that kind of decision. But aren't there a lot of situations in which you do accept that responsibility? What about a situation in which either your life or the life of someone you love is being threatened? Suppose an armed man breaks into your house and you believe he's going to kill you and your family. You have a gun and you know how to use it. Wouldn't you accept responsibility for making a decision about whether to save the intruder's life or the lives of your family members? Or what about war? If our country were in imminent danger of being destroyed, would you refuse to decide whether we should fight back, even though that would mean killing a lot of innocent people? And what about capital punishment? Don't you have an opinion about that? If you do have an opinion, then whether you're for it or against it aren't you accepting responsibility for deciding whether a person who commits a brutal murder should be put to death?

Participant 2: Well, I'd have to think some more about those kinds of cases, but let me see if I can articulate my intuitions about why I would distinguish them from the hypothetical case of the pregnant girl. For one thing, the examples you've given involve powerful human instincts. The examples of the intruder and war have to do with self-preservation. That's such a powerful motivation that, almost universally, I think, societies make it an exception to the general prohibition on killing. As for what God expects of me, I have a hard time believing he would expect me not to react in this very human way in order to protect innocent people, especially ones close to me. I hope—and I want to believe—that he'd forgive me for acting on my understandable human desire to protect innocent lives, even if that means I have to take the life of a person who isn't innocent. And that raises a second point about your examples. Intruders and aggressors aren't innocent. They're consciously and deliberately malevolent. I think that matters. By their own action they condemn themselves to suffering the consequences. That's why I can support capital punishment as a general principle, at least for certain types of cases. Making a decision about who should live and who should die is a lot easier for me when there's an innocent victim and a killer who should be held accountable for his actions.

Participant 4: Without getting into particular arguments for your views about self-defense and capital punishment, it still seems to me that you're accepting responsibility for making a decision in those cases about who will live and who will die. You may be able to justify your response, but that's not the point. The point is, you don't say, "I can't decide, only God can decide." You accept—in fact, you seem to willingly embrace—the necessity of a choice, which you then go on to make. It just seems to me that you're not being consistent. You say you can't support a policy that would permit an abortion in the case we've been talking about because you can't accept responsibility for deciding which life to save. But then you *do* accept responsibility for this decision in the cases of self-defense and capital punishment. So it seems to me that not being able to take responsibility isn't the real reason, or isn't the main reason, why you don't want to support a policy that would permit abortion in our hypothetical case.

Participant 2: Well, maybe. But I still feel there's something qualitatively different about the two kinds of cases, something that's morally significant. I keep coming back to the fact that, in our hypothetical case, both the lives at stake are innocent. In your examples, the killer is not innocent. He's morally responsible for his actions, and he should be held accountable for them. So I don't have as much difficulty accepting responsibility for making a decision in those kinds of cases. Morally speaking, I feel I'm up to the task. But I'm not up to it in a case where both the lives are innocent.

Participant 4: But isn't that just another way of saying you can't make up your mind? You don't want to make a decision—and I think that's understandable, by the way, because I feel the same way about the death penalty—you don't want to make a decision because you know that whatever you do will have terrible consequences. So you justify your reluctance to choose by in effect making up and asserting a principle of nonresponsibility.

Participant 2: Well, I'm sorry it seems that way to you. I really don't feel I'm avoiding responsibility. To me, it feels like I'm acting judiciously. Maybe it's a matter of personal perspective—you call it avoiding responsibility and I call it being wise enough to know I'm not wise enough to make the right decision. It doesn't change the fact, in my estimation, that your examples and our hypothetical case are moral horses of different colors.

Facilitator: I think we've probably taken this particular line of inquiry as far as we can usefully take it right now. Let's see if anyone else has questions.

Participant 5: I have a question. If you want to decline personal responsibility for making a decision, that's fine. But I suspect you would object if other people accept it. It's all right with me if you want don't want to decide; I can respect that. But I think you should respect my willingness to face up to the hard decision.

Facilitator: So what's your question?

Participant 5: My question is, Will you grant me the moral freedom to make my own decision, which is to accept responsibility for facing up to the dilemma in this case and making a decision about what to do?

Participant 2: You're certainly free to make your own decision. And I can respect your willingness to face up to the hard choice. But I reserve the right to take issue with the decisions you make, and with the reasons you give for your decisions. I can respect your conviction that you have a duty to make the hard decision, but I don't have to agree that the conclusions you reach are the right ones. We can disagree about who is right and who is wrong. That means you can continue to think you're right, and I can continue to think I'm right.

Participant 5: Okay, fine. But if we're going to engage in argument about our respective conclusions and the reasons we give for them, it seems to me that we ought to disallow certain kinds of justifications—specifically, religious ones. Your reasons, ultimately, have a religious foundation. I don't think it's appropriate for us to make decisions about public policy that rest on religious convictions. That's what the constitutional requirement of separation of church and state is all about.

Participant 2: If my religious convictions were something I just made up for my own convenience or to serve my own, narrow interests, you'd have a point. But they aren't. They're grounded in an authority outside of and greater than myself. I don't think people with purely secular moral views can say the same thing. In fact, I think nonreligious moral judgments are groundless. Ultimately, they come down to one's personal preferences. And because they do, they're by definition self-serving.

Participant 5: I don't think you can characterize the desire to take pity on an abused twelve-year-old as self-serving, but let's leave that aside. What I consider different and troubling about justifying policy in terms of a person's religious convictions is precisely that external source you invoke: religious teaching. I have two basic problems with the impact of religious teaching, one general and one specific. My general concern is that there's so much room for interpretation in scripture that people can read into it whatever conclusions they want. So believers simply reinforce their preexisting beliefs, no matter how misguided they might be. People with a persecution complex will find plenty of support for their conviction that they're being persecuted. People who are vindictive will find plenty of support for their conviction that vengeance is justified. People who want to keep women and blacks in their place will find support for their sexism and racism. The very fact that people's religious convictions are "grounded in an authority outside of themselves," as you put it, guarantees that their worst inclinations will be strengthened. If religious teachings had the effect of enlightening and educating people, I would be the first to welcome religion-based viewpoints into our public discourse. But they have just the opposite effect, it seems to me.

My specific concern is that religion tends to generate a paralyzing fear in people that keeps them from changing and adapting to new conditions. Perhaps I'm mistaken, but I suspect that your reluctance to take responsibility for making a tough decision in a case like the one we're discussing stems at least partly from your fear that you'll make the wrong decision, and that God will hold you accountable and punish you. No wonder you want to beg off making a decision. My guess is that at some level you feel your immortal soul will be safer if you cling to a few hoary, simplistic commandments than if you take the risk of thinking for yourself. That wouldn't be so bad if those rules weren't so far removed from and so irrelevant to conditions in modern America. They have their roots in the anxieties and insecurities of a primitive, unsophisticated culture whose members could not have imagined the kinds of moral situations we are facing today. I think a contemporary morality based on such an outdated, parochial worldview is worse than irrelevant. I think it's dangerous. It puts a paralyzing fear into people who ought to be taking responsibility for putting the world to rights. And it's innocent twelve-year-old victims of rape and incest that suffer because of it. At least secular morality doesn't let people off the hook. That makes it superior in my book.

Participant 2: I guess you've had a much more negative experience with religion than I have. What you say about the effect of religion might be true of some people. I don't think it's true of most, and it's certainly not true of me. If anything, I think my religious beliefs give me more sympathy and compassion for other folks than I would have otherwise.

Facilitator: I'd like to make a point here that might help us as we continue our discussion. Even if it were true that religion in some way contributes to people's inability or unwillingness to think through difficult moral situations and to make judgments that intuitively seem at odds with their fundamental principles, it's unlikely that we will reduce their fear by criticizing those principles. Even if people hold beliefs that we consider groundless or misguided, it's unlikely that we will

change their minds about those beliefs in the course of our deliberations about specific policy issues. I believe we'll have a more constructive and more productive discussion if we try to just understand,
appreciate, and acknowledge the needs, or fears, or other feelings
that people have. That doesn't mean we have to accept them as well
founded or persuasive. We don't have to agree with them. But if we
can treat them as just facts, as "the way things are," like the weather,
without lamenting them or denigrating them or attacking them, I
think we'll make much better progress toward a policy decision we
can all support. So if you don't mind, I'd like to ask you to accept
this suggestion as a guideline for the remainder of our discussion. Are
there other questions?

Participant 6: I think the suggestion that there's a tough moral dilemma in
the hypothetical case of the twelve-year-old girl is overstated. Personally, I'm inclined to the view that the fetus is not a life at all, at least
not yet. But even if we assume it is, I don't think it's equal to that of
the pregnant girl. First of all, she's got a long life ahead of her—if we
don't make her go to full term. So we may end up robbing her of the
thing that's most precious to us all—and the thing that presumably
only God has the right to take away. The fetus, in contrast—assuming it turns out to be viable—isn't expected to survive beyond a year.
What we deprive the fetus of is not the experience of life as most of
us think of it, but the experience of uncomprehending pain and suffering. Second, the girl is conscious of the fact that she's alive. Forcing her to put her life in jeopardy to bear a child she didn't want and
that she can't take any satisfaction in having is unspeakably cruel. It
says, "we're going to give you a possible death sentence for a crime
you didn't commit." I can't imagine a good and loving God would
deliberately inflict such cruelty on any creature.

Participant 2: All I can say is that, while I'm not insensitive to the kinds of
considerations you raise, I still believe it's not up to me to decide. I
just have to hope for the best and reconcile myself to the outcome,
whatever it is.

Facilitator: Does anyone have a point that hasn't already been made? . . .
If not, let me ask what we, as a group, would recommend as a policy
for cases like the hypothetical one we've been discussing. Have we
made any progress, or not? What still has to be resolved?

Participant 1: It seems to me we're back where we started. Some of us
clearly think it's too restrictive to permit an abortion only if the
mother's life can't be saved without sacrificing the child. This formulation might work for the case of the twelve-year-old girl. But because that's such an extreme and rare case, such a policy would
amount to a total ban on abortion.

Participant 6: Actually, I think we've made some progress. It's true that we haven't reached agreement on the best policy for dealing with extreme cases such as our hypothetical one. But at least we're discussing the matter. We're working through a specific, concrete case. That gives us a chance to refine our positions, not just assert and defend them, which is what we end up doing when we debate an abstract principle that's so broad that our only choice is to accept or reject it. We're identifying and exchanging reasons for our different views. That allows us to open up the discussion instead of closing it down at the outset by simply claiming "I'm right and you're wrong."

Participant 4: There's something else that's important about our discussion. At a couple of points we've been able to dig pretty deeply beneath our surface opinions. We've gotten a lot closer than ordinarily happens to the real motivations that people have for the positions they take. Personally, I now feel somewhat better about you (participant 2) and your view on abortion. I think your stance on responsibility is mistaken. But I don't find it wildly irrational or incomprehensible. I can understand how you feel about it. It's a scary business making decisions that have possible life-or-death implications. Believe me, if I thought we could relieve ourselves of responsibility for making these kinds of decisions, I'd be all for it. But in all sincerity, I don't think we can. God may speak to us, but he doesn't do so directly. If he does, it's through the conclusions we reach when we struggle to determine what's right—or, to put it in religious language, when we pray fervently that he'll reveal to us his will. I guess I take some consolation from believing that if all of us make a good-faith effort to arrive at the soundest, wisest judgment possible, we'll make the best decision. And that decision, even if it's only the best that's humanly possible, will have to do. I don't think God expects us to be passive in the face of moral challenges. If he did, we'd never make any moral or spiritual progress. Moral dilemmas are the engine of our moral and spiritual growth. Without them, we'd stagnate. I think God expects us to struggle with our moral judgments, and then to act on them. If we do that, he can't be displeased with us. Indeed, I think that's what he wants from us more than anything else.

Participant 2: I guess I feel somewhat better, too, about the people in this group who disagree with me. Right now, I don't think I'm going to change my mind. But you've got me thinking. I can appreciate why you've reached a different conclusion. And I find it a little bit unsettling, to be honest. It makes me want to go over my reasons again, if only to reassure myself about my position. I doubt I'll conclude that anything less than a blanket ban on abortion will do for the vast majority of cases. But maybe in this one particular case we've been talking about, it would be best to make an exception. I don't know. I'll have to think about it.

Participant 1: I think we've actually made progress, not just in terms of the *process* of working toward a policy that might win widespread support, but also in terms of the *substance* of such a policy. If we look back at the variety of considerations we've entertained, I think we'll find that we've addressed quite a few issues. We've talked about certainty, about moral responsibility, about the sanctity of life and the relevance of its quality, respect for divergent viewpoints, the importance of making noninterference a presumption in our relations with others, the relevance of religious views and the status of religious reasons, the grounds for nonreligious moral views, and so forth. I think if we were systematic and thorough in trying to assign weights to these considerations, we would find that we're a lot closer to a sound judgment that most people would support than we were when we started out. I don't think there are any "knock-down" arguments on either side of the abortion issue. I don't think anybody's going to come up with a logically valid argument that'll trump or defeat everybody else's arguments, leaving theirs standing alone in the field, victorious. But I do think we can combine the various threads of the arguments we've considered into a "cord" that might provide us pretty strong support for a policy.

Facilitator: That's a good observation. But before we move on to another case, one at the opposite end of the spectrum, let me pose this question: If even the hypothetical case we've been considering is a hard one for us to reach agreement concerning, and if all other cases are at least as hard for us to agree on, what should we do? Suppose it's not possible, through the kind of dialogue we've been engaged in, to build a strong "cord" that will support a widely supported policy. How should do we deal with the fact that we don't agree, and may not ever agree? What should we do?

Participant 5: I don't think we'll have much success agreeing on what to do unless we continue the substantive dialogue. I don't think we could know what policy is best without going through the process of painstakingly discussing detailed cases such as the hypothetical one of the twelve-year-old girl and carefully considering the kinds of arguments that we've offered in trying to work our way toward a conclusion. I think our ability to agree on what we should do if in the end we can't agree depends on our first making the effort to reach a substantive judgment we can all share in.

Facilitator: What do the rest of you think about that? (General nodding and murmurs of assent.) I think that's probably an accurate prediction. So why don't we turn, now, to a hypothetical case at the other extreme?

Notice how the other participants in this hypothetical dialogue try to comprehend the motivating beliefs, reasons, and values underlying the viewpoint expressed by participant 2. Through respectful but close questioning, they're able to reach a point where they can see the "understandability," the "not unreasonableness," of the beliefs and values that motivate participant 2, which they are then able to acknowledge. Having accomplished this, they can begin deliberating—assessing and weighing the reasons that participant 2 offers to explain and justify her assertions. If the participants can sustain their efforts to comprehend each other and to deliberate together over a variety of specific cases, in time they will reach a shared judgment about how they, as a community, should respond to the problem posed by the issue of abortion.

At this juncture the group should proceed to discuss the case of the well-educated, happy, and healthy thirty-year-old professional woman who wishes to begin a family with her husband. (Five months into the pregnancy the couple learns that the child will be a boy. Both prospective parents prefer a girl. So they want to terminate the pregnancy.) After thoroughly examining this case, which represents the extreme opposite point on the spectrum of hypothetical situations, the group should then take up some of the truly difficult cases—the ones in the "gray area" between the extremes. By this process of "successive approximation," the group can bring itself closer to a policy that everyone can live with or go along with, even if it doesn't represent the ideal solution. This outcome is less than consensus, but more than a mere *modus vivendi,* as we will see in chapter 9 when we consider further the idea of public judgment.

### Conclusion

Deliberation is the process of assessing and weighing conflicting motivating beliefs and the reasons that support them in order to establish a (new or revised) prioritized order among those beliefs. To deliberate is to reconcile conflicting opinions in order to reach a sound judgment about which of the valuable outcomes we should give priority.

If we carefully and patiently struggle with the task of applying our initial opinions to a variety of factual circumstances; if in the course of doing so we "comprehend"—that is, understand and appreciate (and acknowledge)—the motivating beliefs and values that underlie the opinions and positions we hold; and if we deliberate together, carefully weighing our motivating beliefs and the reasons we give for them, we will make surer and swifter progress toward a satisfactory resolution of the issue that divides us than we could achieve by any other means.

# 8

# Fourth Principle: Cooperation

*It is our task—our essential, central, crucial task—to transform ourselves from mere social creatures into community creatures.*

—M. Scott Peck

---

**Fourth Principle: Cooperation.** Don't fight with each other—work with each other. If winning the battle today is all you care about, you may end up losing the war. Disregard the concerns and interests of your fellow citizens, and they won't forget it—they will try to make you pay for it later. Cooperation is less costly and more productive than competition, especially over the long run.

NOT in AMERICA

### Collaboration and Cooperation

To some degree, in every community—no matter what its size—the public is fragmented. People are divided along lines created by their different perceptions of who they are, what the world is like, what goods we should seek and what priorities we should have, and who should do what, when, and how. Whatever the source of such perceptions—cultural, economic, psychological, experiential, generational, sexual, ideological, ethnic—the fact is that community members rarely assign the same priority initially to the same goals.

Recent research suggests that only in unusual circumstances are people able to break out of their habitual preoccupation with their particular interests. Disasters, for example—the San Francisco earthquake of 1989, Hurricanes Hugo in South Carolina and Andrew in south Florida, the flooding of the Mississippi River in the summer of 1993 and of the Red River in the spring of 1997—create what we might call the "practical political equivalent of war." Specifically, they produce several conditions not normally present in contemporary public life: (1) everyone's priorities are rearranged, with the same shared interests (e.g., physical safety, shelter, water and power, food) taking the top positions on everyone's list; (2) securing these interests cannot be achieved by individuals operating independently—people have to work together; (3) isolation breaks down—the shared predicament brings to the fore what people have in common, not what differentiates them; and (4) the problem that prompts realignment of priorities is evident to everyone. When these conditions are present, people *collaborate*— they work together for the shared purpose of securing things everyone needs.

The beneficial side-effects of crises such as those cited above seldom last, however. When the crisis passes, life returns to normal, and shared interests having the same priority for everyone fall back down on everybody's lists. Seldom does a serious problem last long enough to effect a permanent change in the nature of a community's political relations. Problems may be severe, but they don't produce a sense of "the community in crisis" and so don't motivate people to reconcile their narrower, particular aims with the goal of pursuing a shared interest having high priority for everyone. People revert to the norm of competitive or adversarial political interaction.

To explain the nature and importance of cooperation as a principle of practical politics, I want to distinguish, somewhat artificially, between cooperation and collaboration. The dictionary treats the two as synonyms: "working together toward a common end or purpose." I'd like to reserve this definition for collaboration. "Collaboration" implies something stronger than "cooperation," a readiness—perhaps even an eagerness—to work together in pursuit of a shared interest, as when, for example, two scholars collaborate on an article. ("Collaboration" also carries a decidedly negative connotation in certain circumstances: for example, when it means "to work with an enemy or opponent.") In contrast, "cooperation" implies a weaker form of working together. It suggests that the parties who are cooperating are merely not working at cross-purposes. They have modified their actions only to the degree necessary to avoid provoking resistance from each other. They've done so precisely because their purposes, goals, or interests are not identical.

*Cooperation*, then, is "working together for mutual benefit"—not "working arm-in-arm for the common cause." This distinction provides an important reminder that in politics the goods we seek and our interests in obtaining them can conflict, and often do. It reminds us as well that we can, and often must, work together because it is in our own interest to do so—not because we want the same thing as the folks we disagree with, but because we stand to gain more from a pragmatic decision to work together than from a mutually harmful competition.[1]

## Why Should We Cooperate?

In chapter 1 I suggested that democratic politics "doesn't work"—doesn't "produce results," doesn't "solve problems"—in large part because in our minds the civic realm resembles a political "market." Politics, we assume, is the process by which groups and individuals self-interestedly and competitively try to advance their particular visions of what's good and right. These visions, and the interests to which they give rise, constitute "political goods." We endeavor to "buy" those goods from government, which has the authority and (we believe) the power to produce and deliver them (if only by getting out of the way). We have come to think of ourselves, not as citizens, but as consumers of what government can deliver.

In a "consumerist" democracy, just as in an economic market, the best result is the one that comes closest to satisfying every individual's and group's desires. Note that in this view there's a hidden assumption, one we're all familiar with but rarely talk about. It's summed up best in Charles Wilson's well-known (albeit somewhat misinterpreted) remark that what's good for General Motors is good for the country. Substitute "me" for "General Motors," and the assumption stands out clearly. As the editors of the *New Republic* put it a few years ago, "The genius of democracy, like the genius of the market, is supposed to be that it orchestrates the individual selfishness of individual men and women into a larger pattern that serves the good of the whole."[2] In other words, if each of us will simply pursue his or her own interest, then the collective result of all our self-interested actions will be a state of affairs that is best for all of us.

In the economic realm, this identification of individual interest with collective interest poses fewer problems, at least where exchanges can be presumed to be for mutual benefit. (Even in the economic arena, however, we find plenty of examples of rational self-interest leading to undesirable collective outcomes. For example, it might be "rational" and "in one's interest" for each of us to dump untreated waste into a lake or to release pollutants into the air—at least for a time; eventually, the costs will catch up with us.) In the political realm, however, the disjunction between self-interest and the public interest is more frequent and more apparent. The "budget crisis" of the federal government over the past quarter century provides a good illustration. Essentially, voters have been presented with four choices: (1) pay higher taxes; (2) pay lower taxes; (3) enjoy adequate public and social services; (4) put up with inadequate services. Being rational and self-interested, voters have consistently chosen (2) and (3). But because it is not possible to have (from a collective point of view) both substantially lower taxes and truly adequate services, the result has been inflation, growing annual deficits and a mounting total debt, prohibitively high interest rates, or some combination thereof—clearly a state of affairs that as a society we do not want.

Theorists of collective choice call this phenomenon (of individual actions based on rational self-interest leading to outcomes that are, from a collective point of view, in no one's interest) "the tragedy of the commons." The phrase comes from the example that Garrett Hardin gave, in his article of the same name, to illustrate it.[3] Hardin asked the reader to imagine a pasture on which any herdsman might graze his animals—a commons. Being rational and self-interested, each does so, with the result that, before long, the pasture no longer has enough grass to sustain anyone's herd. Because each herdsman gets a direct benefit to his own herd from using the pasture but bears no cost in doing so, his action, when added to the actions of the other herdsmen, leads to an outcome that is in no one's interest.[4]

The tragedy of the commons has been recognized as a conundrum for more than two millennia. (Plato and Aristotle knew of it.) It has been used to clarify a host of social and political problems, including the federal budget crisis. Not much progress was made toward solving it, though, until a simpler version of it was formalized in the quasi-mathematical language of "game theory." The simple version is known as "the prisoner's dilemma."[5] (Technically, the tragedy of the commons is an "$n$-person prisoner's dilemma game.")

Here's a whimsical example of the way the dynamic of self-interested behavior works in the prisoner's dilemma. Suppose you and other members of your Oz tour group have to pass through the domain of the Wicked Witch of the West on your way to the Emerald City. Unaware of WWW regulations, you've been arrested for trying to smuggle illegal bottled water through customs. You are being held prisoner in the witch's castle. Half of you are billeted on the Flying Monkey level of the castle dungeon, the other half on the Magic Broomstick level. The witch knows that someone in your group has been plotting to melt her with an economy-size Evian. She just doesn't know who. Being a vindictive sort, she wants to punish the culprit. So she offers each of you the same deal: If you finger the folks in the other half of your group, you go free immediately. But if the others finger you, you can forget about seeing Kansas again for a long, long time.

Specifically, here's what the witch is offering:

—If each group accuses the other one, each group gets ten years.
—If neither group accuses the other one, each group gets five years.
—If the Monkey-level group accuses the Broomstick-level group, but the Broomstick group does not accuse the Monkey group, the Monkey group goes free, and the Broomstick group gets twenty years.

—If the Broomstick group accuses the Monkey group, but the Monkey group does not accuse the Broomstick group, the Broomstick group goes free, and the Monkey group gets twenty years.

Table 2 gives the options for each group, along with their "payoffs." As you think about what you're going to do, keep in mind one important fact: You're confined to separate levels of the dungeon and so can't communicate with the other group. That means you don't know what the other group is going to do— you will just have to make the best decision you can. What should you do?

*Table 2.*

| "Payoff" | Monkey Group | Broomstick Group |
|---|---|---|
| Best (go free) | Accuse B but not be accused by B | Accuse M but not be accused by M |
| Next best (5) | Not accuse B and not be accused by B | Not accuse M and not be accused by M |
| 2nd worst (10) | Accuse B and be accused by B | Accuse M and be accused by M |
| Worst (20) | Not accuse B but be accused by B | Not accuse M but be accused by M |

In this exercise, accusing the other group is the equivalent of not cooperating with them, and not accusing them is the equivalent of cooperating. The rational thing for each group to do is to accuse the other one of plotting to melt the witch. Why?

—Each group knows that the other one will either cooperate or not cooperate.
—If the other group cooperates, your group shouldn't, because the witch will let you go.
—If the other group doesn't cooperate, your group still shouldn't, because if you do, the witch will keep you locked up for twenty years.
—So no matter which course the other group chooses, yours shouldn't cooperate—you should accuse them of harboring the culprit behind the melting plot.

Where's the dilemma? If both groups act rationally and self-interestedly— that is, they don't cooperate—*both* sit in the dungeon for ten years. If each makes the rational choice, each ends up with the second-*worst* result. So rational, self-interested action—accusing each other, or not cooperating—leads to an outcome that is in the best interest of neither group. The dilemma is, do you do the rational thing and suffer the second-worst result, or do you do the irrational thing and take your chances that you will get the second-*best* result and not the worst?

The prisoner's dilemma shows why, in the real-life political situations it resembles, we often end up with results that are irrational—not in anyone's best interest. In effect, we reason like this: "My fellow citizens will either cooperate with me or not cooperate with me. If they cooperate, then I shouldn't cooperate with them, because that'll give me an advantage over them. On the other hand, if my fellow citizens don't cooperate with me, then I still shouldn't cooperate with them, because if I do cooperate and they don't, they'll have an advantage over me. So no matter which course my fellow citizens choose, I shouldn't cooperate." When most people (or at least a lot of them) reason this way, the result is worse (for most) than it would be if they cooperated.

Is there a solution to this conundrum? Is our only choice between self-sacrifice (cooperating even when others do not) and ceaseless, costly competition (never cooperating)? In computer simulations conducted a number of years ago, Robert Axelrod discovered that in $n$-person prisoner's dilemma situations the most successful strategy was a strategy he calls "tit-for-tat."[6] This strategy has four characteristics that account for its success: (1) It's "nice"—the player who uses it always offers initially to cooperate and never acts unilaterally to maximize his or her self-interest. (2) It's "retaliatory"—the user punishes noncooperation immediately. (3) It's "forgiving"—the user remembers only the previous move, not the ones that have occurred previously; he or she is always ready to cooperate with another player who is also willing to do so. (4) It's "clear"—the player using it leaves no doubt about how he or she will behave, thereby minimizing uncertainty and mistrust and making cooperation less risky and more attractive.

Significantly, tit-for-tat is a strategy for producing the best results *in the long run*. It is not the best strategy if one's goal is to *win*. In Axelrod's simulations, tit-for-tat never won outright. In fact, less-cooperative strategies were better at winning particular games. But tit-for-tat proved best if the user took the long view— accepting, in effect, that it's better to lose the battle and win the war. Tit-for-tat produced the best results over a large number of games with an opponent. This is significant because, in real life, we rarely play just a single "game" with an opponent—we play multiple "games" with him or her over a period of time.

Playing games with others repeatedly over time is another way of saying we have a *relationship* with them. Having a relationship with others doesn't mean we agree with, get along with, or even cooperate with them. A relationship can be good or bad, friendly or unfriendly, competitive or cooperative. What makes our interactions a relationship is the fact that we interact repeatedly over time. As a result, we have a substantial and enduring effect on each other's lives. The important point here is this: *if* we see ourselves as existing in a relationship with each other, we will be more likely to cooperate. Why? Because each of us will see that the strategy that will produce the best overall results is the one based on the realization that we will have many "games" over time. We will understand that not cooperating may win a few "battles" but is unlikely to win "the war." Cooperation is the strategy of rational self-interest for dealing with others *with whom one has a relationship*.

Now, the interesting question: If it's rational to cooperate only if we can count on others to cooperate as well, and if cooperation is the strategy of rational self-interest for dealing with others with whom one has a relationship, does it make a difference what kind of relationship one has with them? For example, in the exercise above, does it make a difference whether the other group is composed of people you get along with or is made up of people you don't get along with? Probably. Why? Because the former are more likely to care about your well-being in addition to their own. Odds are, they'll cooperate. And that makes it more rational for you to do so as well.

### Relationships: The Infrastructure of Civic Life

#### COOPERATION AND THE ATTENUATION OF CIVIC RELATIONSHIPS

The dearth of cooperation that characterizes our political interactions is a symptom of the difficulty we have in seeing that, for good or for ill, every one of us is enmeshed in a web of relationships that are as indispensable to a healthy community life as the air is to our physical survival. As Robert Putnam suggests, we are increasingly a society composed of solitary individuals who have retreated into the privacy of their homes and families.[7]

I have seen this first-hand in a burgeoning new suburb of Denver. There, the presidents of the community's several homeowners' associations told me that most residents of the suburb's new housing developments have not met their neighbors and do not even know their names. In such circumstances a minor irritation over a dog barking in the middle of the night can lead to a persistent dispute marred by puerile behavior on both sides. Instead of responding to each other's needs and concerns, as neighbors who enjoy a good relationship readily would do, the residents of adjoining lots resort to lobbing epithets and bottles across the fences that separate them. In America in the 1990s, it seems, neighborliness of the sort portrayed by Wilson and Tim "the Tool Man" Taylor in the television sitcom *Home Improvement* is mere nostalgic idealization. In reality, neighbors are more likely to behave like doughboys and the kaiser's troops, sniping at each other from their respective trenches.

Politics-as-we-know-it—what I have termed "consumerist politics"—not only fails to bridge these differences, it actually exacerbates them. It weakens our disposition to cooperate because it obscures our relationships with one another. In the quasi-economic consumerist political world we inhabit, we tend to lose sight of the fact that we are bound to each other in ways that will endure over time. The truth is that we resemble members of an extended family—we can't choose whether to be related to each other, and we can't escape the relationships in which we find ourselves. We have grown too interdependent to remain unaffected by what each of us does or fails to do. Indeed, today we require good working relationships with each other in order to safeguard our individual interests. Remaining preoccupied exclusively with those interests weakens or even damages our relationships, thereby making it harder to resolve disputes and protect our interests over the long run. Such preoccupation leads us to view each other as potential obstacles or adversaries rather than as partners in a relationship that affects the ability of each party to advance its vital interests. In short, it impedes cooperation.

## INDIVIDUALISM AND INDIVIDUALS

In *Habits of the Heart*, Robert Bellah and his colleagues note that one of the greatest sources of unhappiness for Americans is the sense of being trapped in constraining social relationships.[8] Not surprisingly, therefore, we strongly assert the value of self-reliance and autonomy. Bellah and his coauthors point out, however, that the term "individualism" has several meanings. The sense of the term that is most prevalent and most familiar is that of *moral* individualism. Used in this sense, "individualism" expresses the belief that the human person has inherent dignity and moral worth. Moral individualism is the basis for our claims about individual rights and Values such as freedom and equality. It lies at the core of American civic culture.

But "individualism" has another meaning as well. Although less familiar and prominent than the moral sense, *ontological* individualism is historically, culturally, and psychologically linked to the former. Ontological individualism is the belief that the individual is the primary or ultimate reality in the human world.[9] As such, the individual is the basic conceptual building block for all other human entities, including families, communities, nations, and societies. In this view, the latter are second-order, derived, or artificial constructs; they're not "real." We talk about them as if they were real things, but they aren't. If we ask ourselves what a community or a society "really is," the argument goes, we always end up talking about individual persons. Here, the analysis seems naturally to stop. Social entities can thus be "reduced" to collections of individuals.

The fact that social entities such as communities lack the tangible quality of individual human beings should not blind us, however, to their importance in the scheme of things. Nor should we allow it to mislead us into imagining that the reality of the individual person stops with the physical outer limit of his skin. Individuals are more than just brains and bodies. They're complex systems, not only of biophysical structures and biochemical processes, but of thoughts, experiences, memories, beliefs, habits, attitudes, desires, dispositions, abilities, values, sensitivities, needs, priorities, attachments, principles, and emotions. Strip away these intangible but real features of a person and what remains is not an individual but a mere human body.

Although some of what constitutes an individual is bequeathed to her by heredity, it's evident that her individuality—her uniqueness—is the consequence of the interaction between her inheritance and the conditions of the world she resides in throughout her life. If a person's life is the series and sum of those interactions over time, then the individual is, in large measure, the (ever-constant but ever-changing) result of those interactions. And if this is so, then an individual is not a thing or object per se but a *relationship* (and a dynamic one at that) between the physical person and all that exists and occurs in her environment—other human beings and their actions not least of all.

This becomes clear when we consider that a relationship is essentially a (dynamic) communication structure. Brent Ruben, for example, defines a relationship as "a social unit consisting of reciprocal message processing," that is, two or more human beings mutually taking account of each other's verbal and nonverbal behavior.[10] Try to imagine what a person would be like without any of the interactive communicative behavior he engages in with other human beings. If he had no such interactions, he would not be a person. (Aristotle said he would be either a beast or a god.) In an important sense, he would not "exist." Equally, if the nature, character, or quality of his interactions were other than they are, he would be a different person than he is. (It is a common experience, for example, that we are "different persons" in different situations, at different times, and with different people.) Because the individual is the ever-changing, ever-accumulating product of the interactions between his physical self and the world around him, he is affected profoundly and continuously in his very being by the world he inhabits. A person's relationships with other human beings are not just important to the individual—they are constitutive of who he is. It might be more accurate to say, not that I *have* relationships, but that I *am* my relationships.

## GROUPS AND COMMUNITIES

In our examination of cooperation, the fundamental reality we need to concern ourselves with is not the individual per se but rather the *individual-in-relationship*. The individual-in-relationship is an integral component of the social unit that is the relationship. A relationship is the smallest form of a *group*. What is real (and hence interesting and important) is not "a mere aggregate of interacting individuals but . . . individuals connected to one another in some patterned fashion"—that is, groups.[11] A group, in the sociological sense, is "any collection of people bound together by a distinctive set of social relationships."[12] It is "group" in this sense that is relevant to our discussion of civic infrastructure and cooperation.[13]

Sociologists distinguish further between two different types of groups. A *primary group* (such as the family, clan, army platoon, church congregation, or multigenerational ethnic neighborhood) is one "in which members have warm, intimate, personal ties with one another. . . . Primary groups exhibit an identity of goals among members who share a similar worldview and strive for shared goals. Because of their close ties, each person in the primary group is concerned with the welfare of all the others. Belonging to a primary group is thus an end in itself; relationships among members are valued in their own right rather than as means to another goal."[14] In contrast, and "unlike primary groups, secondary groups [apartment and neighborhood associations, schools, business corporations, unions, professional associations, municipal districts, cities] are characterized by few emotional ties among members and limited interaction involving only a part of the person. Furthermore, the goals of participants . . . may vary. Formal relationships replace the informal spontaneity of the primary group."[15]

The distinction between primary and secondary groups is similar to the classic typology of *Gemeinschaft* and *Gesellschaft*. Ferdinand Tönnies, the German sociologist who employed these terms, used them to describe two types of relationship. *Gemeinschaft* (usually translated as "community") exists in social settings characterized by many primary group relationships. In *Gesellschaft* ("society"), relationships are more businesslike and contractual. People associate voluntarily and out of a self-interested desire to achieve a particular goal or set of goals. As Hess et al. observe, "in general, the development of modern societies can be seen as a progressive replacement of *Gemeinschaft* by the impersonal, fragmented, goal-directed relationships of *Gesellschaft* settings."[16]

This historical fact presents a conceptual problem for anyone wishing to describe the kind of social entity that would result if the relationships constituting it were the sort that permit and encourage cooperation between citizens. Although in the end we may have little choice but to continue using it, the term "community" is far from ideal for this purpose. First, "community" often means simply a collection of people living in the same geographic locality—an "aggregate," in sociological terminology. Other times it is used to designate secondary groups—the "academic community," the "business community," the "defense community," the "black community." It can even be applied to the largest and most diverse groups to which people belong—as a synonym for "the public," for example, or even society as a whole. At the opposite end of the social spectrum, "community" often refers to a primary group, such as a "community of faith." To compound matters, "community" is often used in a normative, prescriptive, or aspirational sense, as in the "need for stronger (healthier, closer) community" or the importance of "restoring" or "preserving" a feeling of community. Such usage conveys the sense of loss that has accompanied the advent of modern society (*Gesellschaft*), which is dominated by secondary group relationships.

For purposes of our discussion of civic infrastructure and cooperation, it is less important to label the social entity that would result if the relationships constituting it could permit and encourage cooperation than to gain some clarity about the features of those relationships. Let's just stipulate that we'll call the resulting social entity a "civic community." The question we need to address is, What kind of relationships does a civic community require?

## Healthy Civic Relationships

### THE IDEA OF CIVIC "FRIENDSHIP"

An article about Aristotle's notion of "civic friendship" by Sybil Schwarzenbach provides a starting point for thinking about the kind of relationships a civic community requires. Because Aristotle uses the term "friendship" (*philia*), which has connotations in English of personal closeness, affection, and similarity, our first task is to distinguish civic friendship from its personal form. As Schwarzenbach points out, Aristotle makes civic friendship a subcategory of friendship relationships in general. He defines such relationships as those in which I wish for you what I believe to be good things, not for my own sake but for yours, and in which I am inclined to help bring those things about. A civic friend is one who feels this way toward others and stimulates those feelings in return. Each person treats the other as an "end," not as a "means" to be used for his own advantage or satisfaction. Among civic friends intimate knowledge and close emotional bond are absent.[17]

As sociologists and social psychologists point out, whenever individuals interact, elements of exchange characterize their relationship. In a relationship between you and me, for example, each interaction between us will be an exchange in which I give up something (time, energy, affection, approval) in return for something I want (love, money, attention) that you can provide.[18] The same goes for you. This process of exchange, and the principle (both psychological and normative) of reciprocity it embodies, is a feature of interactions between human beings that has been exhibited in every culture in human history.

In civic friendships, Schwarzenbach says, the relationship from the start is based on a narrower notion of reciprocal exchange than is true of personal friendships. By "narrower" she means that the base on which the civic friends stand isn't as broad—there is less commonality of experience, outlook, and interest to hold the relationship together. Put another way, the relationship isn't on as firm a footing; inequalities, perceived injustices, resort to coercion or manipulation, and so forth will weaken or break a civic friendship much more quickly than they will a personal friendship. This is a way of saying that the reciprocal exchanges in civic friendships more closely resemble the kind of cooperation for mutual benefit that characterizes the interactions in secondary groups than they do the relationship-oriented interactions in primary groups.

Civic friendships, however, are not characterized by the sort of purely self-interested, instrumental behavior that characterizes, say, negotiations between business enterprises or between partisan political adversaries. The point here is not that civic friends must be impartial between their own well-being and that of others, still less that they must be altruistic; indeed, they need not even like each other. What they must do is adhere to and uphold certain public standards—civility, reasonableness, fair-mindedness, honesty, integrity, reliability, accountability, and so forth—that permit and encourage cooperation for mutual benefit. In Aristotle's view, then, civic friendship is evidenced, not by every citizen liking every other citizen, which is impossible, but, as Schwarzenbach says, "by a general concern and attitude in the everyday lives of . . . citizens . . . ; it is recognized in . . . social norms regarding the treatment of persons . . . [and] in the willingness of citizens to uphold them."[19] Civic friendship is created and sustained through our public (political) speech and actions toward our fellow citizens.

### HEALTHY CIVIC RELATIONSHIPS AS "CIVIC PARTNERSHIPS"

What, then, does a healthy civic relationship look like? First, in a healthy civic relationship people don't view each other as adversaries. They do not preoccupy themselves with winning. But equally, they don't imagine that they're the best of friends, bosom buddies who have so much in common that they will never disagree. In the best sort of civic relationship, people take the pragmatic view that they're "partners-of-necessity," equally responsible for solving problems or meeting challenges that affect them both. For this reason, it might be helpful to characterize healthy civic relationships as "civic *partnerships.*" "Partnership," I believe, works better for relationships in the sort of secondary group that a civic community is than does "friendship," which is a primary group relationship.

Accepting the role of a civic partner means treating one's fellow citizens in the manner recommended by Roger Fisher and William Ury: being "easy" on each other but "tough" on the problem, rather than easy on both or tough on both.[20] This approach doesn't require that people trust each other implicitly. Nor, on the other hand, does it require them cynically to expect the worst from each other. As I said in chapter 6, what is required is "mutual comprehension." If people comprehend each other, they will realize and accept that certain differences are unbridgeable. Nevertheless, they will try to identify a range of actions that everyone can live with, that everyone can go along with, even if those actions aren't ideal. They will do so because they know that this is the most effective and surest way, over the long run, to advance their own interests, and because they know that maintaining a good working relationship with each other is the *sine qua non* for doing so. Accordingly, they won't dig in and defend their positions, pressure each other to extract maximum gains, refuse to compromise, or insist that their preferred solution be accepted. On the other hand, they won't cave in, collapse in the face of pressure, compromise at every turn, or agree immediately to whatever the other party demands. Instead, they will think together, building scenarios, envisioning possibilities, brainstorming together about how to bring into existence the sort of future that everyone can live with. They won't devise solutions independently and try to sell or impose them but will invent options that previously neither had thought of.

### Building Civic Partnerships

If our civic relationships are in such poor shape that we're unable and unwilling even to talk with and listen to each other, we stand little chance of achieving the mutual comprehension upon which the formation of a public perspective, a public judgment, a public choice, and public action depend. It might prove necessary, therefore, to do some preliminary work to get our civic relationship to the point where we're prepared to make the effort to comprehend each other. This requires finding partners who realize that the relationship is at a point where it demands special attention. In some especially difficult relationships, "getting to the table" may require persistence and creativity.[21] For example, many communities today are so deeply divided along racial lines that it is uncertain whether people will ever be able to live and work together. Dayton, Ohio, is one of those communities. Dayton is divided literally as well as figuratively. The west side of the city is predominantly black, the east side predominantly white. But the vision, commitment, and goodwill of a handful of Dayton's citizens have given the city hope in the face of persistent racial tension. Several years ago pastors and church members from several congregations, black and white, saw that they could do something themselves to improve race relations in their city. They undertook an effort, which they call the "Vineyards Project," to reach out to one another. They realized that, whatever their differences, they were bound together by shared spiritual and moral values that obliged them to show concern and respect for their fellow human beings. Project members began to meet for the purpose simply of enjoying each other's company—as believers, as citizens, as human beings—in the context of what they share: a common faith, common values, and a common home.

Of course, in this age of unbelief the religious common ground enjoyed by participants in the Vineyards Project participants does not, by itself, provide a foundation on which to build the sort of democratic communities to which most of us, at least in theory, aspire. But that is not the point. The Vineyards Project depends less for its success on specifically religious values and principles than on value commitments that most people share. The project shows what can be achieved by a few concerned citizens who have the courage of those convictions. Of all the troubles that afflict America today, racial conflict is arguably the most serious. If a few ordinary citizens with the ability to see that good civic relationships are the precondition for solving political problems can begin to build bridges across the racial divide, then there is hope for a solution. But a solution can emerge only when our civic relationships are healthy enough to permit us to talk and act together to create one.

To be sure, healthy civic relationships are not sustained on goodwill alone. People keep them alive by doing the difficult political work of recognizing the hard choices they face and by struggling, together, to find a way forward that everyone can live with. Participants in the Vineyards Project prepared the ground for this work by making the effort to reconnect themselves to one another, by deliberately bringing back into focus the civic relationship that they cannot escape and that they must mend and fortify in order to carry out the hard work of practical politics. Gradually but steadily, they came to terms with the fact that their political differences stem not so much from who they are as from the very nature of the problem they jointly confront. The tensions they experienced are less those between black and white than those between freedom and equity, between justice and prosperity, between individualism and community. Dayton's Vineyards Project is extraordinary only in the ordinariness of the people who conceived it and the things they do to keep it alive. Building bridges requires no special talent, no special training, no special conditions. It is an exercise, not in moral heroism or saintliness, but in political practicality.

### Coercion versus Cooperation

Sometimes, using one's superior political strength to compel or pressure others to act in accordance with one's wishes is unavoidable. There are circumstances in which we may have no choice but to use political force, situations in which, faced with an implacable foe, we may not be able to avoid "playing hardball." For example, in chapter 4 I cited Martin Luther King Jr.'s recognition that legal coercion would be necessary to bring an end to institutionalized racial discrimination in the American South. King understood that moral appeals and political persuasion alone would not suffice, that there was a limit to how much could be achieved through noncoercive methods alone.

But resorting to pressure tactics sometimes can be justified in situations less extreme than those that prevailed in the South in the early 1960s. Sometimes this is the only way to get the attention of people who are overlooking or ignoring a problem they have a duty to help solve. I once spoke with residents of an urban community who had tried in vain to get their city government to do something about the drug use, drunkenness, and crime that occurred as a result of a day-labor firm operating at the edge of their neighborhood. They tried working with the company to find a solution. They went through the proper channels to get help from their public officials, all to no avail. When their representative on city council accepted a job with the day-labor firm, and no one in a position of authority saw this as a conflict of interest, they were left with no choice but to resort to coercion: they recalled their councilperson, generated publicity through the news media, and threatened the day-labor firm with a lawsuit.

Although coercion is sometimes unavoidable, we should never lose sight of the fact that it is usually ineffective and often counterproductive. The reason for this is that coercion is essentially punitive. Bruno Bettelheim argued that punishment teaches a person only that those who are stronger can force others to do their bidding.[22] Punishment makes the punished person so angry that he fails to reflect on his action and to take responsibility for its consequences. Punishment diverts his attention away from his motivation and any harm his action might cause and redirects it to the pain he will suffer as a result of being punished. This makes punishment—and by extension, coercion generally—a weak deterrent of undesirable behavior. It teaches a person only to avoid getting caught. The control that others exercise through punishment makes it unnecessary for the punished person himself to learn to evaluate the consequences of his actions and to regulate his conduct accordingly. Punishment disposes him to behave similarly whenever he thinks he can get away with doing so.

According to Bettelheim, most normal persons feel convinced that their desires, intentions, and actions are, on balance, justified. Even when we know what we have done or are about to do will have adverse consequences for someone else, we often feel that what we stand to gain is so important that it overrides all contrary considerations. The problem with coercion is that it reinforces this tendency. It offers me no incentive—in fact, it creates a disincentive—for rethinking whether my behavior is truly, on balance, justified. Like a child anxious to escape punishment, when threatened with coercion I close my mind in self-defense. Coercion merely increases the cost to me of acting as I'm inclined to do. But it often fails to deter because it doesn't raise the cost enough to overcome my powerful desire to proceed as I'm inclined.

Worse, like punishment generally, coercion puts me at odds with others, and so causes our relationships to deteriorate. When I'm coerced, I feel as if I'm being told that I'm bad or unworthy as a human being, not simply that my action might be harmful or otherwise undesirable. I see coercion directed toward me as a person, not at a particular intention or desire I happen to have. If I take to heart the implicit message that I am in some way inherently defective, I may begin to act more frequently in ways appropriate to the sort of person I supposedly am.

Coercion also tells me that others are concerned only with my behavior, not with what I think or feel. If this is so, then why shouldn't I be interested only in what I want? Why should I care about others? Why shouldn't I go along only when it's necessary to avoid unpleasant consequences, but otherwise do as I please—especially if I'm strong enough to get away with it? Coercion implies that, whatever people say, there are no standards of rightness and fairness, no moral rules that all of us should respect and that should guide me in determining how I should act. Coercion tells me that "might makes right."

### RESPONDING TO COERCION

Despite coercion's flaws, it remains a popular strategy for dealing with political disagreement.[23] There will be many times when we are on the receiving end of coercive political action. People who disagree with us, and with whom we do not have a strong working relationship, may regard us as hostile, ill-intentioned, weak, or unapproachable. As a result, their first inclination may be to threaten us or otherwise assume an adversarial stance. In such situations "playing hardball" may be forced upon us.

Responding to coercion by behaving coercively ourselves—"fighting fire with fire"—is apt to prove counterproductive, however. Most likely, it will simply escalate tensions, raise the psychological stakes of backing down, and lock people into positions that require them to win. How, then, should we respond to coercion? What can we do to take the heat out of a dispute and give our adversaries an opportunity and an incentive to cooperate for mutual benefit?[24]

Recall my discussion concerning mutual comprehension and what Maurice Friedman, following Martin Buber, calls (identity) "confirmation."[25] Psychologically, each of us throughout our lives seeks recognition or acknowledgment of who we are, as individual persons. As adults, however, and especially outside of intimate relationships with family and close friends, such confirmation is often hard to come by. (Paradoxically, to be confirmed as an individual, to discover and validate what is unique about myself, I need to be recognized by persons whose identities and values contrast with my own—precisely the people I'm most likely to disagree with, and hence most likely to find myself in an adversarial political situation with.) As a general proposition, therefore, the most desirable (because the most effective, in the long run) response to coercion is to follow the second principle of practical politics: comprehend the people you disagree with. Listen to them in order to understand, appreciate, and acknowledge the needs, desires, hopes, fears, and other emotions that motivate their political behavior. Because comprehension is psychologically more "confirming," in Friedman and Buber's sense, than competitive or coercive strategies, it is more likely to elicit cooperation.[26]

From this general proposition a few general guidelines follow: First, as soon as there's a hint of a possible dispute, respond immediately. Don't expect it to go away on its own. Second, always keep lines of communication open. Always be willing to hear different ideas and views. Third, keep discussion focused on the problem and on people's underlying interests and motivations, not on their positions, personalities, attitudes, or behavior. Fourth, find a way to give everyone who is party to the disagreement a "stake" in developing a solution that has win/win consequences for everyone. Try to invent options that will have such consequences. Finally, never cause anyone to "lose face." Let them hold on to their pride and their dignity.

### WHEN ALL ELSE FAILS: "TIT-FOR-TAT"

Recognizing that reverting to politics-as-usual is not in our own interest, we should make every attempt to draw our opponents into the cooperative process of practical politics. Only when their actions leave us with no alternative should we "fight fire with fire"—and then only to the extent necessary (a) to protect ourselves from being forced to act against our own interests, and (b) to restore a "balance of power" from which we can once again invite our opponents to work with us rather than fight with us.

Earlier in this chapter I mentioned Robert Axelrod's discovery that in $n$-person prisoner's dilemma situations the most successful strategy is one he calls "tit-for-tat." Tit-for-tat is a good strategy for dealing with adversarial political behavior because it allows us to "fight fire with fire" only when it's necessary to protect ourselves from being forced to act against our own interests or we need to restore a "balance of power" in our relationships with others. Think back to the scenario involving the Wicked Witch of the West. Imagine that the Wizard of Oz is trying to arrange a meeting with the witch to secure the release of your tour group. After he drops a hint about some feminine footwear that's in his possession, the witch agrees to get together with the wizard. The appointed hour comes and goes, however, and the witch doesn't show. Because he's heard nothing from her, Oz picks up the phone and calls her.

> Witch's Personal Assistant: Good afternoon, office of the Wicked Witch of the West.
> Oz: Hello, is she in?
> WPA: May I ask who's calling, please?
> Oz: Yes. This is Oz, the Great and Terrible.
> WPA: Just a moment, please. I'll have to page her. . . . I'm sorry, sir. She's busy right now. May I take a message?

Oz: Would you remind her, please, that we had a meeting scheduled for this morning? Tell her I'd like to know whether she's still interested in having a discussion.

WPA: Yes, sir. I can see your appointment right here in her Day-Minder. May I put you on hold for a moment?

Oz: Only for a moment. I'm very busy . . .

WPA: Sir? I can put you through now.

Witch: Oz! How are you? Listen, I'm terribly sorry about this morning. I got caught up in "entertaining" our guests. They're *so* fascinating—the time just got away from me.

Oz ("retaliating"): Listen, WW, I told you this was an important meeting. I was counting on your keeping our appointment. A friend of mine who was visiting from Kansas recently left some ruby slippers I thought you might like. But if you're not interested enough to keep a meeting about an important matter like locking up tourists who were on their way to the Emerald City, you can forget about the shoes. I'm going to call the Smithsonian first thing in the morning. I'm sure the folks there will be delighted to take them off my hands.

Witch: Oh, Ozzie, I *am* sorry. I truly am. Can you ever forgive me?

Oz ("forgiving"): Okay, we all get sidetracked. I know how it is. Let's just get back to the business at hand.

Witch: Wonderful! How can I make it up to you?

Oz ("nice"): Is there a time when you can be sure to be free? I'll try to re-arrange my own calendar if it'll help you.

Witch: Lovely! How about tomorrow? Want to do lunch?

Oz ("clear"): Lunch'll be fine. Let's say twelve sharp, shall we? Listen, WW. I want to keep the tourists coming. I'd prefer to work with you on this. But I have to be able to rely on you. If you don't hold up your end, I'll have to go ahead and do what I need to do without you.

Witch: Anything you say, Ozzie. I'll fly on over soon as I finish my meeting with the Disney execs. Did I tell you they want to do an animated movie with me? There's a merchandising tie-in with McDonald's. Could be big, Oz.

Oz: Yeah, good for you. Fill me in at lunch. See you tomorrow. Goodbye.

Witch: See ya, Ozzie.

## The Political Practicality of Civic Relationships

Practical politics depends on healthy working relationships with our fellow citizens—relationships that are strong and resilient enough to weather the inevitable stresses and strains of the democratic decision-making process. "Communities that work" are ones that have developed healthy civic relationships. They do not have these healthy relationships because they can solve their problems—they make progress toward solving their problems because their civic relationships are healthy. In the absence of such relationships, efforts to respond to problems, opportunities, and challenges invariably prove ineffective.

The importance of healthy civic relationships doesn't mean we have to make their improvement the focus of politics. We can, and should, focus on the substantive matters that concern us. Nor does the fact that healthy civic relationships are imperative mean we should subordinate our respective needs, convictions, and interests just for the sake of agreement, in order to accommodate each other or to get along better. It means only that we should place these in the context of the inescapable long-term association we will have with each other. Viewing our communities as a web of civic relationships in which all of us are enmeshed, rather than seeing it as an aggregate of independent individuals who interact, can help us generate a new sense of possibility that will release previously untapped energy for seeking and devising effective responses to the work that has to be done.

## Cooperation and "Public Work"

In *Community and the Politics of Place,* Daniel Kemmis contends that the inhabitation of the great open spaces of America in the nineteenth and early twentieth centuries fostered not only individualism but also cooperation. When most of us lived on farms, Kemmis says, we couldn't avoid people we disliked. We needed them. We had to cooperate, out of self-interest. This led us to accept and tolerate one another. (Kemmis gives the example of how his mother was compelled to tolerate neighbors she disliked because the Kemmis family had to rely on them for help in matters such as building a new barn.) But having to cooperate out of self-interest taught us more than just acceptance and tolerance. The repeated experience of working together taught us that we could rely on each other, and that by doing so *we could accomplish difficult and important tasks together.*[27]

We have largely lost this sense. As our communities grow large and people become more transient, even the memory is fading of a time when mutual reliance and cooperation connected us with other members of our community. Because we no longer experience such reliance and cooperation, we are losing the understanding that our ability to live well as human beings depends on our ability to live well in community—with people, especially those having a different approach to life and different priorities, who occupy the same physical space that we do.[28] Consumerist politics, with its fragmenting and competition-fostering tendencies, further obscures the reality that our fates are interwoven, that the good life for each of us depends on our fellow citizens' being secured in the good life as well.[29]

Kemmis notes that classical republican thinkers from Montesquieu to Jefferson understood that healthy democratic communities can be constructed only by affording citizens the *repeated experience* of successful cooperation with their fellows. Citizens have to learn through their own personal experience that, together, they can enrich their own lives through enriching the life of their community.

Before people become citizens, Kemmis says, they are neighbors. Neighbors are people who find themselves living in the same place.[30] Because each of them is in the place, they are brought into relationship with each other—just as strangers milling about at a cocktail hour become dinner companions when they take their places at the table. But what holds people together long enough to discover their potential as citizens is not just their physical proximity, but their "inhabiting" together the place where they live.[31] By intentionally saying to themselves, "this place is home, this place is ours," they commit themselves to it and resolve not to be driven or seduced away from it. It is this intentional "inhabiting" that affords neighbors the opportunity to become citizens.

Inhabiting a place is only the beginning, however. In order for the interplay of physical space and human action to yield genuine democratic community, Kemmis says, there must be an important element of the concrete, the tangible. Public goods remain mere abstractions, and hence elusive, unless they are given concrete form, unless, like a barn that people have raised together, they can be seen and sensed and felt. It's this element of concreteness that renders goods objective, and hence truly public. If democratic community requires activity by citizens in which the coincidence of personal concern and the common welfare can be experienced concretely, what can we do and experience together that we all will find to be good? What, in short, is the contemporary political equivalent of a barn-raising?

In general, I believe, the cause of fostering cooperation, and hence the building of a healthy democratic community, is advanced by any undertaking that produces a result that members of a community can point to with satisfaction and say, "We did that," and which would not have come into existence without their joint effort. For example, in Daniel Kemmis's home town of Missoula, citizens joined in the project of restoring and assembling a disused carousel. But the public good a community creates through cooperation can be less directly tangible. For example, the citizens of Trinidad, Colorado, who participated in their community's first annual Community Convention in 1995 shared the conclusion that

> the key to achieving the kind and degree of growth and development that is consistent with the quality of life we want for our area is to make our area a truly desirable place for anyone to live. . . . By making our community into the kind of place we want to live in, we will take an important step toward making it attractive as well to tourists, new employers, and new residents. . . . We should therefore concentrate our time, money, and energy on making the

best of what we have. [Among the things we have are the historic buildings that reflect] the history and cultural influences that give our area an identity and sense of uniqueness. [We should restore and preserve this physical legacy of our past.] Our slogan might be, "Rebuild it and they will come."[32]

Like the community effort to restore the carousel in Missoula, the Trinidad community's commitment to save its historic buildings is a public good, something having value for all community members that can be generated only through the efforts of citizens who willingly work together to benefit themselves and each other. Like the barn in Kemmis's anecdote, such public goods embody community for the people who inhabit those places. Like the barn, a carousel that a community builds or a historic building it restores is more than a utilitarian structure. It's a physical representation of community. It's a public creation and as such a reminder that people benefit from their ability to rely on each other and work together.

Harry Boyte calls such cooperation the doing of "public work." He contends that people become citizens, not by speaking a sentimental language of community building, but by taking on common civic tasks. For his book *Building America: The Democratic Promise of Public Work,* coauthored with Nancy Kari, Boyte interviewed surviving participants in the Depression-era Civilian Conservation Corps.[33] He believes their strong sense of citizenship was forged through their experience of doing with others what was widely regarded as important public work. Throughout the nineteenth century and well into the twentieth, says Boyte, democratic citizenship in America was linked to what he calls the "commonwealth" view of democracy. Citizenship was understood as the down-to-earth labors of ordinary people who created goods and undertook projects of public benefit. Citizenship was public work.[34]

What both Kemmis and Boyte recognize is that cooperation is self-fulfilling. Whenever cooperation occurs—even when entered into purely out of self-interest—people find themselves taking responsibility for their community and their fellow citizens in ways that, because they have not been experienced before, come as a pleasant surprise. Cooperation is rewarding, both in itself and for the good things it makes possible. As people learn to cooperate, Kemmis observes, they discover in their new pattern of relationship a new competence, an unexpected capacity to get things done.[35]

# 9

# Public Judgment and Action

*Don't just do something; get out there and talk.*

—Willis Harman

Suppose for a moment that people in your community are concerned about your public schools. In particular, they're concerned that standardized test scores, the graduation rate, and the percentage of graduates continuing their education beyond high school are not as high as they could be and should be. You and others have spent many hours over the past six months addressing these matters. If your community is typical, you might hear comments such as these from people who haven't been involved in the discussions—or even from your fellow participants:

> We've had six meetings, each with forty or fifty people. We know what people think.

> We've involved everyone—teachers, parents, and school officials.

> The board of education has been very receptive to our ideas, and a lot of teachers agree.

> We need a new superintendent. We're devoting our energies to getting one who shares our outlook on the problem.

> The community people are unified, but the people in the schools won't listen.

> We agree on the goal. But agreeing about how to get there is hopeless. Our priorities are just too different.

> People won't listen to reason. They're bound and determined to get their way, come hell or high water.

> My concerns were just brushed aside. They didn't really listen to me.

> What's being proposed is too risky, too controversial. It'll never fly.

> We've talked about this for half a year. Now we need to put together a package to present to the board.

We've decided the real issue is school-based management.

We've selected three or four specific changes to work on. These items are more concrete and people understand them better.

I don't see what we've accomplished. All we've done is talk, and we haven't even reached a consensus.

The people who have been involved aren't experts. What do they know?

Unless our elected officials decide to do something, we're not going to get anywhere.

The group isn't representative of the community as a whole. Most of them are middle-class white folks who see things pretty much the same.

This group isn't any different from any other group that has its own point of view, its own interests, and its own solution to the problem.

The only way we're going to come to a decision is to vote on it. If you aren't in the majority, that's too bad. You'll just have to live with it.

I'm not going to put a lot of time and energy into working on this problem until I know enough people are committed to solving it.

If you look closely at these statements, a couple of things become clear. First, each statement either makes an unstated assumption or is a preface to a conclusion that remains unspoken. In each case, what has not been said has something to do with *action*. In some instances, the tacit implication is something along the lines of "we're ready now to take action," or "let's get on with it." In other instances, the implication is that, in spite of all that's been done, "we're no closer to taking action than we were before," or "we still don't know what to do." Second, these are the statements of people who have been disappointed—or who are about to be. Like you, they want to see the community take action. Unfortunately, their statements provide evidence that your community is not yet able to act.

## The Prerequisite for Action: Public Judgment

Ultimately, democratic politics must issue in some form of action. We can't solve problems, meet challenges, or seize opportunities through talk alone. If our public decision-making process doesn't produce effective action, it's of little use to us.

We do ourselves a disservice, however, by holding our communities up to the same standards we apply to individuals. When you or I make a decision about what to do, action follows naturally and easily. I decide to run for city council and I soon find myself knocking on people's doors. It works more or less the same way for communities—*but only after a genuine collective decision has been made.* Collective decisions are far more difficult for communities than individual decisions are for people. As I've noted previously, if we were to compare communities to individuals, the individuals in our analogy would be persons who suffer from an impossibly extreme case of multiple personality disorder. Imagine how hard you would find it to act if the thousands of "personalities" that are "you" couldn't reach a decision about what to do! (As Leland Kaiser has quipped, "if your brain was connected the same way your community is connected, you couldn't get up off your chair.")

As an individual, I can find it difficult to make a decision, especially when I'm genuinely pulled in different directions. But I have a big advantage over a community: in the end, the "me" that "loses" the battle is more easily reconciled to my decision. Because "he" is part of the "total me"—a member of the team, as it were—the "losing me" can console himself with the thought that he, too, will gain from the decision. What's good for me-the-whole-person is good as well for him-the-part-of-me. My good, on balance and all things considered, is also his good. A community isn't so lucky. If some part of it—some number of its individual members—disagrees with a "decision,"[1] reconciliation is a lot harder to come by. Because they don't accept that the community's good is, on balance and all things considered, also their good, at the very least they are unlikely to act in a way that helps move the community in the direction of the objectives for which action is required. And it's possible they will act in a way that thwarts or undermines such action.

Throughout this book I have emphasized that the essential political task for a democratic community is that of constructing a shared, public perspective on a matter of public concern; deliberating alternative responses to it; forming a shared, public judgment about priorities; and collectively choosing a way to proceed that everyone can go along with. If—and it's by no means a small "if"—a community is able to carry out this task, then the further task of enabling and encouraging people to act together will pose little difficulty. Such action will be as natural, automatic, and sustainable as the action you or I take after having made a firm decision. Strategic or tactical questions may arise about timing, appropriateness, effectiveness, efficiency, and the like. But because the basic end to be achieved and the general direction to take have won general assent, those questions are unlikely to persist as substantial obstacles to progress.

In order to approximate individual rationality in our collective decision making—and it can only be approximated—we must begin by combining our individual perspectives into a shared, *public perspective*. A public perspective emerges when we *comprehend*—understand and appreciate—the needs, values, fears, angers, perceptions, sensitivities, dispositions, and beliefs about what is good and bad, right and wrong, true and false, that give rise to our fellow citizens' motivations. When we've achieved a perspective that incorporates each other's motivations, we have a foundation—common ground—on which to weigh the considerations that count in favor of and against each of the courses of action that are open to us. *Deliberation* is the activity of determining, for different sets of factual circumstances, what it would be best, all things considered, to do.

The conclusion we reach, as a public, about what it would be best, all things considered, to do, is our *public judgment*.[2] To grasp this concept, it's essential to recall that mutual comprehension, while necessary for achieving a public judgment, does not require that we give up or subordinate the motivations that underlie our political outlooks and dispositions. Rather, it requires that, in addition to holding our own motivating beliefs and values, we understand and appreciate each other's motivations so that they become quasi-real for us. It is mutual comprehension that permits us to deliberate as if we were a single decision maker. (See my discussion of mutual comprehension in chapter 6, especially figures 6 and 7.)

## PUBLIC JUDGMENT: AN EXAMPLE

The example I've cited in preceding chapters—the issue of abortion—can render the idea of public judgment more concrete. What follows is purely hypothetical; indeed, it's highly speculative. There is no way to predict the judgment that might be reached by a given group of people who have comprehended each other and who have deliberated together about this issue.[3]

In the fictional deliberation in chapter 7, the participants considered the case of a twelve-year-old girl who faced the prospect of bearing a child in some of the most extreme circumstances imaginable. The participants discussed several matters, including personal responsibility for making difficult decisions in situations that are morally complex and ambiguous. Let's suppose that this issue of personal moral responsibility continued to feature prominently in the group's discussions, with the result that a point was reached at which it became clear to everyone that a satisfactory resolution of the issue would require that the group find some way to reduce the salience of the agonizing question of whether to end a life process. Could the group make headway toward a shared judgment by devising a way to keep to a minimum the number of cases in which this question would arise?[4]

Using a diagram (fig. 8), we can summarize this aspect of the issue. The preeminent motivation ($M_1$) for those participants (represented by $V_1$) who are inclined to take the position ($P_1$) that there should be a total ban on abortion is their belief that they must honor the moral duty to safeguard the sanctity of life by denying that we have the moral authority to make a decision that would terminate a life.[5] In contrast, the preeminent motivation ($M_3$) for those participants (represented by $V_2$) who are inclined to take the position ($P_2$) that abortion should be available "on demand" is their belief that they must honor the moral duty to minimize suffering, which entails that we have the moral authority (because we have the moral responsibility) to make a decision that would achieve this aim by terminating a life.[6] The participants have succeeded substantially in comprehending each other's motivation, however, and as a result have been able to deliberate together as if they were a single decision maker. Their mutual comprehension can be depicted as in figure 9.

What collective judgment, then, might emerge from the participants' deliberations? Specifically, what conclusion might they reach that would keep to a minimum the number of cases in which there would arise the agonizing question of whether to end a life, and that would consequently permit them to reduce the degree of disagreement between them? Here is one (hypothetical) possibility:

> To terminate the human life process is, in all circumstances and situations, a matter of the utmost moral gravity. We must not approach the termination of that process lightly. We must agonize over it. We must do everything within our power to find an alternative to it. We must permit only the most compelling moral considerations to move us to a reluctant acceptance of its necessity. Accordingly, we agree that abortion is, in itself, a practice to be strenuously avoided. Even for those of us who believe it must remain legally

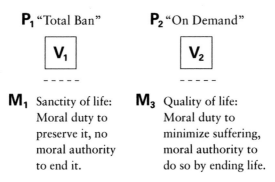

*Figure 8.* Viewpoints and Motivational Priorities
in Opposition: The Abortion Issue

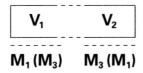

*Figure 9.* Mutual Comprehension of Viewpoints and
Motivational Priorities: The Abortion Issue

available, it is admittedly at best a necessary evil, a concession we make to reality in the interest of preventing a greater harm from being done.

*Resolution:* We hereby assent to the following statements and recommendations, which constitute our considered judgment:

1. We must endeavor to discourage the life process from being initiated in circumstances that might lead persons ultimately to desire or seek an abortion. In our effort to prevent conception in such circumstances, we should employ every reasonable and humane method that can be expected to contribute to the prevention of pregnancy, including but not limited to moral exhortation, sex education, contraception, legal deterrents, financial and material incentives and disincentives, counseling, social approbation and disapprobation, religious education, therapy, and early intervention. Recognizing that we may have to establish priorities and choose among the various methods available to us, we resolve nevertheless that we will not allow this to undermine, impede, or deflect progress toward our agreed goal.

2. If we can begin now to make progress toward preventing pregnancy in circumstances that might lead persons ultimately to desire or seek an abortion, we should begin, in direct proportion and by painstaking calibration, to progressively "close the window" of ready access to abortion services. Taking care not to discriminate against persons because of their income, education, race, age, social status, religion, moral beliefs, health, or abilities and faculties "outside the statistical norm," and always with a view to minimizing hardship and suffering, we should begin gradually to withdraw the mandates and resources that currently afford anyone, irrespective of circumstances, to readily obtain an abortion. Beginning with those circumstances that provide the least justification, we should begin to reduce the number of factual situations that would authorize both *de jure* and *de facto* access to the medical and social services required for the safe termination of pregnancy.

3. We must begin now, with all deliberate speed, to remedy those social, economic, psychological, cultural, political, and other factors that give rise to circumstances that might lead a person ultimately to desire or seek an abortion. Equally, we must remedy those factors that put children at risk of growing to physical and sexual maturity without acquiring the familial, social, economic, emotional, and intellectual abilities, strengths, skills, values, desires, and aspirations that will enable and encourage them to postpone pregnancy until such time as they are thoroughly prepared to give the children they bear the security, love, and support needed to grow into healthy, happy, responsible, productive, and independent adults.

4. Having dedicated ourselves to the foregoing courses, we hereby resolve that, as a result of our sustained efforts, within twenty-five years the legal guarantee afforded persons by the judicial decision of *Roe v. Wade* will be *de facto* unnecessary for the protection of their freedom, privacy, and physical and emotional integrity. In order to help hold ourselves to this commitment, we hereby pledge our contingent political support for the reversal of that

decision twenty-five years hence, either by judicial action or constitutional amendment, in favor of a ruling proscribing abortion except when the life or well-being of the prospective mother or the child she is carrying is in danger. (Our hope is that by this date the decision in *Roe v. Wade* will be of such irrelevance that it might safely be permitted to stand, to be invoked only with great rarity, thereby freeing us of the political necessity of attempting to reverse this judicial decision.) We agree that the target date for reversal may be extended by mutual consent in increments of five years up to an additional twenty-five years. We further agree that if government, the public, or groups having a social or political agenda relating to abortion policy fail to make a sustained good-faith effort to comply with the provisions of paragraphs 1, 2, and 3, our pledge of support for reversal of *Roe v. Wade* will be null and void.

Is this too complex? One-sided? Confusing? Unclear? Morally compromised? Politically unworkable? If it seems so, bear in mind that you are viewing this hypothetical judgment from the perspective of someone who has not participated in the process of forming a shared perspective through mutual comprehension and deliberation. Viewed from the outside, as it were, any judgment arrived at through this process will be open to objection and criticism. Because you haven't had the opportunity to participate in its formation, you will not be able to see how objections and criticisms have been dealt with to the satisfaction of the participants. As I have pointed out previously, the "resolution" or "reconciliation" that practical politics achieves is not logical in character, but psychological and interpersonal. Not having participated in the process, you have not been able to experience the transformation that permits people to reach a shared judgment.

In matters such as abortion, moreover, we also must not expect judgments that are neat and tidy. The world in which abortion is a fact of life is itself complex and ambiguous, a place in which it is often difficult to see clearly what we should do; in which difficult moral issues admit of no solution devoid of undesirable—even tragic—consequences; in which political impracticality is routinely offered as an excuse for our failure to make the effort to replace consumerist politics with a practice of democratic decision making characterized by the principles of inclusion, comprehension, deliberation, and cooperation. We shouldn't expect our political judgments to exhibit the precision, simplicity, clarity, and elegance of a mathematically expressed scientific law. It is not possible. Human affairs do not admit of such order.

What we may expect to achieve, if we work for it, is something more unwieldy, perhaps, but even more valuable: a shared sense—a widespread, general assent—that certain conditions and consequences are acceptable to us and certain others are not; that we are prepared to accept tradeoffs that cannot be avoided; that we can and must establish priorities. This is a public judgment. It is not the same thing as complete agreement or consensus. It is not the same thing as what we would prefer to have in the best of all possible worlds. But nor is it simple compromise—the negotiated giving up of something in order to obtain a reciprocal concession. Rather, a public judgment is a broadly shared conclusion about what is best—on balance, all things considered, and in the circumstances— for our community or society as a whole. A public judgment never loses sight of the importance of the good things that may have to be assigned relatively less emphasis in order to make a decision that authorizes and initiates collective action. Accordingly, it insists that they be validated, acknowledged, and respected as far as possible. A public judgment points to "a way forward that everyone can live with." It indicates a general policy direction or a range of policy responses that all members of the community, if they are people of honesty, integrity, and goodwill, will assent to, even if they disagree with it in particular details.

Imperfect though it is, that is what, with respect to the issue of abortion, the public judgment sketched above aspires to be.

## Paving the Way for Action

### THE COMMUNITY CONFERENCE REVISITED

Collective action poses a problem for communities for two reasons. First, in most communities the only mechanism available for authorizing, initiating, and sustaining action is the institutional structure of local government. As we have seen, the institutional decision-making process, which reflects and reinforces the competitive character of consumerist politics, attempts to "resolve" political disagreement—and thereby to "make decisions"—by applying the principle of majority rule, aided by norms such as equality ("one person, one vote") and compromise, and constrained by various constitutional rights. The institutional decision-making process (at least currently) is not suited to the formation of a public perspective and the reaching of a public judgment through deliberation. As a consequence, it is unable to produce genuine collective decisions that authorize actions having strong, widespread, durable support. Without a *civic* decision-making structure and process mechanism that parallels and complements the official *governmental* decision-making structure and process, the community as a whole cannot carry out the essential political task of forming a public perspective and reaching a public judgment through deliberation.

Second, collective action typically poses a problem for communities because in most communities the absence of a parallel civic decision-making structure and process prevents action from being taken by the community as a whole. The only types of action that can be taken are those authorized, initiated, and sustained by government or those taken by individuals or organizations acting in an ad hoc and loosely coordinated manner. Hence the desirability of an innovation such as the council of neighborhoods, which serves as the kind of parallel civic decision-making structure and process a community needs.

In chapter 5, we considered how, with respect to a given matter of public concern, a community might initiate and sustain the kind of discussion that will lead to a public judgment "of, by, and for" that community. I suggested that, broadly speaking, there are two ways to go about this: the "contagious" approach and the "concerted" approach. In the former, groups of citizens convene informally to discuss a matter of public concern and then encourage participants to convene additional groups. The process expands, spontaneously, as far as people are willing to take it. I noted, however, that this approach doesn't provide links between the outcome of any one group's discussions and those of other groups, nor does it connect directly with the governmental policy-making process. For these reasons, the contagious approach does not lead directly to community action. I therefore recommended a more highly coordinated, "concerted" approach to public decision making: the "community conference." If a public judgment is a prerequisite for a genuinely collective decision, and if a genuinely collective decision is a prerequisite for effective community action, then something like the community conference will be needed as a vehicle for public discussion.[7] Whatever that vehicle is, it must embody and exhibit the principles of inclusion, comprehension, deliberation, and cooperation.

## ASSESSING YOUR COMMUNITY'S READINESS FOR ACTION

In order to maximize your community's prospects for responding effectively to a problem, need, or opportunity, you and your fellow citizens should take stock of how well prepared the members of your community are to think, talk, and work together. Although you might wish to have this discussion as part of a community conference, it would be prudent to have it before embarking on such an undertaking. Here are some questions you should ask yourselves:

1. On what occasions in the past have citizens in our community worked together on solving a public problem or resolving a public issue? What was the problem or issue? What was accomplished? Who took the initiative? What did they do? Was it successful? Who participated? What did different people contribute? Who didn't participate, and why? How did that affect what was accomplished? Did government officials participate? Why or why not? What was the effect of their participation or nonparticipation?

2. Do we know of any current problems or issues that citizens are working together to solve? What is the problem or issue? What is being accomplished? Who is taking the initiative? Is it proving successful? Who is participating? What are different people contributing? Who is not participating, and why? How is that

affecting what's being accomplished? Are government officials participating? Why or why not? What is the effect of their participation or nonparticipation?

3. Can we identify one or two important problems or issues that we believe our community won't deal with effectively unless we find a better way as a community to talk about them, understand them, and evaluate different options for responding to them? (Write the items you've identified across the top of a sheet of paper or chalk board. Beneath each one, indicate whether in your estimation one of the obstacles listed below is an important factor keeping your community from making progress toward solving it. Suggestion: you might simply want to place a check mark next to the obstacle. Or you might want to use a rating system. For example, you could place a "3" next to it if it's "very serious," a "2" if it's "somewhat serious," a "1" if it's "not very serious," and a "0" if it's "not an obstacle" at all.)

> —*Fragmentation:* No one's taking an overall view of the matter, a comprehensive look at it. Different groups, organizations, and persons are focusing on different aspects of it, and they either don't coordinate their efforts or deliberately work at cross-purposes.
>
> —*Misframing:* People see the concern as being of a certain kind, but it's really a problem of a different sort, or it's just a symptom of a deeper problem. For example, "bad schools" may be a misframed problem. The real problem may be a poor total learning environment that includes family life and social or economic conditions in the community.
>
> —*Solution Wars:* People are caught up in arguments or debates about the best plan or policy response. Advocates for different solutions lobby for their preference and dismiss all other solutions. There's little or no discussion of what the problem really is, how it got to be that way, and the difficult choices and tradeoffs that have to be made.
>
> —*Elitism:* Ordinary citizens are passive spectators. The actors are government officials, individuals, or organizations pushing their preferred solutions.

4. What is the state of our community's "civic infrastructure"? Do we have places where community members can gather, as citizens, to discuss (analytically and civilly) the problems we face? Does our community have genuine "public spaces" where practical political discussion can take place? Do we have institutions that permit, enable, and encourage a real exchange of views? Do our newspapers, radio and TV stations, government, and civic organizations foster the habit of practical political discussion among members of the public? How many town

meetings or other kinds of public forums have citizens convened in our community over the past three years? Were they well attended? Why or why not? How were they conducted? Were they productive? Why or why not?

5. What is the "civic landscape" of our community like? Who is part of our community? What groups and organizations make it up? Which members of our community have some impact or influence on the decisions we make and the action we take? Do people in our community talk with each other? Who does and who doesn't? Do people work together? Who works together and who doesn't?

6. What conclusions should we draw from the answers we've given to the foregoing questions? What are the implications for our ability as a community to make decisions and act? What lessons have we learned?

### OBTAINING WIDESPREAD, ACTIVE PARTICIPATION IN YOUR COMMUNITY

Let's imagine that, like most places in our country, your hometown, River City, is finding it difficult to guarantee everyone high-quality medical care at an affordable price. You believe that ensuring universal access to such care is one of the most important challenges facing your community. Unfortunately, an even greater challenge is engaging the interest of enough of your fellow citizens to have a productive discussion of what to do about your community's health care needs.

Ask yourselves: What incentives do people have for accepting personal responsibility, taking the initiative, and getting involved in addressing the problem? What impediments or disincentives do we have to overcome in order to get more citizen involvement? How can we begin to overcome them? Research and experience suggest that citizens won't become and remain engaged in efforts to solve problems, meet challenges, or seize opportunities facing their communities unless seven conditions—what we might call the "Citizen's Seven Cs"—are met. As you undertake to organize a process of public discussion, keep these conditions firmly in mind and take steps to ensure that they are addressed.

—*Connection*: People must see a direct connection between the problem and their personal concerns or needs. If they don't see how a problem affects what they care about, they won't make an effort to contribute to its solution.

—*Control*: People must have, and believe that they have, some genuine control over their situation. If they don't have power and authority to act on the problem, they'll conclude—correctly—that whatever action they might take will be thwarted or deflected.

—*Context*: People want to know what the problem is, why it's a problem, and how it got to be one. They want sound, coherent explanations that illuminate the problem, that help them understand the situation.

—*Consultation:* People want to hear what others have to say. They want to examine different perspectives on the problem and what to do about it. They want more room to engage in give-and-take discussions, to ask questions, and to build confidence in what they think by testing their views against those that others hold. In short, they want to consult one another.

—*Choice:* People want to identify, examine, and evaluate several solutions and make a choice among them. They do not want a simple "up or down vote" on one or two courses of action that someone else has identified and presented to them.

—*Change:* People must believe that whatever they do will make a genuine difference—that their action will produce change. If their action won't have a substantial impact on the problem—if they can't make it budge—they won't waste their time and energy.

—*Co-action:* People must be persuaded that enough of their fellow citizens will join with them to ensure that their own efforts are not for naught.

### TAKING A STEP BACK TO MAKE A NEW BEGINNING

Sometimes a community will find itself immersed in a controversy that it seems unable to resolve. People cling to their positions and show little readiness to talk constructively with each other. At other times, people may be willing to work together but genuinely do not know how to break through the impasse they've reached. In such circumstances it can be helpful to take a step back from the problem or issue. Going back to fundamental questions such as, What kind of community do we want to have? can help people get a fresh perspective on a troublesome matter and can stimulate new thinking about it.

Here is a short exercise for taking a step back to make a new beginning. It poses questions that will help you determine what you and your fellow citizens want for your community. It asks you to identify the things you must have or the obstacles you must overcome in order to keep or achieve what you want for your community. It asks you to figure out how the particular matter of concern you're trying to respond to fits with your community's vision of the kind of community its citizens want it to be.

1. What do we value most about our community, as it is today? What do we really like about it? What do we care about that we don't want to lose?

2. What do we value for our community that we currently *don't* have? What do we care about that we would like to see in our community? For example: What

kinds of things would we like to read about, or not read about, in our local newspaper? What would we like to hear about, or not hear about, on radio or television? What would we like to point to with pride when telling strangers about our community? What do we want to see and experience when we're out—when we go shopping, when we go out for the evening, when we're out on weekends, when we go to public events and gatherings, when our family members go to school or work?

3. What should our priorities be? Let's look at the list we've made of the things we value, the things we like about or want for our community. We need to learn what's important to different people and at the same time get a sense of what people in general care about most.

To identify what we value, let's assume that each person has ten points that he or she can assign to any of the desirable things that have been mentioned.[8] Each individual can give all of his or her points to just one thing or distribute them among several things. Take five minutes or so to think about your priorities. Then record each person's points next to the things he or she cares about most.

Let's discuss the results of our scoring. What do they tell us about our priorities as a community? Is there a lot of agreement, or not very much? How do we feel about the results? Can we understand and appreciate why each of us gave different things different scores?

4. What are the necessary conditions for keeping or achieving the things we value for our community? What has to exist or happen first, before we can have the things we care about? What are the obstacles to keeping or achieving what we value? What are the impediments, the blockages, the missing elements? What is absent or lacking? For example, if we want access to a lake, we've got to get permission from the owner to cross the land that surrounds it. Also, we'll have to build a road or a path. Then we'll need the labor, materials, and money to construct and maintain the road. Perhaps most important, we'll need the support of everyone who'll be asked to pay for it—especially people who won't benefit directly or who might even be affected adversely. Finally, we've got to be able to let those people know what other members of the community want and why they should support it.

For every condition or requirement you identify, you should ask, What is the necessary condition or requirement for *that?* In other words, keep "peeling the layers of the onion" until you've identified *everything* that has to exist or happen before your community can achieve what it values.

5. Given the things we care about and want for our community, what is the real problem we're facing? How does the problem as we currently understand it relate to what we value for our community? Does thinking about what we want suggest a different view of the problem? For example, suppose that, initially, the

problem is that our children aren't getting the sort of education we think they ought to have. When they finish school they still aren't prepared adequately for their roles as adult members of the community. They don't have the skills they need for employment and they aren't ready to start contributing to the community. We conclude that the schools aren't doing their job. Now, suppose that one of the items on our list of things we want for our community is independent, self-reliant, responsible citizens who contribute to making our community a good place to live. We might start by asking ourselves what enables a young person to grow up to be this sort of citizen. This might lead us to reflect on what in our own lives helped us acquire experience, wisdom, and maturity. In turn, we might discover that the most important influences on our personal growth came not from school, but from other sources: family, friends, neighbors, the local grocer, the police officer whose beat included our block, a local religious leader.

After thinking about the problem in connection with what we want for our community, we might discover that our preliminary definition of the problem isn't quite accurate. We might conclude that the real problem is that we expect our schools to do too much. We expect teachers to do what only we—parents, business people, public officials, clergy, members of civic associations—can and must do together: provide the examples, opportunities, standards, expectations, incentives, rewards, and so forth that our young people need in order to develop fully into competent, responsible, knowledgeable, effective adults.

6. Without getting into specific solutions or policies, what, in general terms, would we say the answer is? What, very broadly speaking, is the remedy? What general approach do we need to take?

7. What are some of the proposals that people have made to solve the problem? Are these proposals likely to help us keep or achieve what we care about, what we value? What effect would they have on the problem, as we now understand it? What effect would they have on what we want for our community? If the proposals and solutions people have offered won't help us achieve what we value for our community, what consequences will they have? Will they affect adversely what we care about? What are the real purposes of these proposals? What motivates people to make them? Ultimately, what do their proponents care about or value?

8. How do these purposes and values compare to the values we've listed? What are the similarities and differences? Are there values that we didn't list before that we now think should be included?

## NEGOTIATING A COURSE OF ACTION

Even after members of a community have formed a public perspective, deliberated together, and reached a public judgment, important differences may persist.

Choosing a course of action that everyone can go along with may therefore require some negotiation. To succeed, however, negotiation must take place in the context of the public perspective that people have formed and the public judgment that they've reached. People mustn't lose sight of each other's understandable motivations, the tradeoffs that can't be avoided, the points they disagree on as well as those they agree on, and the priorities they have established for themselves as a community.

Such negotiation may, and probably will, require multiple steps, just as in a chess game. In contrast to the chess game, however, the "players" in the sort of cooperative negotiation that practical politics calls for do not try to think ahead to block the each other's efforts or to gain a competitive advantage. Rather, they think ahead together in order to determine what each might do to improve the other's ability to address their fundamental concerns and needs. They explore together the actions that each might take to help their fellow citizens obtain what they need. In other words, the players in the chess game of practical political negotiation in effect operate as a team. They sit on the same side of the chess board, working together to solve the problem before them by addressing each other's concerns and helping each other meet their respective needs.

Negotiating for the purpose of setting a general direction that everyone can go along with may prove to be reasonably straightforward. More likely, however, such a direction will not be immediately evident. It will have to be crafted out of various imagined possibilities. If initially there doesn't seem to be a way forward that everyone *will* go along with, the question becomes, Is there nevertheless a way of proceeding that everyone *would* go along with, provided that certain conditions are met? To answer this question, participants may find it useful to pose the following questions to each other:

—What do *we* (who favor this direction or way of proceeding) want that we need *you* (who favor a different direction or way of proceeding) to help *us* achieve?

—What could *we* (who favor this direction or way of proceeding) achieve more readily if *you* were to take some action that you might be willing to take?

—What can *we* (who favor this direction or way of proceeding) offer *you* (trade you, do for you) in return for what we want to accomplish?

—What will you accept from us that will help us accomplish what we want?

—What can we (who favor this direction or way of proceeding) do to make it easier for you (who favor a different direction or way of proceeding) to obtain what you hope for?

—What can we (who favor this direction or way of proceeding) do to reassure you about your concerns, worries, or fears?

Successful negotiation depends as much on the way people behave toward one another as it does on the intellectual skill they bring to bear on their discussions. When trying to negotiate a direction that everyone can go along with, therefore, it's helpful to follow certain guidelines for interacting with each other. For example:

—*Inquire and solicit:* Instead of stating your demands, instead of staking out a position and defending it, inquire and solicit information from each other that will clarify your respective concerns, needs, aspirations, hopes, and fears.

—*Stop and think:* Instead of rejecting, denying, contradicting, or making counterassertions in response to what others say, make observations and ask questions that prompt them to stop and think, to reconsider. Draw out implications. Explore consequences. Do your fellow citizens accept these? Ask them questions such as: If this is so, and this happens, then where will we be? What will our situation be? How will our relationship be affected? Will each of us be better off? What responses are likely to be provoked?

—*Stimulate and support:* Instead of shooting down ideas, suggestions, and proposals, encourage them. Promote brainstorming. Support and reinforce use of imagination, flashes of creativity. Ask, "What if . . . ?" "How about . . . ?" "What do you think of this?" Respond with, "That's interesting." "That might work." "Good idea!" "That's worth exploring." "That has some potential." Express appreciation for every sincere and serious new idea.

—*Facilitate and "pro-act":* Try to predict and anticipate the consequences of different actions that people might take, not for the purpose of opposing them or finding fault with them, but for the purpose of finding ways to facilitate them. Instead of *re*acting to each other's ideas and suggestions, "pro-act"—get out in front with ideas and suggestions designed to help others take action that will promote their interests as well as yours.

### AFTER THE CONFERENCE

Few community conferences, especially when they are being tried for the first time, will truly represent the community. Perhaps the biggest challenge that participants will face, therefore, is how to connect with their fellow citizens and public officials who did not participate in person. Although there always will be a danger that some participants in the conference will treat their conclusions as something that they have to "sell" to others, the greater danger by far is that people who do not participate will regard those conclusions as the conclusions of a particular group, not those that the community as a whole would arrive at. This is why participation must be as widespread and as representative of the community's diversity as possible. The more representative the participant group is of the community as a whole, the less difficult it will be to assure nonparticipants that the judgment arrived at by the conference can be regarded as the judgment of the community.

Even in the best circumstances, however, there will be persons who, because they chose not to participate or because they disagree with the conclusions reached, will question the representativeness of the delegates and the legitimacy of the process. (This is especially likely in the case of persons who have narrow agendas or who do not wish, for whatever reason, to take into account the concerns and interests of their fellow citizens.) How should conference participants approach nonparticipants? What should they say and do? How might they move the judgment they've reached and the general direction they've arrived at outside of their group into the larger community?

Conference participants have a number of options. One is to *promote* the way of moving forward—the general direction for action—that they have settled upon. They might encourage public officials or others to take steps consistent with the direction they've set. (Because of the unresponsiveness or resistance that a strategy of "tell and sell" is likely to evoke from people who have not participated in the process, this option is not recommended.) A second possibility is to *work with* other individuals, organizations, and public officials to identify actions that the community might take. Conference delegates might select emissaries from among their number to work in partnership with representatives of other organizations and with public officials to develop and implement a strategic plan that is consistent with the conclusions reached by the conference. A third option is for participants to content themselves with *publicizing* the judgment they've reached, sharing it with government, organizations, and members of their community without asking them to act on it. Fourth, participants might elect simply to *continue their discussions,* refining the direction they've set and developing strategies for pursuing it. As they do so, they might make opportunities for others to join them. In this way they might catalyze similar discussions elsewhere in the community. As "mini-conferences" proliferate, a steering group might be established to consolidate the process. In time, proliferation might produce a "critical mass" in the community that will result in concerted action.

Even in the course of a one- or two-day discussion (let alone a discussion lasting a couple of hours), it is unlikely that participants will be able to do more than begin working toward a judgment and choice of action. Working toward a collective decision takes time; it requires more thought and discussion than is possible in the relatively short periods of time that people are accustomed to and that test their patience for political talk. If you and your fellow participants believe you have reached a sound public judgment and have identified the course of action that will enable your community to respond effectively, bear in mind that you represent only a small portion of your community as a whole. As I've suggested above, if you simply try to "sell" your fellow citizens on the conclusions you've reached, you may be perceived, with some justification, as just another "interest group" promoting its favorite solution. You shouldn't jump to the conclusion that the "voice" articulated in the conference is the same as that of the public as a whole. It is better to treat it as *a* community voice, or as the preliminary (tentative, or provisional) voice of your community. You should continue to invite nonparticipants into the process of deliberation, constantly expanding the circle of citizens engaging in practical political deliberation.

While realistically and soberly accepting that much work remains to be done, you should be able to see how important and substantial your progress has been, though it may seem modest. A community in which a small group of persons has begun the process of practical political deliberation has turned the corner in its political life. A politically healthy community is not one that has solved all its problems, met all its challenges, and settled all its issues, but one that has the ability and the will to conduct its civic business according to the five principles of practical politics. The challenge is to bring ever-greater numbers of one's fellow citizens into that process. Any progress in this direction is significant for the community as a whole because it is the process by which political choices are considered and made that is the key to responding effectively to matters of public concern. The quick fix is doomed to failure. Only a sustained process of practical political talk and action stands a chance of producing effective and widely supported public policies.

## The Need for Citizens' Organizations

It's hard for a community to make decisions if the public isn't organized sufficiently to do so. That's why we need civic structures such as the council of neighborhoods and discussion vehicles such as the community conference. It's also why we need citizens' organizations.

In most communities, there is no institution, organization, or group that takes responsibility for facilitating practical political discussion and action. Even those entities whose missions bring them closest to this role—colleges, the League of Women Voters, service clubs (Kiwanis, Rotary, Sertoma, or others)—either shy away from the potential for controversy that public discussion carries or are forced by lack of time, energy, and money to focus on a narrow aspect of the community's civic needs and activities. By default, the responsibility for facilitating practical political discussion and action falls to government, which in most cases is happy to monopolize everything political. Unfortunately, most public officials share with their constituents the mistaken notion that the civic life of a community is the same thing as the institutional decision-making process and the culture of political consumerism that supports it.

Communities need citizens' organizations—organizations made up of individual citizens who take it upon themselves to find ways to enable and encourage the members of their community to think, talk, and work together. Such organizations should be committed to

—creating opportunities for *participation* that permit all citizens to have a meaningful and beneficial impact on the decisions that affect the future of their community and the quality of life it affords;

—promoting clear and constant *communication* between organizations, between citizens, and between each of these and their representatives in government;

—fostering the growth of healthy working *relationships*—characterized by understanding, respect, and good will—between organizations, between citizens, and between each of these and their representatives in government;

—facilitating *cooperation* between citizens, and between citizens and public officials;

—urging *proactive responses* to the problems, challenges, and opportunities confronting the community; and

—encouraging and developing *leadership* that unites and inspires.

In general, a citizens' organization should exhibit the following characteristics:

1. *It must be inclusive.* Whether or not particular individuals or groups choose to join in the organization's efforts, their perspectives must find clear and persuasive expression in the group's membership.

2. *It must be open.* People must feel that they can join and participate at any time, should they feel it important to do so, provided that they recognize the work the group has already done, the need to reach closure and make decisions, and the importance of making progress and producing results.

3. *It must be public-minded.* There is such a thing as the common good and the public interest. In addition to acknowledging and respecting the needs, concerns, and values of particular groups within the community, the organization

must seek to articulate and honor that elusive but nonetheless indispensable sense of what is good for everyone, for the community as a whole.

4. *It must take responsibility for the whole.* Someone has to make sure that all the necessary connections are made, all the essential relationships are established and maintained, all the lines of communication are opened and kept open.

5. *It must maintain continuity.* A citizens' organization must have a membership large enough to permit individual members to transfer their responsibilities to newer members as they reach the limits of their time and energy.

6. *It must be flexible and adaptable.* Stubbornness, rigidity, dogmatism, the inability or unwillingness to admit and learn from mistakes—all doom a citizens' organization to failure.

7. *It must produce results.* This doesn't mean eliminating problems. Nor does it mean making spectacular progress in a short time. Such expectations are unrealistic. It does mean modest, early successes and a steady chipping away that is apparent to everyone.

8. *It must have legitimacy.* The organization must achieve and demonstrate that it has the moral and political authority to speak and act in the name of your community. If it is inclusive, open, public-minded, responsible, continuous, adaptable, and effective, it will win legitimacy in the eyes of your community and public officials.

# 10

# Fifth Principle: Realism

*Democracy is the worst form of government, except for all the others.*
—Winston Churchill

---

> **Fifth Principle: Realism.** Have no illusions—following the principles
> of practical politics won't be easy. You will always encounter obstacles and
> resistance. Accepting that difficulties are inevitable, and that they can't al-
> ways be fully overcome, will let you work without getting discouraged. A
> healthy realism will keep you from naïvely expecting swift and dramatic
> change. And it will give you something that will serve you even better—
> hope.

We come now to the fifth principle of practical politics: realism. "Realism" means
understanding and accepting that a number of obstacles—some small, some
large—stand in the way of a more effective response formulation process. We
should have no illusions about the ease of overcoming these obstacles. Accordingly, we should have no illusions about the ease of responding effectively to the
problems and opportunities that confront our communities today. Realism permits us to proceed nonetheless.

## Impediments to Practical Politics

### THE ILLUSION OF AN APOLITICAL LIFE

One impediment to practical politics is the illusion that we can avoid politics
altogether. This misconception is particularly troublesome in American culture,
with its emphasis on what I have termed ontological individualism, its decidedly
libertarian philosophical bent, its tenuously constrained economic competition,

its historical legacy of hostility to governmental power and authority, and its incessant corrosion of established practices, conventions, and institutions in the name of freedom, profit, or progress. In part because of the malign effects on our life of consumerist politics, but also because of the historical, cultural, economic, and ideological currents just cited, probably most Americans believe politics is worse than a necessary evil—it's just plain evil.

Like life more generally, we can approach politics in a variety of ways. We can treat it as a burden to be borne or as an adventure. We can practice it for a variety of purposes: to promote our respective interests, to make the world a better place, to safeguard our rights and liberties, to settle the disagreements that inevitably arise between us. But there's one thing we can't do—we can't avoid it. We can steer clear of particular forms of politics; more precisely, we can avoid allowing a given form to predominate. But we can't avoid politics per se. Why not?

We can't avoid politics because, first, politics is part of living. At its most general, politics is simply the way we interact with each other over time as we try to fashion the sort of community, society, and world we wish to live in. When we try to make the world we inhabit into the sort of place we want to live in, invariably we end up at cross-purposes with others. We find ourselves disagreeing with our fellows. Often these disagreements break out into disputes. If we could ignore our differences with each other, of course, there would be no disputes. But we can't. Each of us is motivated to act in order to fulfill needs, satisfy desires, pursue interests, carry out obligations—in general, do the things we consider worth doing. These include our desire to live in a community, society, or world of a certain sort. We can't sit back passively and expect life to harmonize itself with our personal preferences. Like it or not, we must decide what kind of society we will be. Not to act is not an option. It is this inescapable necessity of acting in order to bring about the kind of social environment we want to inhabit that brings us into disagreement with each other, and hence into the realm of the political.

A second reason why we can't avoid politics is related to the fact that we can't avoid having to act. No matter what you or I want to accomplish in life—especially if it has to do with making our community, society, or world into the sort of place we want it to be—we can't accomplish it alone. Each of us needs the cooperation of others, even if that cooperation amounts only to not interfering with our efforts. None of us is rich enough or powerful enough or smart enough to achieve anything substantial without the assistance of others. Without the assistance of others I couldn't get an education, I couldn't earn a living, I couldn't feed myself, I couldn't have a warm, dry, well-lighted, and safe place to live. Still less could I build a road, or a sewage treatment plant, or a factory. And I certainly couldn't solve problems such as violent crime, poverty, child abuse, pollution, consumer fraud, unfair business practices, racism, or traffic congestion. Nor could I enjoy the rights I think are mine, or the pleasure of living among others whom I can rely on to deal with me civilly, respectfully, and honestly.

### THE CONCEPTUAL BOX OF CONSUMERIST POLITICS

Our current practice of politics—what I call "consumerist" politics—has accustomed us to thinking of politics as simply the means by which we try to get government to respond (or not respond) to the desires we happen to have, as individuals or groups. In this view, politics is a competition between private interests. So long as people find it hard to envision an alternative form of democratic politics—one that engages ordinary citizens and enables them to respond effectively to the problems, challenges, and opportunities facing their communities, we will continue to experience both persistently stubborn problems and growing disenchantment with the political process.

### DIVERSITY AND DISTRUST

Sociopolitical fragmentation is a byproduct of the growing diversity of our society and the belated recognition that the pluralistic character of our country cannot be papered over. American society is riven with divisions that follow fault lines where friction occurs between people of different socioeconomic classes, levels of educational attainment, occupational specializations, geographical regions, ethnic and racial subcultures, and ideological outlooks. Our identification with and loyalty to these groups, necessary and desirable though they might be, compete with our identification with and loyalty to the shared, universal role of citizen. Inevitably, fragmentation has been accompanied by fear and mistrust of—and even hostility toward—others whom we think are substantially or fundamentally different from us. We are apprehensive about encountering those persons in situations where we must talk about things that highlight the differences between us.

### FEAR OF FEELING

We fear expression of powerful feelings, especially anger. So we try to ban them from our social and political interaction. Talking about the reality of life in our communities might mean reviving tensions we've put to rest. It might mean delving into matters that most people would rather not know about. We don't want to open old wounds that would make people angry at each other all over again.

### THIS IS WORK

Responsible public participation is not entertainment. It's not recreation. It consumes one's time, patience, and energy. In current circumstances, the demands placed upon people by their careers or jobs, family responsibilities, and personal difficulties and needs, not to mention the general overwhelming character of modern life, deter them from shouldering fully their duties as citizen decision makers in the communities where they live. Such demands weigh even more heavily on the large and growing number of persons who lack the time, resources, confidence, and skills that many middle-class people take for granted.

## NOT YOU, NOT ME, NOT THEY—WE

Good working relationships, sustained and strengthened over time, are the key to achieving progress toward solving problems, seizing opportunities, and meeting challenges. "Realism" means "relationships before results." Including the large and diverse number of our fellow citizens in the decision-making process; endeavoring to comprehend the needs, desires, and feelings that underlie their perspectives; deliberating together to reach a sound judgment about what to give priority; and building good working relationships—all this takes time, energy, and sustained effort.

## OUT OF PRACTICE

Citizens need opportunities to develop and hone the skills that practical politics requires. Because it asks so little of people, consumerist politics has "de-skilled" ordinary citizens. Generations of Americans have grown up without having acquired the know-how of democratic self-government. They're not incapable of governing themselves, but they're out of practice. Like learning how to play baseball, or paint a picture, or play a musical instrument, or drive a car, or write, or teach, or practice law or medicine, learning how to engage in democratic politics is not something that can be achieved simply by reading a book or by having other people tell you about it. In the end, we learn the dispositions and skills of democratic politics by *doing*. We need to reacquire these dispositions and skills through practicing the art and craft of democratic politics.

## THE SHRUNKEN TOWN SQUARE

The difficulties posed by the foregoing obstacles to practical politics are compounded by a lack of psychologically safe, politically neutral spaces where people feel welcome, where they feel they have a right to be, and where the "playing field" is level. Most of the places where politics occurs today—legislatures, city council chambers, hearing rooms, school board meeting rooms—are the sites of official or quasi-official decision making, the domain of consumerist politics in its institutional setting. Such places are ill-suited to the inclusion, comprehension, deliberation, and cooperation that practical politics requires. Neutral public spaces simply do not exist in most communities today, or, if they do, they are severely underdeveloped. Unfortunately, most of the institutions that might create space for people to engage each other about matters of public concern—libraries, churches, schools, newspapers, community colleges, foundations, service organizations—accept no responsibility for promoting the practice of practical politics. They do not see this public purpose as part of their institutional missions.

## DEPENDENCE ON "THE MAN"

The workplace—perhaps the single most important public space in terms of the time and energy we spend there—is notoriously undemocratic. Even in the bastions of outspoken democratic rhetoric—universities, foundations, news organizations—democracy stops at the door. The demands of efficiency, control, profitability, and public relations require, we are told, that responsibility and authority rest with the privileged few who purportedly know best. Most of us are, and will always be, utterly dependent for our livelihoods on institutions, organizations, and persons that resist and rationalize the absence of real democracy. This is a serious problem, if for no other reason than that the corrosive irony of democratic rhetoric belied by undemocratic reality demoralizes, renders cynical, and ultimately enervates us.

## THE POWERS THAT BE—AND WANNABE

Another source of resistance to practical politics is the massive investment that elites—established, emerging, and aspiring—have in the structure and practice of consumerist politics. Elected officials, political parties, the major news media, and (especially) interest groups—all have a huge stake in perpetuating the great game of competition for power, influence, status, and money that has so alienated most ordinary citizens. Practical politics may be perceived as a threat by persons, groups, and organizations who enjoy influence and power within the system whose flaws we gloss over by defending it as "representative" democracy. Our fellow citizens who direct the agencies, departments, foundations, associations, universities, corporations, lobbies, and political action committees that have the wherewithal to affect the conditions in which the rest of us live may be content with the status quo. Experts and persons in positions of authority are particularly prone to suffer from this fear because they have the most to lose (though less than they imagine).

As for public officials, most believe they bear the responsibility for "leading"—for coming up with and implementing solutions. Their job, as they see it, is to bring the public along. That involves building broad-based support for a solution. But leadership so understood is a euphemism for managing the public so that people will accept the plans that officials develop. This is the conventional approach to community governance, and it goes by names such as "tell and sell" and "decide, announce, defend." It is increasingly obvious, however, that this approach does not work very well in current conditions. The community is likely to feel manipulated or even coerced. More and more, the public can't be managed. People refuse to be treated as consumers who must be sold a solution, as clients who must accept without question the medication that their political physicians prescribe.

Public officials and experts aren't the only elites who, often with the best intentions, push the public to the sidelines. Some established civic leaders—heads of service organizations, voluntary associations, neighborhood groups, chambers of commerce, leadership organizations, and so forth—think *they* are the public. They see themselves as a microcosm of the public. They see citizens outside their elite circle as their constituencies, not as members of the public with whom they need to work as partners. They believe they speak for members of the community who aren't actively involved in trying to influence the policy-making process. As a result, they don't feel a need to engage the community as a whole. Practical politics may appear uncongenial as well to persons and groups who previously have been excluded or marginalized. Folks who hope for or are on the verge of obtaining political power within the existing system may feel cheated by the transformation of our political practice just at the moment when they are about to gain an advantage.

## Some Practical Precepts for the Political Realist

In the next chapter, I offer some thoughts that will help us sustain our commitment to the principles of practical politics in the face of resistance, disappointments, and setbacks. Here are some "rules to live by" that, if we follow them, will keep us from setting our sights unrealistically high.

*Expect sinners, not saints.* Human beings aren't perfectible. In fact, they're improvable only to a limited extent. Yes, people can grow and mature. And in the right circumstances we can bring out the best in each other. But we're never going to be angels, so we shouldn't expect perfection even as we strive to make ourselves better.

*Expect size to matter.* In most communities it isn't feasible to assemble hundreds or thousands of people in one place for the purpose of deliberating the community's options and reaching a public judgment about what to do. That makes coordinated action difficult to achieve. We need to develop structures and processes that provide opportunities for sustained, face-to-face discussion.

*Expect discomfort.* A lot of people feel uncomfortable when faced with ambiguity, lack of structure, uncertainty, open-endedness, and "endless discussion." They want to see decisions made and actions taken. Other people are unable and unwilling to make decisions and choices because they're afraid they'll make mistakes; they're afraid they don't have enough information to make a sound decision. These people may procrastinate and engage in avoidance behavior—anything to avoid the risk of acting.

*Expect to benefit from opposition.* We need people who will challenge us in our civic life, just as athletes require competitors in sports. Conflict helps keep us from getting lazy and complacent and from becoming rigid in our beliefs and behavior. We don't have to love our enemies, or even like them. But we should *value* them, because they help *us* become better. Corollary: We shouldn't caricature our opponents. We should grow stronger by taking on their soundest arguments, not their weakest.

*Expect to be painted partisan.* Sometimes, some people don't want to solve problems and get things done. They want to win. For these folks, if you're not for them you're against them. There's no middle ground. If you try to position yourself as neutral, they'll still think you oppose them. Their reasoning goes something like this: "We're right. Anybody who's right is on our side. You're not on our side. So you're wrong."

*Expect self-interest to be pervasive.* Self-interest is okay. In fact, it's unavoidable. Everyone—yourself included—is motivated by the prospect of achieving something that he or she believes is good. So look for people's self-interest and try to address it.

*Expect "intolerance."* Tolerance implies not only that we are obliged to put up with something we find objectionable but that we must be "neutral" (indifferent) with respect to it. What we should practice is not tolerance but forbearance—that is, patience, self-control, and restraint.

*Expect to find something beneath the surface.* Objectionable behavior doesn't necessarily mean objectionable motivations. Distinguish the person from his or her position. Also, don't accept "simple" or "obvious" explanations—you may be projecting your own experience or feelings onto your adversary.

*Expect to bear your share.* Don't imagine you're an innocent victim. In any dispute all parties bear some responsibility. Even if you're 99 percent in the right, you're responsible for the remaining 1 percent. So hold up your end. Corollary: Don't sink to your adversary's level. Conduct your political efforts with passion and zest, but also with integrity. Don't cheapen your cause and degrade your character by turning an honorable struggle into a petty contest for the moral high ground.

*Expect "grayness."* Nothing is ever "either/or." Everything human admits of degree: physical strength, intelligence, beauty, skin color, power. Even truth is a matter of degree.

*Expect chaos.* Remember Churchill: Democracy is messy, time-consuming, turbulent, frustrating, and exasperating. But it's the safest way to organize our public life. As Sir Winston said, "Democracy is the worst form of government, except for all the others." Like it or not, we're stuck with each other. It's in everyone's interest to play by the democratic rules of the game. Corollary: If you live by the sword of undemocratic action, eventually you'll be wounded by it as well.

*Expect the use of force.* There will always be situations in which some people are not responsive to reasoned appeals, will not cooperate, and persist in doing things we consider unacceptable. There are circumstances in which we may have no choice but to use political force, situations in which we may not be able to avoid "playing hardball." There will also be times when you're on the receiving end of coercive political action. People who disagree with you, and with whom you don't have a strong working relationship, may regard you as hostile and unapproachable. As a result, their first inclination may be to threaten you or otherwise make demands that put them in an adversarial stance in relation to you. In such situations "playing hardball" may be forced upon you. But you should always keep the door open for dialogue. Only when there is no alternative should you "fight fire with fire"—and then only to the extent necessary to (a) protect yourself (or others) from being forced to act against your own interests, and (b) restore a balance of power from which you can once again invite your opponents to work with you rather than fight you.

*Expect to "settle."* A problem can be so complex, so deeply rooted, or so pervasive that it can't be truly solved, but can only be contained, moderated, or lessened. Some problems aren't solvable. The best we can do in those circumstances may be to make them less severe. We shouldn't let the best be the enemy of the good. We should take what improvement we can get and not hold out for an ideal outcome. Our motto should be, "mitigation, not elimination." Moreover, some disagreements are not resolvable. The best we can do may be to make them less intense, divisive, and harmful. In such circumstances, "compromise" shouldn't be a dirty word. What compromise gets us may be the best we can reasonably expect.

*Expect to be in it for the long haul.* Showing people that following the principles of inclusion, comprehension, deliberation, and cooperation are in their interest will take a lot of explaining and demonstrating. Don't give up. Be patient. More than anything else, realism means patience and perseverance.

# 11

# Leadership, Practical Politics, and Hope

---

*Human hope is such a miracle that it is not surprising if at times it glows within one for no earthly reason. The main thing is that afterwards it continues to lift one's life on its great velvet wings.*

—Jean Giono

### Leadership and Change

It is ancient wisdom that nothing endures but change. "There is nothing in this world constant," wrote Swift, "but inconstancy." Two thousand years earlier, Diogenes anticipated Swift: "All is flux," he said, "nothing stays still."

Were these sages of the past alive today, they would think themselves even more solidly confirmed in the wisdom of their words. The twentieth century has seen, especially in its last decades, the most rapid and pervasive change in all human history. Nothing in current circumstances suggests that our future will not continue the trend.

It has long been the desire of humankind to master change, to harness and control it—sometimes for the purpose of improving our situation, more often in order simply to survive. Change thrusts itself upon us. In its wake it trails problems and crises. It provokes conflict and prompts resistance. But it also stimulates progress. For when change appears to be for the worse, it is precisely change that we want—change for the better. Change is the engine of our development, and as such is as indispensable to human life as the air we breathe. How we meet change—the nature and quality of our response to it—determines how well we live. One way to think of leadership is to see it as a creative and effective response to change and the need for change. The oft-expressed and widely felt need for public leadership in our day can be understood as a desire for action designed to achieve change for the better in response to change perceived to be for the worse.

If leadership is creative and effective action designed to bring about desired change, we might immediately ask, Change of what sort? Change in what direction? Often, the answers to such questions are supposed to be supplied by "leaders." Many of us think leaders are those exceptional persons who by definition know what needs to be done and how to do it. The purpose of leadership, in this view, is to define and present a policy agenda for the community and to move the public to support that agenda. Leaders are the few who possess the ability to understand problems and to come up with ideas for solving them. They're the individuals who can rally us behind their ideas. By their self-assurance and decisiveness they inspire the confidence, trust, and optimism we require in order to go along with them.

But it would be a mistake to think that leadership is the exclusive province of a chosen few who just happen to have the right traits or the right ideas for making things better. To change communities as large, complex, and diverse as ours is more than we can expect from even the most exceptional individuals. Imperfect though our democracy might be, the power and authority to change things for the better does not—should not—reside in the hands of a few. To effect change in contemporary America is a task beyond the capabilities of a few individuals, no matter how talented and heroic they might be. If we stop to reflect, it becomes plain that the only potentially effective agent for change in our public life is the public itself. We, together—the citizens of our communities and country—have the ability, the right, and the responsibility to produce the change we desire.

## Leadership and Consumerist Politics

It is not possible to talk meaningfully about leadership except with reference to the social, cultural, and institutional setting in which leadership is to be practiced. To understand what leadership is (or ought to be) in a democratic community (as opposed, say, to a business corporation, a government, or a school system), we need to begin with an understanding of democratic politics.

That is what we did in the early chapters of this book when we examined the practice of politics that prevails in most communities today, which I call "consumerist politics." When people talk about public leadership, the settings they usually have in mind are institutional decision-making arenas such as Congress, state legislatures, city councils and county commissions, and school boards. The kind of leadership that is appropriate in these settings is directly related to the rules that govern the activity that occurs there. In formal political decision-making institutions, the cardinal rule is the principle of majority rule. Implicit in this principle is a division of decision makers—and hence the constituents whom they represent—into prospective "winners" and "losers." When a vote is taken, those who find themselves in the numerical majority "win," those in the numerical minority "lose." This division is reinforced by the two-party system of government that has been an enduring feature of American politics throughout the country's history, and by the tendency of public opinion to coalesce around two poles representing opposing responses to a given problem, opportunity, or state of affairs.

It's not surprising that public leadership should be conceived in a way that reflects the bipolarism of majority rule decision making in formal political settings. As I pointed out in chapter 1, the goal to be pursued in such settings is "winning"—getting enough votes to achieve a numerical majority for a particular response to the question at issue, and thereby to "defeat" those whose support of an alternative response confines them to a numerical minority. Winning entitles those in the majority to exercise the authority to make policy decisions that are binding on everyone. Leadership, accordingly, is treated as the act of assembling and maintaining a numerical majority for the purpose of obtaining the authority to make such binding decisions.[1]

The emphasis on decision making in formal institutional settings also contributes to another sort of division. It divides people not only into prospective winners and losers, but into those who are able and willing to perform the task of assembling and maintaining a numerical majority, and those for whom or on whose behalf this task is performed. It thereby reduces the latter to passive "consumers" of the policies that the wielders of political authority craft in consonance with what the (majority of the) public supposedly wants.[2] Hence my suggestion, in chapter 1, that politics as we currently practice it can be understood best by comparing it to the self-interested behavior of consumers. In this analogy, citizens are political "consumers." They are assumed to have particular interests and desires, which they try to satisfy by "buying" the political goods and services supplied by "producers"—elected officials and other policy makers, experts, analysts, consultants, and commentators.[3]

This bifurcation of the political population into "producers" and "consumers" corresponds to a conceptual division in our "social map" noted by John McKnight, whom I cited earlier: a division between individual persons, on the one hand, and institutions, on the other.[4] McKnight believes that this social map is inaccurate because it excludes the domain of "the community," its associations, unions, houses of worship, neighborhood organizations, and other social structures of ordinary people.[5]

Consumerist politics denigrates the capabilities of ordinary citizens and privileges political elites in the decision-making process. Its rise has gone hand-in-hand with the ascent of political professionalism. McKnight challenges the claim of *soi-disant* "experts" to superior political knowledge. He argues that democratic community rests on the "recognition of fallibility." Democracy assumes that the best idea is the sum of the knowings of the collected fallible people who are citizens.

McKnight's critique has been echoed by Charles Anderson, who has written that, although all theories of policy science recognize that public decision is a social process, the clear implication of their teaching seems to be that the best course of action can be ascertained within the mind of any single person who analyzes the situation logically and dispassionately.[6] In other words, political "experts" assume that it is possible apolitically to determine what is best for society. But as I endeavored to show earlier, this is not possible. What Douglas Torgerson has called "a dream of the abolition of politics—of putting an end to the strife and confusion of human society in favor of an orderly administration of things based upon objective knowledge," is in truth a pipe dream.[7] Such knowledge as we may have of political matters can be obtained only through a practice of democratic politics marked by the principles of inclusion, comprehension, deliberation, cooperation, and realism.

Unfortunately, the predominant view of leadership derives from a model in which the world is divided into "producers" and "consumers," "institutions" and "individuals," "professionals" and "clients," "experts" and "laymen," "advocates" and "victims." The way we typically think of leadership, I believe, grows out of our dividing the world (erroneously) into doers and those-for-whom-things-are-done. As a result, the very idea of leadership has become an obstacle to practical politics.

## Leadership for a Politics That Works

### THE PROBLEM WITH LEADERSHIP IS THE PROBLEM WITH POLITICS

If we are dissatisfied with the quality of public leadership today, it is because we are dissatisfied with the prevailing practice of making public decisions and policies. If we think of leadership as the act of assembling and maintaining a numerical majority for the purpose of obtaining the authority to make binding decisions, and therefore of being responsive to the opinions and preferences of the political "market," then to say there is something wrong with our public leadership is to say there is something wrong with the public decision- and policy-making process. What is wrong is, first, the failure of that process to produce effective policy responses to the problems, challenges, and opportunities that confront our communities and country, and second, the failure of the public to accept responsibility for resolving the conflicts that inevitably arise with respect to the question of how best to deal with these matters.

How do we remedy this situation? The short answer is, we must change the way we practice democratic politics. The fundamental weakness in that practice is its disregard of the essential task of democratic politics, which is to enable the public to make sound decisions, *as a public*. To be able to make decisions as a public, citizens must form a common perspective, reach a shared judgment, and make a collective choice about how they will respond to the problems and opportunities their communities encounter.[8] Moreover, because every course of action we might pursue carries negative as well as positive consequences, and because there is no single objectively correct answer to the question of what to do, we invariably face a dilemma. The wisest and most effective solutions to such dilemmas emerge from a process in which the public as a whole weighs the costs and consequences of the available options and reaches a collective judgment about what to do.

Democratic politics is not about which individual or group gets how much of what he or it wants. It is about how citizens decide what they will do, as a community, in response to problems, challenges, or opportunities they face. Instead of viewing political community as a quasi-consumerist aggregate of individuals having their own interests and desires, we should think of political community as a commonwealth—a diversely constituted but enduring association of persons and groups united for mutual benefit.[9] In this view, citizens are not consumers but producers—indeed, the primary producers—of political goods. Political goods are not just those things that satisfy the desires and serve the interests that individuals and groups happen to have. Rather, they are also things that people need and aspire to that they have to create—and create together. Political goods include conditions that everyone has an interest in but that he cannot secure by himself. They include such goods as a healthy community life, a high material standard of living, wise and prudent political decision making, a habitable environment, civility in public encounters, and effective solutions to problems that affect everyone.

If we view democratic politics in this way, how should we think of public leadership? The conventional view makes effective public decision making a function of good leadership: if we get good leaders, we will have good politics. Practical politics suggests an alternative conception that reverses the equation: good leadership is a function of good public decision making—if we build a good practice of politics, we will have good leaders. In the conventional view, the purpose of leadership is to define and present a policy agenda for the community and to motivate people to support that agenda. A leader is a person who knows what needs to be done and who persuades enough people to go along so that it gets done. In the alternative view, the purpose of leadership is to improve the public's ability to understand the hard choices confronting it and to contribute to its ability and readiness to form a public perspective on the problem, to reach a public judgment, and to make a choice that sets a direction for the community that everyone can go along with.

Democratic political leadership cannot be confined to having the authority to make public decisions. There is abundant evidence today that having such authority doesn't guarantee that public policies will be effective or widely supported. What is required today is the ability of the citizenry as a whole to respond effectively to the problems and opportunities it encounters. "Communities that work"—that is, communities that respond effectively to the problems and opportunities they encounter over time—are ones in which the "response formulation process" (i.e., politics) is characterized by the five principles: inclusion, comprehension, deliberation, cooperation, and realism. If the purpose of politics is to enable a community to respond effectively to the problems and opportunities it encounters, then the purpose of leadership is to improve the public's ability and readiness to form a common perspective, to reach a shared judgment, and to make a collective choice that sets a direction for the community that everyone can go along with. And if an effective "response formulation process" is one that is characterized by the five principles, then leadership is the activity of promoting adherence to those principles as a community undertakes to respond to the problems and opportunities it encounters. In short, *leadership is the activity of promoting inclusion, comprehension, deliberation, cooperation, and realism in a community's politics.* It is the activity of promoting practical politics.

### WHO WILL LEAD?

No individual or group of individuals—no matter how talented, visionary, or exceptional—can do for the public what only the public in its entirety can and must do for itself. A community needs many leaders—perhaps as many leaders as citizens. Everyone has a contribution to make: ideas, experience, time, skills, personal contacts, energy, principles, knowledge.

The more widespread the ability and willingness to take initiative in a community, the more effective the public will be and the less pressure there will be on particular individuals to take on more than their share of the responsibility. Not everyone can or should contribute in the same way. Different persons will have different contributions to make at different times. This means that leaders and followers are, and should be, to a substantial degree interchangeable. On any given occasion, of course, a few persons will have to take the first step. One aspect of public leadership, and an important one, is the ability and willingness to take that first step. We might say, then, that a leader is any citizen—any member of the public—who takes it upon himself or herself to enable and encourage his or her fellow citizens to bring their abilities, skills, and energies to bear on the task of forming a common perspective, reaching a shared judgment, and making a collective choice about what to do.

### HOW DO WE DEVELOP LEADERSHIP?

Democratic politics is a practical activity. It's an "art," and like other arts it rests on knowing *how* to do something. "Know-how" is what citizens need. The five principles are practical guides for democratic political decision making and action. As such, they can't properly be learned simply by reading about them in a book. For a person to learn the dispositions and skills—the "know-how"—needed to practice the kind of political involvement that leads to effective community responses, he or she must participate in the process of responding to real problems or opportunities in actual situations. The task of helping a community form a common perspective, reach a shared judgment, and make a collective choice about what to do and the task of acquiring the know-how of public leadership are one and the same. Leadership education is "on-the-job training."

### On Hope's Velvet Wings

Is there reason to hope that we can transform the way our communities conduct their public life? Although Americans express irritation and dismay about public life, many remain actively involved in addressing the matters that concern them. This isn't surprising. As the political analyst William Schneider has observed, most Americans are "pragmatists." They believe that "what works is right."[10] And at some level they understand that, in the end, only citizens can make a democracy work. As a recent political cartoon put it, "We the People of the United States . . . are still in charge of making it work." The leaders we seek are among us already. *We* are the leaders our communities require.

Even so, transforming politics as we know it into a practice of public decision making that issues in effective responses to problems, opportunities, and challenges—and is effective because it is characterized by inclusion, comprehension, deliberation, cooperation, and realism—clearly will prove a herculean undertaking. At some time, in some way and to some degree, we will encounter every one of the impediments to practical politics I described in my discussion of the principle of realism. Knowing that we will meet stubborn resistance, what can we say to ourselves to sustain us? What reasons can we give ourselves for pressing ahead nevertheless, remaining faithful to the principles of inclusion, comprehension, deliberation, and cooperation?

First, let us be patient. Like all habits, political habits are hard to break. We must bear in mind what John Adams said about change: "All great changes are irksome to the human mind, especially those that are attended with great dangers and uncertain effects." We're not going to change overnight the political practices and attitudes that have been with us for decades, perhaps generations. We have to be in it for the long haul.

Second, let's recognize that we have more assets, resources, and advantages than we sometimes think. This is especially true in today's society, where power is becoming fragmented and widely dispersed, creating more opportunity for people who know how to work together. No single group, individual, or organization has the ability by itself to make substantial inroads into the conditions that most concern us. For this, we need not only each other's cooperation, but each other's contributions: energy, time, experience, insight, creativity, and resilience. That gives every one of us leverage. If something is important enough to enough people, it'll get done. We should concentrate on what we *can* do. The more we in fact do, the less we'll be unable to do.

Third, let's appreciate that nothing we do is truly futile, insignificant, or done in isolation. As Richard Flacks observes, every action we take in every day of our life has a ripple effect that is magnified beyond our ability to see. Something as small as a phone call "can initiate a chain of action and events that fundamentally reshape the lives of millions."[11] This is the so-called butterfly effect, a metaphor that illustrates a central theme in highly complex systems: that the overall behavior of the system is extremely sensitive to small fluctuations in small areas within the system. The little things we do in the life of our communities *do* have an effect, even if we can't readily see it. We are justified in taking it on faith that, if we follow the principles of inclusion, comprehension, deliberation, and cooperation, in time our action will have a meaningful impact.

Fourth, even if it were true that the principles of practical politics do not lead to better success in solving the problems, meeting the challenges, and taking advantage of the opportunities we encounter, following those principles would still be the right thing to do. Why? Because they ask us to show greater concern and respect for our fellow citizens than do other approaches to political life. The practical approach, although this is not its aim, bids us become better people, irrespective of what we get out of it.

Finally, let's not lose sight of what's at stake. It is nothing less than the American experiment itself. It is as true today as it was in 1789, when George Washington, in his first inaugural address, said that "the destiny of the republican model of government [is] . . . deeply, perhaps . . . finally staked on the experiment entrusted to the hands of the American people." As I noted in the previous chapter, it is unclear whether in a society as large, diverse, and complex as ours we will ever be able to realize fully the promise of democracy that germinated in the practices of ancient Athens and the towns of eighteenth-century New England. It is—fortunately—too soon to tell. As James Fishkin has noted, "We have only a brief history of experimenting with the adaptations of democracy to the large-scale nation-state."[12] But surely it is worth pondering, particularly in this day of disenchantment with and disengagement from democratic politics, what the consequences might be, should we fail in our attempt to adapt democratic ideals and practices to the social and economic conditions of our time. My own belief is that our failure to fulfill democracy's promise can have only harmful effects on the well-being of our families, our communities, and our country as a whole.

Whether in the end our politics becomes more practical, in the sense I have used that term in this book, depends on whether enough of our fellow citizens answer the call. Naturally, uncertainty about their readiness to respond and to commit themselves to this undertaking makes us wary of investing our time, our energies, and our emotions in what might prove to be a failed endeavor. What we need, above all, is hope. Obviously, there are no guarantees. There is only belief in the goodness of our cause, commitment to the work that must be done, faith in our ability to make a difference, and the example of history.

Small victories keep us going. They bolster our faith, sustain our commitment, and urge us on in the face of frustration and failure. It's small successes, then, that we require to succeed—small but heartening examples that show democracy at its best. This, finally, is where practical politics can help most, because a practice of public decision making marked by inclusion, comprehension, deliberation, cooperation, and realism works best on a small scale—the scale of our immediate neighborhoods and communities. It's at the local level of public decision making that we most need people who understand why the way we currently practice politics is unsatisfactory, and who know how to go about enabling and encouraging their fellows to deliberate, judge, choose, and act—together.

Hope may be a marvel, but it's no mystery. It's the natural product of sustained effort, hard-won progress, and a stubborn refusal to give up despite disappointments and setbacks. We need citizens—members of communities who are prepared to take the risks and make the effort to produce successes, however small they might be, that will give hope to the rest of us. We need citizens to show by example that politics can be practical, and hence effective. We need citizens to lead their communities to small victories in the way of life we call democracy. We need citizens who will lift their own lives, and those of their fellows, on the great velvet wings of hope.

# Notes

## Introduction: The Work of Democratic Communities

1. Lawrence Susskind and Jeffrey Cruikshank, *Breaking the Impasse: Consensual Approaches to Resolving Public Disputes* (New York: Basic Books, 1987), 3.

2. Ibid., 8.

3. Robert A. Levine, "The Empty Symbolism of American Politics," *Atlantic Monthly*, October 1996, 81.

4. William Schneider, "An Insider's View of the Election," *Atlantic Monthly*, July 1988, 55–56.

5. There is some evidence that current members of Congress are less willing to communicate and work across party lines than were their predecessors. But they probably are not as disinclined to talk and work together as the news media portray them—or compel them—to be.

6. See Sidney Blumenthal, *The Permanent Campaign* (Boston: Beacon, 1980).

7. Alasdair MacIntyre, *How to Be a North American,* Publication No. 2–88, November 14, 1987 (Washington, D.C.: State Federation of Humanities Councils), 17.

8. James Fallows, "Why Americans Hate the Media," *Atlantic Monthly*, February 1996, 45–64.

9. Jonathan Schell, "The Uncertain Leviathan," *Atlantic Monthly*, August 1996, 70.

10. We are most apt to do so when the problem or issue is a matter of both local and national concern (crime and welfare, for example), less inclined to do so when it is clearly either local (zoning and street repair) or national (the federal budget deficit and foreign policy).

11. Dirk Johnson, "Civic Civility Disappearing," *New York Times*, December 13, 1997. Johnson reported that, "during a fiery debate on financing education, the president of the [Rockford, Illinois] school board . . . chose a rather dramatic way to express his disagreement with a fellow board member. He grabbed him by the throat." The incident, Johnson said, "is only the latest example of incivility in American civic life, as the work of town councils, county assemblies and school boards becomes increasingly nettled by behavior that is boorish, menacing, and even violent." Johnson notes that in 1997 the National League of Cities made the problem of unruliness at local meetings its top focus, and that *Governing* magazine, a publication for state and local officials, had expressed concern about a nationwide "epidemic of incivility."

12. Ibid.

13. Notice that we tend to think of ourselves as *taxpayers* rather than as *citizens*.

14. Holly Heyser, "Citizens Uniting to Solve Problems," *San Jose Mercury News*, September 29, 1996, 1A.

15. Michael Joyce, speech delivered to the Board of Trustees and Founders of the Heritage Foundation, Washington, D.C., December 1992.

16. The Harwood Group *Citizens and Politics: A View from Main Street America* (Dayton, Ohio: Kettering Foundation, 1991).

17. To be precise: I believe experience supports the contention that the five principles are jointly necessary (and perhaps jointly sufficient) for a community to respond effectively to a problem, challenge, or opportunity. An "effective" response is one that, in the view of any (not every) adult member of the community who participates actively and in good faith in the community's attempt to respond, is more successful and satisfactory than what the community reasonably could be expected to have achieved using other principles, strategies, and methods.

18. From time to time, however, I will offer suggestions about how to apply the five principles—how to translate them into concrete steps a community might take.

## Chapter 1: Impractical Politics

1. As I pointed out in the introduction, the public's perception that politics doesn't work is strongest with respect to politics at the national level. In general, people regard their local political decision-making processes more favorably. In view of the different sorts of problems, challenges, and issues dealt with at the two levels, the public's perception of greater effectiveness at the community level is probably justified. However, there are important similarities between the decision-making processes at the two levels. These similarities make community politics vulnerable to the same criticisms and attitudes that national-level politics elicits from Americans today.

2. Schell, "The Uncertain Leviathan," 70.

3. Ibid., 77.

4. Nobody, of course, cares about one thing and one thing only. Everyone has multiple interests. But in particular times in particular situations, one interest usually takes priority over others. The priorities of different persons can conflict, and often do, thereby giving rise to political disputes.

5. People may pursue the same political goods (i.e., "favorable results"), of course. If they do, the goods they seek, and hence their interests, are *shared*. Typically, however, not everyone seeks the same political goods. For example, two persons, A and B, might each believe it is desirable to have the freedom to use the property he owns as he sees fit. They share a belief: personal freedom to use one's property is good. But if A's exercising his freedom were to have unwelcome consequences for B, and vice versa, the political goods they seek, and hence their respective interests in obtaining those goods, would not be shared. The good that A seeks ("having the freedom to do what I want with my property") conflicts with the good that B seeks ("having the freedom to do what I want with my property").

6. See Harold Lasswell, *Politics: Who Gets What, When, How* (New York: P. Smith, 1950).

7. The differences between the "political market" and an economic market, of course, are important and obvious. In the latter, typically there is more than one producer. Ford isn't the only company that builds cars. People can buy from General Motors or Toyota or Volkswagen. Precisely for this reason, buyers in an economic market usually do not have to compete with each other to win a favorable decision from the producer. They can simply turn to another one.

8. Indeed, "the market" is sometimes more than a metaphor. In some ways—in the way lobbyists for interest groups "buy" access (and perhaps influence) through campaign contributions, for example, or the way political campaign directors "buy"

votes with slick political ads that draw on the same principles and make use of the same techniques as commercial ads—politics literally *is* a market.

9. For a compelling example of how the consumerist mentality pervades our thinking about matters of public concern, see John Doble, *A Factory Mentality: The Consumer Mindset in American Public Education: A Report for the Kettering Foundation* (Dayton, Ohio: Kettering Foundation, 1998).

10. Michael J. Sandel, "America's Search for a New Public Philosophy," *Atlantic Monthly*, March 1996, 58. In this article and in the book from which it is excerpted (*Democracy's Discontent: America in Search of a Public Philosophy* ([Cambridge, Mass.: Harvard University Press, 1996]), Sandel describes the historical development of the consumerist form of democratic politics. He notes that "the central idea of the public philosophy by which we live is that freedom consists in our capacity to choose our ends for ourselves" (58). Sandel traces the preeminence of this idea to the triumph of Keynesian fiscal policy in the aftermath of the Second World War: "[U]nlike the various proposals for structural reform, such as vigorous antitrust action or national economic planning, Keynesian economics offered a way for the government to control the economy *without having to choose among controversial views of the good society.* Keynesians . . . proposed simply to *accept existing consumer preferences* and to regulate the economy by manipulating aggregate demand" [emphasis added] (63). The triumph of the Keynesian theory of political economy thus paved the way for the triumph of consumerist politics. "Americans of the postwar decades found their way to a new understanding of freedom"—and of democratic politics. "According to this understanding, our liberty [indeed, our overall well-being] depends not on our capacity as citizens to share in shaping the forces that govern our collective destiny but rather on our capacity as persons to choose our values and ends for ourselves" [i.e., our ability, as individuals, to get, have, or become whatever we happen to want] (66).

11. The epitome of irrationality, perhaps, is California's notorious Proposition 13. Peter Schrag ("California's Elected Anarchy," *Harper's*, December 1994, 50–58) describes the nightmarish conditions that have been created by the decision of California voters in the late 1970s to limit the rate of property taxation to 1 percent, roll back assessed property values to 1975 levels, prohibit assessed value from rising more than 2 percent a year unless ownership changed, and require a popular vote—in many instances a two-thirds majority—in order for local governments to levy a new tax or increase taxes for a designated purpose.

What began as an exhilarating exercise in "citizen power" (more precisely, *taxpayer* power) designed to provide relief from property taxes that were skyrocketing as property values soared in the 1970s has turned out to be a disaster. California government has become a "Rube Goldberg machine" of pointless, unproductive complexity. The state, Schrag says, "is now spending its scarce revenues not through a comprehensible legislative process in which priorities are evaluated against one another but through a crazy quilt of ad hoc decisions that frustrates healthy development and defies rational budgeting, intelligent policy formation, and civic comprehension" (55). All the while, costs and expenditures keep rising as taxes remain constant. In their simple-minded, short-sighted lust for low taxes, Californians are quickly destroying the economic, physical, and civic infrastructure of what once was in many ways the most successful, progressive, and well-run state in the Union.

12. Eric Dexheimer, "Spaced Out: Colorado Residents Take the Initiative in Slowing Growth," *Westword*, September 11–17, 1997. For a discussion of the consequences of "government by plebiscite," see Peter Schrag, "California, Here We Come," *Atlantic Monthly*, March 1998, 20–31.

13. Steve Farkas and Jean Johnson, *Divided Within, Besieged Without: The Politics of Education in Four American School Districts* (New York: Public Agenda Foundation, 1993), 1.

14. In his *Community and the Politics of Place* (Norman: University of Oklahoma Press, 1990), Daniel Kemmis makes essentially this point in his discussion of the public hearing process. In public hearings, Kemmis observes, not much real hearing occurs. In particular, members of the public don't hear each other.

15. Benjamin R. Barber, "America Skips School: Why We Talk So Much About Education and Do So Little," *Harper's*, November 1993, 40.

16. Ibid., 46.

17. Compare another teenage problem: pregnancy and the consequent failure to complete school. In a syndicated report on teenage pregnancy published on May 25, 1997, Robert T. Cooper of the *Los Angeles Times* cited a study conducted by V. Joseph Hotz, a professor at UCLA:

> Hotz has found that being a teenager has almost nothing to do with the problems that afflict most [teen-age mothers] and their children. Teenage pregnancy is a symptom, he says, not a cause. Teenagers do not have problems because they have babies; they have babies because they have problems. . . . The problems they suffer from [poverty, dysfunctional families, physical and sexual abuse . . . , poor school performance and behavioral problems] are so severe and began so early in their lives that it makes little difference whether they have babies as teenagers or a few years later. Focusing on their age diverts attention from the real causes of their problems . . . and makes solutions harder to achieve. . . . Hotz's message . . . implies a need to help [teenagers] develop more stable lives.

See also Barbara Dafoe Whitehead, "The Failure of Sex Education," *Atlantic Monthly*, October 1994, 55–80.

18. When people talk about a community's "vision" for itself, they're getting at questions such as: Do we want our community to be a good place to raise kids? A good place to retire? A good place to do business? A place with a high quality of life? These are things we can't create as individuals. We can only create them together.

19. Alexis de Tocqueville, *Democracy in America* (1835; New York: New American Library/Mentor, 1956), 70.

20. Alan Ehrenhalt, *The United States of Ambition: Politicians, Power, and the Pursuit of Office* (New York: Times Books, 1992), xxii.

21. J. Mac Holladay, *Economic and Community Development: A Southern Exposure* (Dayton, Ohio: Kettering Foundation, 1992), 35.

22. Ibid., 17.

23. See *Clues to Rural Community Survival* (Lincoln, Nebr.: Heartland Center for Leadership Development, 1987), which is based on the center's Entrepreneurial Case Study Project. Cited in Holladay, *Economic and Community Development*, 19–20.

24. Holladay, *Economic and Community Development*, 40.

25. Michael Kinsley, "You Still Can't Have It All," *Time*, September 21, 1992, 72.

26. Schell, "The Uncertain Leviathan," 76–77.

27. Ibid., 77.

28. It is worth noting that even formal theories of social (i.e., collective) choice, which attempt to derive choices for a society (or any large group) from individual choices, have run into difficulties. The best known of these is Arrow's (Impossibility) Theorem, developed by the Nobel Prize–winning mathematical economist Kenneth J. Arrow. Arrow demonstrated that if there is any degree of variety in individual preference orderings, there can be no "social welfare function"—i.e., no set of rules for transforming the desires of individuals into a choice for a social group—that meets the four axioms he posits as conditions for such a function. Although some critics have taken issue with the conditions Arrow assumed, the interpretation of those conditions, or their applicability to politics, other theorists have taken Arrow's results as evidence that it is fundamentally misguided to think that individual preferences per se can serve as the basis for, or be translated into, a coherent social choice that is consistent with each individual's preferences. (They have argued, for example, that interpersonal comparisons of intensity or significance must be taken into account.) The assumption of a social or collective analogue of individual utility or preference function appears to be at best problematic. See Roger Scruton, *A Dictionary of Political Thought* (London: Macmillan, 1982), and Robert Audi, ed., *The Cambridge Dictionary of Philosophy* (Cambridge: Cambridge University Press, 1995).

## Chapter 2: The Inescapability of Choice

1. To be precise, we encounter three types of difficult choices: those among options the consequences of which are all positive—"good/good" choices; those among options the consequences of which are all negative—"bad/bad" choices (a.k.a. the "lesser of evils"); and those among options the consequences of which are mixed, some positive and some negative—"good-bad/good-bad."

2. The standard model of public policy making, which derives from micro-economic theory, also emphasizes tradeoffs between painful alternatives. This model assumes that there is too much demand for scarce goods. However, we should exercise caution and not accept this assumption uncritically. The point is not that scarcity does not exist. Rather, the danger is that we might treat some scarcities as natural or inescapable. "False scarcities" are shortages that we assume without question are necessary or inevitable. "False scarcities" occur when we take for granted that the way our community or society happens to be organized at a given moment in its history is the only way it can or should be organized.

It is important, therefore, to be clear that a "practical" approach to politics does not imply that we may simply take the social world as it is, that we may get on with the business of solving problems without having to raise fundamental questions about our value priorities, our principles, and our social practices. "Practical" should not be interpreted to mean doing what we can *given the way things "are."* We must guard against the danger that people will pay lip service to the ideal of democracy while allowing their actual political practice to fall far short, justifying it as "practical." "Practical politics" as I use the term is "radical" in the literal sense that it enables and encourages us to get at the roots of our problems, precisely by *not* assuming that the way things are necessarily is the way they must or should be.

3. Willard Gaylin, "Faulty Diagnosis: Why Clinton's Health-Care Plan Won't Cure What Ails Us," *Harper's*, October 1993, 57–64. All quotations from Gaylin in this chapter are from this article.

## Chapter 3: Alternatives to Impractical Politics

1. See, for example, Boyte's "Neither Intimates nor Innocents: Citizen Politics and the Public Sphere," *Civic Arts Review* 4 (Summer 1991): 4–9.

2. Ibid., 6.

3. Christopher Lasch, "For Shame," *New Republic*, August 10, 1992, 34.

4. Eugenie Gatens-Robinson, "Beneficence and the Habilation of People with Disabilities," *Contemporary Philosophy* 14, no. 2 (1991): 8.

5. Leslie Lenkowsky, letter to the editor, *Chronicle of Philanthropy*, March 9, 1995, 35–36.

6. For an excellent and compelling historical account of the ideology of progress that provided the cultural context for professionalism, see Christopher Lasch, *The True and Only Heaven: Progress and Its Critics* (New York: Norton, 1991).

7. Sandee Brawarsky, "The Politics of Knowledge: Foundations and Public Policy," *Carnegie Quarterly* 17 (1992): 8–11.

8. John McKnight, "Regenerating Community," *Social Policy* 17 (1987): 54–58. See also his book *The Careless Society: Community and Its Counterfeits* (New York: Basic Books, 1996).

9. McKnight, "Regenerating Community," 57.

10. Tocqueville, *Democracy in America*, 70.

11. Gatens-Robinson, "Beneficence and the Habilation of People with Disabilities," 8–11.

12. For example: Most young people today would benefit from greater contact and interaction with mature, experienced adults. Most senior citizens would benefit from greater contact and interaction with young people. Granting that there is much to be gained from bringing the two together, it has to be acknowledged nonetheless that there is likely to be an element of artificiality in efforts to do so, particularly if one group feels the other is there just to "help" or "do good" for the other. A more natural basis for interaction between members of age groups that have been separated by the structure of contemporary community life is the intersection of self-interests. Where might the self-interest of youngsters and seniors intersect? One possibility is personal safety. Creating opportunities for the two groups to work together on the challenge of securing *everyone's* personal safety might accomplish more than opportunities for "service." Self-interested cooperation is a more promising basis on which to build and sustain civic relationships than are motives that are, or appear to be, essentially altruistic.

13. The most effective grassroots efforts today, such as those of the Industrial Areas Foundation, are far more sophisticated and multidimensional than those of earlier organizers, whose stance toward their fellow citizens was often unrelentingly adversarial.

14. Ilene Philipson, "What's the Big ID? The Politics of the Authentic Self," *Tikkun* 6, no. 6 (1992): 52, 54.

15. William Connolly, *Identity/Difference: Democratic Negotiations of Political Paradox* (Ithaca: Cornell University Press, 1991), 9.

16. Christopher Lasch, "The Communitarian Critique of Individualism," paper presented at the "Search for Civic Community" conference sponsored by the University of San Francisco, Grace Cathedral, and Congregation Emanu-El, San Francisco,

November 1989. A version of Lasch's remarks was printed in *Harper's,* April 1990, 17–20.

17. Shelby Steele, "The New Sovereignty," *Harper's,* July 1992, 52–53.

18. Philipson, "What's the Big ID?" 51.

19. Lasch did not live to see his contention supported by the activities of right-wing militias, whose paranoid sense of victimization has led them to preach—and, in some cases, practice—violent rebellion against legitimately constituted and broadly supported public institutions. Less worrisome but perhaps an even better illustration of Lasch's contention is an example provided by Jonathan Raban in the August 1993 issue of *Harper's.* Raban describes the civic sculptures he encountered while driving through the timber towns of the Pacific Northwest: "The sculptures . . . were part of the counter-preservationist movement. . . . They made the assertion that timber-industry workers, like the Indians, had . . . a unique and historic *culture.* Deny me my job, and you deny me my culture, my past, my ethnic identity. So the logging communities were busy manufacturing craft objects that gave them a tribal history and the right to be regarded as yet another beleaguered minority threatened with extinction." Raban, "The Next Last Frontier: A Newcomer's Journey through the Pacific Northwest," 45.

20. Steele, "The New Sovereignty," 48–50.

21. Ibid., 53.

22. See, for example, Robert Bellah et al., *The Good Society* (Berkeley: University of California Press, 1995). See also those authors' earlier work, *Habits of the Heart: Individualism and Commitment in American Life* (Berkeley: University of California Press, 1985). Other important sources include two essays by Christopher Lasch: "The Communitarian Critique of Individualism," and "Communitarianism or Populism?" in Lasch, *The Revolt of the Elites and the Betrayal of Democracy* (New York: Norton, 1995): 92–114. See also the symposium proceedings, "The Communitarian Debate," *National Civic Review* 82, no. 3 (Summer 1993): 217–54, especially the contribution by William A. Galston, "The Promise of Communitarianism." Notable books with a communitarian theme include Jane Mansbridge, *Beyond Adversarial Democracy* (Chicago: University of Chicago Press, 1983), and Benjamin R. Barber, *Strong Democracy* (Berkeley: University of California Press, 1984). For an anthology of writings with a communitarian theme, see Markate Daly, ed., *Communitarianism: A New Public Ethics* (Belmont, Calif.: Wadsworth, 1994).

23. Julius Kovesi, *Moral Notions* (London: Routledge and Kegan Paul, 1967).

## Chapter 4: Value, Needs, and Conflict

1. Milton Rokeach, *The Nature of Human Values* (New York: Free Press, 1973), and idem, "Stability and Change in American Value Priorities: 1965–1981," *American Psychologist* (May 1989): 775–84.

2. Abraham Maslow, *New Knowledge in Human Values* (New York: Harper, 1959), and idem, *The Farther Reaches of Human Nature* (New York: Viking, 1971).

3. For more on this point, see chapter 6.

4. Political disagreements usually involve disagreements over facts. Factual disagreements often prove difficult to resolve because the parties hold strong motivating beliefs about their respective values and priorities. The ability and willingness of people to accept or reject factual assertions depend on the implications of doing so for their

values and priorities. If an alleged fact is at odds with one or more of a person's strong motivating beliefs, he or she is unlikely to accept it. Faced with a choice between accepting the alleged fact and abandoning the motivating belief, on the one hand, and rejecting the alleged fact and maintaining the motivating belief, on the other, he or she is apt to favor the latter.

5. Robert J. Samuelson, "The End of Economics?" *Newsweek,* July 24, 1989, 53. For evidence of the importance of "values" based on polling data, see William Schneider, "The New Shape of American Politics," *Atlantic Monthly,* January 1987, 39–54, and idem, "An Insiders' View of the Election," *Atlantic Monthly,* July 1988, 29–57. See also Norman J. Ornstein, *The People, The Press and Politics: The Times Mirror Study of the American Electorate* (Reading, Mass.: Addison-Wesley, 1988). For a more interpretive approach based on interviews and direct observation, see Mark Gerzon, *A House Divided: Six Belief Systems Struggling for America's Soul* (New York: Tarcher Putnam, 1996).

6. Samuelson, "The End of Economics?" 53.

7. Ibid.

8. John W. Burton, "Conflict Resolution as a Political System," *Working Paper 1* (Fairfax, Va.: George Mason University, 1988), 7.

9. Charles Case, a New York cultural anthropologist, has devised a system of "personal anthropology" that enables persons to identify their deepest motivations and consistencies or inconsistencies between them. At the heart of his system are "the whys." A barrage of "why" questions—some forty to fifty in a row—compels the client to "burrow deeper into his or her belief system." The process leads inexorably to its end-point: an unanswerable question. At the end-point are a person's "core beliefs," of which what I call "motivations" or "ultimate values" are one kind. Everyone has a personal philosophy composed of such core beliefs. See also Daryl Bem, *Beliefs, Attitudes, and Human Affairs* (Belmont, Calif.: Brooks/Cole, 1970).

## Chapter 5: First Principle

1. I have changed the names and some of the details to protect the identity of the community and its citizens.

2. Research and experience suggest that citizens won't become and remain engaged in efforts to solve problems, meet challenges, or seize opportunities facing their communities unless seven conditions—what we might call the "Citizen's Seven Cs"—are met. See my discussion of these in chapter 9.

3. There will be times, of course, when some stakeholders refuse to participate and instead persist in their efforts to compel the other stakeholders to accede to their demands. Or, if they do participate, they may refuse to cooperate, instead using their place at the table to "play hardball," or even to sabotage the process. In such situations, the best course is to turn to the strategies and techniques of nonadversarial dispute resolution. Writers such as Roger Fisher and William Ury (see their book *Getting to YES: Negotiating Agreement Without Giving In* [New York: Penguin, 1981], and, especially, Ury's *Getting Past NO: Negotiating with Difficult People* [New York: Bantam, 1991]) offer sound advice on how to deal with people who do not grasp that it is in their own interest to be guided by the principles of practical politics and who refuse to make a good faith effort to collaborate for mutual benefit. But see also chapters 8 and 9 in this book.

4. Kemmis, *Community and the Politics of Place,* 52–53.

5. It is unclear whether, given the scale on which contemporary life is organized, we will ever be able to achieve complete face-to-face political interaction. Efforts such as the National Issues Convention conceived by University of Texas professor James Fishkin and conducted for the first time in the United States in January 1996 may help. Whether emerging electronic technology will allow a large number of persons to participate in public discussion remains an open question at this point. As Howard Rheingold observes in *The Virtual Community* (Menlo Park, Calif.: Addison-Wesley, 1993), "Perhaps cyberspace is one of the informal public places where people can rebuild the aspects of community that were lost when the malt shop became a mall. Or perhaps cyberspace is precisely the *wrong* place to look for the rebirth of community, offering not a tool for conviviality but a life-denying simulacrum for real passion and true commitment to one another. . . . You can be fooled about people in cyberspace, behind the cloak of words. . . . In some ways, the medium will, by its nature, be forever biased toward certain kinds of obfuscation. [Yet] it will also be a place [where] people often end up revealing themselves far more intimately than they would be inclined to do without the intermediation of screens and pseudonyms" (26–27). See also the special section devoted to "electronic democracy" in *Whole Earth* 71 (Summer 1991).

6. The community conference is an adaptation for the local level of an idea originated by the political scientist James Fishkin of the University of Texas: a national "deliberative opinion poll." (Fishkin's plan, which was first aired in the *Atlantic Monthly* and later was described with approval in *Time,* the *Washington Post,* and the *New York Times,* has been adopted by all nine presidential libraries, which co-sponsored the first National Issues Convention in January 1996. See his book *Democracy and Deliberation* [New Haven: Yale University Press, 1991].) Fishkin's plan calls for a "convention" attended by a randomly selected representative sample of the public. Delegates would spend two days deliberating with each other in small groups. The expectation is that the interactions among citizens, and between them and public officials, will be considerably more thorough, constructive, rigorous, and pragmatic than that which usually characterizes our public discourse.

7. The sort of random sample required is a "stratified" random sample. This is a subset of the public whose members are selected at random within predetermined categories, such as race, ethnicity, age, education, income, partisan identification, religion, and so forth.

8. Although we cannot say with certainty that whatever conclusions emerge from the conference are precisely those that the community as a whole would reach if literally everyone were able to deliberate together, we can have greater confidence in the validity, reliability, and generalizability of those conclusions than we can in information obtained in any other manner—including opinion polls and surveys. See note 9.

9. Permitting participants to "self-select" leads invariably to unrepresentativeness because the persons who are most inclined to participate are those who have the time, self-confidence, and interest to do so. Although we should not want to deny anyone the opportunity to participate, we also need to know what the public as a whole thinks. In order to serve both these important values, we should supplement the self-selected group with a group consisting of persons who are selected randomly to represent the community in its full diversity.

10. I am not suggesting that the delegates continue the discussion, in the sense of picking up where the participants in the previous round left off. Rather, in each round the delegates from the preceding round will start over at the beginning, just as they did in earlier forums. Naturally, to the extent that participants have been over this ground before, they should be able to make better progress. But such progress, if it occurs, must be the result of growing familiarity with the way the public as a whole views the subject being discussed, not the result of a few citizens being able to reach agreement among themselves that enables them to move forward. Allowing delegates to "go off on their own," to avoid their responsibility to carry forward with them the "group voice" of the forum(s) that have designated them to continue, would undermine the genuinely public and democratic character of the emerging "community voice." (Incidentally, the way of proceeding recommended here minimizes the need for public "feedback" after each round of forums. If delegates carry out their responsibility to the forums that delegated them, the "group voice" of those forums will emerge uncompromised at the culminating event.)

11. A random sample of fewer than around four hundred persons does not permit us to generalize with a small margin of statistical error (i.e., the plus-or-minus four percentage points achievable in well-constructed opinion polls) from the group's judgment to a conclusion about what the community as a whole would judge, were all its members to undergo the process. Nevertheless, including randomly selected citizens—even if there are only forty to sixty of them—will generate relatively better information about the judgment that would emerge from a fully inclusive community deliberation than could be obtained in any other fashion.

It's important to understand that polls and surveys do not capture what a *community* thinks, because a community is not the same thing as a collection of individuals. A community is not equivalent to the sum of all its individual members. Moreover, there is an important difference between what the sum total of individuals happen initially to think about some question and what the people of a community think as a community after they've had a chance to discuss it together. In contrast to conventional opinion polls, which measure what individual members of the public think—given what little information they have obtained, the modest degree to which they typically have reflected on an issue, and their isolation from each other—a community conference attempts to ascertain what the community *would* think if its members had more information and had the chance to think more carefully and deeply about the issue, especially after discussing it with their fellow citizens. Public *opinion* is what individuals say—more or less off the tops of their heads—when they are asked a question. In contrast, the community's *judgment* does not exist until members of the community have deliberated together.

12. If logistically it seems unworkable to hold any open public forums at all, a community might consider relying exclusively on a random sample (version 7 in the table).

13. Clearly, a community that sets out to hold a community conference will have to be serious about the time and effort required to pull it off. For the most part, a conference can—and should—support itself; there should be little need for public funds or for money from private sources. It is in the interest of every citizen, every organization, and every institution in the community—newspapers, TV and radio stations, churches, libraries, schools, businesses, community foundations, neighborhood groups, humanities councils, professional associations, civic organizations, social service agen-

cies—to contribute time, energy, and in-kind resources (e.g., physical space, employee release time, etc.).

14. As Willard Gaylin observed of the first Clinton administration's health care proposal, "We are told that the President's health-care plan must be 'sold' to the American public. Of course, had the plan been authored by the American public, it would not now have to be sold to it." Gaylin, "Faulty Diagnosis," 64.

15. It is highly desirable to video- and audio-tape the conference in its entirety. The resulting footage can be edited down to a length of perhaps sixty to ninety minutes. Adding suitable "wrap-around" (introductory and concluding) material of thirty minutes in length would yield a broadcast program of one and a half to two hours. Care must be taken to highlight the sorts of exchanges and comments that both illustrate the process of public deliberation and capture substantive outcomes as these have emerged from the process.

16. A complementary, parallel civic structure need not be organized on a geographical basis—it could also be built on an organizational basis. A council of community organizations might be composed of entities such as homeowners' associations, elementary school site-based management committees or PTOs, businesses, unions, churches, service organizations (Rotary, Optimist, etc.), fraternal organizations (Knights of Columbus, Moose, etc.), interest groups (Chamber, Downtown Merchants, etc.), recreation/sports organizations, hobby groups, support groups, service providers, professional associations. The obvious disadvantage of using the organizational basis is that any citizen who does not belong to an organization will not be represented.

17. The Harwood Group, *The Public's Role in the Policy Process: A View from State and Local Policymakers* (Dayton, Ohio: Kettering Foundation, 1989).

18. *Connecting Citizens and Their Government: Civility, Responsibility and Local Democracy* (Washington, D.C.: National League of Cities, 1996), 1–18. All quotations related to NLC in this chapter come from this source.

19. Gene Feldman, *Connections* 8, no. 1 (1997): 8–9.

20. A number of devices are available for creating a partnership between your community and your local government, for example, the "citizens' advisory committee," the "Citizens' Jury™," and the "joint policy committee."

A *citizens' advisory committee* is a body of citizens who, as the name suggests, advise government with respect to either a single problem, challenge, or opportunity or a number of such matters over time. Such a committee can help government by performing certain tasks that government lacks the time, resources, or mandate to do itself. For example, a citizens' advisory committee might take on responsibility for soliciting the views and concerns of a wide variety of people, perhaps by conducting surveys or focus groups. By facilitating communication between the public and government, a citizens' advisory committee can help bridge the gap between citizens and the official decision-making process.

A *Citizens' Jury™* is a device that combines the advisory role of the citizens' advisory committee with the sampling techniques described earlier in this chapter in connection with the community conference. As the name suggests, the Citizens' Jury™ resembles a jury in a legal case. Its purpose is to render an advisory judgment on problems, issues, policy options, or specific proposals. The Citizens' Jury™ differs from courtroom juries in some important ways, of course. The most obvious is that the question to be decided is not a legal fact-finding one, but one of public policy for a community that must decide what action to take. For more information concerning the Citizens' Jury™, see Ned Crosby and Janet M. Kelly, and Paul Schaefer, "Citizen Panels: A New Approach to Citizen Participation," *Public Administration Review* (March 1986), or contact the Jefferson Center in Minneapolis.

A *joint policy committee* is a body whose membership consists of both public officials and (a representative group of) citizens who work together to study problems, develop options, solicit views from the public, and make recommendations for government action. The joint policy committee constitutes a hybrid of the "advisory," "preparative," and "review" committees described by Joseph Rodgers (*Citizen Committees: A Guide to Their Use in Local Government* [Cambridge, Mass.: Ballinger, 1977]). Its role is "advisory" in that it makes recommendations. Its role might also be "preparative"—the committee might take on responsibility for actually crafting and implementing a strategic plan, for example, or even specific policies, programs, or activities. Finally, it might "review" government proposals or actions to ensure that they accord with the community's concerns, needs, and priorities.

21. In a report for the Pew Partnership for Civic Change (*Making Community Coalitions Work* [Charlottesville, Va.: Pew Partnership for Civic Change, 1993]), researchers from the Harwood Group identified a number of obstacles to effective partnerships between the public and government. First, communities and governments often have difficulty agreeing on what to talk about. For example, because of the growing financial stringency to which governments are subject, public officials typically move immediately to a discussion of how much money it would take to carry out a given task and how little of it is available.

Second, it's getting harder to say exactly where "the community" begins and where it ends. Particularly in the suburbs around America's largest cities, it's hard to say who belongs to the community and who doesn't. The growing ethnic, cultural, and socioeconomic diversity of our country also makes it hard to say what the community is.

The third obstacle pointed to by the Harwood report is a shortage of community members with the time, energy, skills, and commitment to partner with government on the community's behalf. These days, if a family has two adults, both probably work. If they work, they probably spend more energy and time on their jobs than at any time in the past twenty years. This fact of life leaves fewer people with less time and energy for their community's affairs.

A fourth observation made by the Harwood report is that it isn't clear who "the public" is. The public often appears to government officials as an amorphous mass from which bubbles arise depending on the latest hot issue. Not knowing who the public is makes it hard to identify one's partner.

### Chapter 6: Second Principle

1. As I have remarked previously, there may be conflicts that are in fact zero-sum. (Disagreements over the values implicit in the question of whether to develop land or leave it as open space come to mind.) But zero-sumness is a feature of fewer conflicts than we tend to think. Mutual comprehension helps us sort out true cases of zero-sumness from those that are only "pseudo-zero-sum."

2. This illustration also shows why "common ground" understood as what we happen (in the absence of mutual comprehension and deliberation) to agree on doesn't get

us very far toward a shared judgment and collective action. "Common ground," as I use the term, does not mean an area of agreement. Typically, common ground is construed as the area of overlap between what you believe or desire and what I believe or desire. Thus understood—and especially when sought too early in the public decision-making process—common ground usually amounts to little more than the "least common denominator." For example, during a videotaped discussion of abortion a few years ago, the spokespersons for the national pro-choice and pro-life groups were able to identify as common ground the fact that people on both sides of the issue care about children. Such common ground is too insubstantial to support a shared judgment. Common ground in this weaker sense would mean either that we happen to have the same set of motivations ($M_1$, $M_2$, $M_3$, and $M_4$) or that we happen to assign the same priority to two motivations (e.g., $M_2$ and $M_4$). It is unlikely in either case that our recognition of "common ground" would, in the absence of mutual comprehension and deliberation, by itself move us substantially toward a shared judgment and collective action. The different priorities we assign to $M_1$ and $M_3$ would probably prevent that.

The achievement of common ground in the weaker sense, while helpful, may be too easy a victory. It may divert the parties from truly comprehending and acknowledging each other's deep motivations. As we shall see, mutual comprehension is crucial to the effort to transform the way the parties view each other and act toward one another. It is this transformation that ultimately provides the solid foundation—the true common ground—upon which a shared judgment can be constructed.

3. The reconciliation that mutual comprehension makes possible is not logical in character—it is psychological and interpersonal. Mutual comprehension disposes each of us to take fuller account of the other's motivations in deciding what *we together* should give priority and what *we together* should do.

4. This emphasis on individuality, which has its roots in the ontological and moral individualism of the eighteenth-century Enlightenment that provided the conceptual context for the founding of the United States, has received a new impetus lately from the political proponents of "diversity" and "multiculturalism." An important casualty, however, of the otherwise commendable reminder of our particularity is our ability to keep in view the fact that, in certain crucial respects, we are all "the same." At bottom, we are all human beings, with the same basic inventory of human needs, and hence basic underlying motivations. It is this sameness that enables us—if we make the effort—to comprehend each other even when we find each other odd or disagreeable.

5. George Watson, "The Fuss about Ideology," *Wilson Quarterly* (Winter 1992): 135.

6. Harold Saunders, "The Concept of Relationship: A Perspective on the Future Between the United States and the Successor States to the Soviet Union," occasional paper (Columbus, Ohio: Mershon Center at Ohio State University, 1993), 16.

7. Maurice Friedman, "Healing Through Meeting, *Tikkun* 3, no. 2 (March/April 1988): 33.

8. Amy Gutmann and Dennis Thompson, "Moral Conflict and Consensus," *Ethics* (October 1990): 76.

9. Andrew Sullivan, "Wouldn't Normally Do," *New Republic*, February 21, 1994, 42.

10. See Richard Bernstein, "Pragmatism, Pluralism, and the Healing of Wounds," *American Philosophical Association Proceedings* 63 (no. 3): 16.

11. Some human motivation is (at least currently) largely beyond our comprehension. For example, we find it hard to understand the psychopath, the obsessive, and the paranoid. The motivational states of fanatics and of persons with severe intellectual impairment are scarcely more accessible to us. Nor can we readily grasp what it is like to be a victim of Alzheimer's disease or a person in a persistent vegetative condition. The subjective lives of dogs and dolphins remain opaque to us, as does the world of the simplest sentient life forms. For most of the questions we need to answer in democratic politics, however, the subjects we need to comprehend are people not fundamentally unlike ourselves.

12. Robert McShea, *Morality and Human Nature: A New Route to Ethical Theory* (Philadelphia: Temple University Press, 1990), 91.

13. Ibid., 15.

14. Ibid., 119. On this point, see also Lionel Tiger and Robin Fox, *The Imperial Animal* (New York: Holt, 1989), and Winifred Gallagher, "How We Become What We Are," *Atlantic Monthly*, September 1994, 39–55.

15. Martha Nussbaum, "Venus in Robes," *New Republic*, April 20, 1992, 38.

16. Evidence of our ability to comprehend one another abounds. For example, in her essay, "On Not Being a Victim" (*Harper's*, March 1994, 35–44), Mary Gaitskill illuminates the motivations of women who feel so insecure and vulnerable that they advocate what to many people (women as well as men) appear to be draconian measures designed to protect women from "sexual assault," whether literal or metaphorical. Similarly, in a penetrating piece of social anthropology ("The Code of the Streets," *Atlantic Monthly*, May 1994, 81–94), Elijah Anderson describes vividly the situational rationality—the "understandability," the "not-unreasonableness"—of the beliefs, attitudes, and behaviors that constitute the "code of the streets" for young inner-city black men (and, increasingly, women). Yet another example, which I cited above, is Andrew Sullivan's review of the motion picture *Philadelphia*, which "insisted on the commonality of the gay and straight experience." Noting that "homosexuality is more stigmatized in black America than even in white America," Sullivan relates how, while watching the picture, he could "overhear a straight, black couple sitting behind me [becoming] completely involved in the fate of a white homosexual." Sullivan, "Wouldn't Normally Do," 42.

Most compelling of all, in my experience, is Rian Malan's exploration (in *My Traitor's Heart* [Boston: Atlantic Monthly Press, 1990]) of the motives of a young black South African murderer, Simon Mpungose, known for his crimes as "the Hammerman." In the most gut-wrenching, heart-rending piece of nonfiction writing I have ever encountered, Malan peels back layers of ostensibly adequate explanation until he arrives at the most authentic explanation of all. When Malan concludes with the words, "his Zulu heart was rent open, and that was what was in it," we suddenly comprehend what previously had seemed opaque—or at least better explained in ways more familiar to our educated Western minds. Malan demonstrates convincingly that even the seemingly most alien thoughts and feelings are comprehensible to us—if we make the effort to understand them.

17. Michael Lerner, *Surplus Powerlessness: The Psychoanalysis of Everyday Life and the Psychology of Individual and Social Transformation* (Oakland, Calif.: Institute for Labor and Mental Health, 1986). Lerner is not alone in emphasizing the importance of dealing with the emotional dimension in politics. John Burton, a dispute resolution theorist and practitioner, observes that "resolving deep-rooted conflicts

frequently requires an escalation of tension and emotion between the parties." ("Conflict Resolution as a Political System," Working Paper 1, Center for Conflict Analysis and Resolution, George Mason University, February 1988, 8.) The escalation is necessary to bring to the surface the strongly felt needs that must be addressed if the conflict and the resulting dispute are to be dealt with productively. Burton writes, "It is often only at the point of apparent impasse that the underlying sources of conflict reveal themselves. Focusing on areas of agreement and smoothing over differences can be a serious obstacle to achieving a lasting agreement."

18. Because people begin their thinking about matters of public concern at the intersection between those concerns and their personal experiences, describing those experiences—telling stories—should be the first step in a practical political conversation. Sharing each other's experiences enables citizens to comprehend each other's motivations. Telling stories helps them see that they have something in common with each other. It begins to revitalize public relationships that have languished or attenuated. People discover that despite their differences they have much in common.

19. See Friedman, "Healing Through Meeting," 33–35, 85–87. See also Martin Buber, *The Knowledge of Man: A Philosophy of the Interhuman* (New York: Harper Torchbooks, 1966), chapter 6.

20. Rokeach, *The Nature of Human Values.*

21. For discussion of these divisions, see, for example, Gerzon, *A House Divided.*

22. In her article "On Civic Friendship" (*Ethics* 107 [October 1996]: 97–128), Sybil Schwarzenbach gives an example (albeit for a different purpose) that illustrates both how we are taught not to comprehend and how we might assist others in comprehending. She recalls a veterinarian telling her of the vet's observations of new slaughterhouse workers on their first day on the job: "The young men were horrified, paralyzed, and tears came to their eyes at witnessing the cruel treatment and death of the animals. Of course, the older men immediately laughed at the neophytes, cajoled them, and whipped them into shape by words, and it was not long before the general house practice was acceptable to many of those who remained. What if such pointed training were exercised in the opposite direction, *against* . . . the killing of cows?" (121).

23. Elijah Anderson, "The Code of the Streets," *Atlantic Monthly,* May 1994, 81–94.

24. In this hypothetical example, the focus is on *one* of the factors that may play a part in the debate over abortion. Certainly, this factor is not the only one that contributes to the debate. It might not even be an important one. But it is a plausible one. It illustrates the kind of mutual comprehension that is possible and essential when political issues turn on deeply felt needs and the motivating beliefs that are related to them.

25. The following questions can help you to determine the feasibility and desirability of different matters that you might want to select for community discussion:

—To what extent is the matter of current concern? How pressing a problem is it? A problem that is not immediate enough will not generate interest and effort. One that is too immediate might prevent people from "taking a step back" from their favored solutions.

—How "public" is the problem? How much of the community is concerned about it? A problem that's not "public" enough won't generate the widespread involvement and eventual support necessary to respond effectively to it.

—How "discussable" is it? Can people talk passionately yet civilly with each other despite deeply felt differences? A matter that's not "discussable" requires time for the long-term building of healthier working relationships, and perhaps efforts at mediation between key players.

—How "accessible" is it? Can people make sense of what's at stake and the considerations that must be taken into account? A matter that's complex or esoteric must be put into terms that most people can understand. This may require considerable time and effort.

—How "tractable" is it? Can people, acting both as individuals and as a community, do something about it? Can they make progress toward solving or at least mitigating it? A problem that is intractable will simply discourage people. They need to feel they can assert some control over the problems they face.

—Which of the foregoing considerations are most important for our community? Which are least important?

—What matter of concern best meets the test of the foregoing considerations?

26. The issue of abortion is one with respect to which people have difficulty comprehending the views of folks on the other side. This is precisely why I have selected it rather than one of the other matters of public concern your community might need to address. Attempting to present the abortion issue in a way that promotes mutual comprehension illustrates both the power and the difficulty of following the second principle of practical politics.

27. Try to dig as deeply as possible into people's motivations. Gently but persistently probe beneath the surface to reach the things that, at bottom, people really care about. Keep asking "why" until it's no longer fruitful to continue doing so. (Recall the example in chapter 4.)

28. Usually, there aren't more than three to five *basic* points of view. (Leave open the possibility, however, that in your group a genuinely distinctive point of view might be overlooked.) Also, because it's difficult for people mentally to hold onto more than three or four points of view at a time, as a practical matter the best guide is to aim for three or four clusters. If you come up with fewer than three clusters or more than five, go back and ask whether the motivations that have been identified are *discrete* (i.e., distinctive, qualitatively different) and *ultimate* (i.e., basic, not a consequence of a more fundamental motivation). If they aren't, you may have to dig deeper to find the real sources of people's beliefs and attitudes.

29. Take care not to define the matter too narrowly or too broadly. A fairly general initial characterization—one that everyone can subscribe to—creates a "big tent" that everyone can come into despite having different outlooks on what the "real problem" is. A broad initial definition enables you to avoid excluding anyone from the discussion. It lets you get the discussion underway without bogging down immediately in a dispute over how to define the problem. "Crime in our community," for example, is probably too broad. On the other hand, "the sale of automatic weapons to persons with criminal records" is probably too narrow. "The growing rate of acts of violence involving deadly weapons" is about right. It's just narrow enough to be manageable for purposes of public discussion. We can "get our minds around it," so to speak. It's not so multifaceted or complex that we feel overwhelmed and can't maintain our focus. On the other hand, it's just broad enough to encompass a variety of particular "takes" on the problem.

30. Characterizing the matter isn't easy. Keep trying out different statements until you get one that will work for anyone, regardless of his or her view. Which formula-

tion best covers all the motivating concerns you've identified? Eliminate any jargon that might have crept into your language. For example, the following statement is jargon-ridden: "The real costs of the system of primary delivery of medical services and third-party payments have reached a level at which they are severely impacting private and public economies. Moreover, gaps in coverage owing to growing financial pressures on third-party payers have exposed a substantial portion of the population to the serious risk of being unable to cope with either routine or catastrophic situations." It's much better simply to say that "Our system of health care is too expensive and doesn't guarantee that everyone who needs medical care can get it."

### Chapter 7: Third Principle

1. The statement "X is good" can be rendered as "It is true that (it is a fact that) X is good." Similarly, the statement, "X is right" can be rendered as "It is true that (it is a fact that) X is right."

2. In the discussion here, I emphasize conflicts between courses of action or end-states each of which carries positive or desirable consequences. The choices we face in life, however, are rarely between alternatives one of which has only good consequences and the other of which has only bad consequences.

To be precise, there are four basic forms of conflict. (See Dennis Coon, *Introduction to Psychology*, 5th ed. [Denver: West Publishing Company, 1989].) The first form is the one I've just cited and will use to illustrate the need for deliberation. It is called "approach-approach" or "good-good." This is a choice between two or more alternatives having positive or desirable consequences. The second type is "avoidance-avoidance," or "bad-bad" (also known popularly as a "Hobson's choice," or a choice between "the lesser of evils"). In this type of conflict a decision has to be made between alternatives having negative or undesirable outcomes. An "approach-avoidance," or "good-bad," conflict is one in which a given course of action has both positive and negative consequences, so that the person faced with it feels ambivalent—simultaneously drawn to it and repelled by it. The fourth type of conflict is the "double approach-avoidance," or "good-bad/good-bad," conflict. In this situation, each of two or more alternatives has both positive and negative consequences. It is choices of this sort that are most common in life. Typically, we are confronted with several dilemmas—hard choices between two or more options, each of which carries good and bad consequences.

3. If I probe deeply enough, I will find that (paradoxically, in view of the connotation of the words "reason" and "reasons") the basic source of my motivation is nonrational. At rock-bottom, there is nothing more I can say to justify my belief that "it is true that X is good (valuable, satisfying, etc.)." At that depth, I encounter mere feeling; in the end, I can say only that "this is how I feel." (Saying "this is how I feel" constitutes an adequate reply to the question of what warrants or justifies a motivating belief *only* after all other reasons have been identified, considered, and still found wanting as a justification.) Deliberation, then, is ultimately a process of deciding whether to permit myself to be moved to action by the prospect of experiencing, say, feeling X (which I expect to experience if I follow course of action X) or feeling Y (which I expect to experience if I follow course of action Y).

That deliberation can involve both the weighing of reasons and the weighing of feelings is clear from the work of Richard Hare (*Moral Thinking: Its Levels, Method and Point* [Oxford: Clarendon, 1981]). Hare distinguishes two levels of evaluative (specifically, moral) thinking and discourse. At the "ordinary" level, evaluative thought and talk consist chiefly of identifying and asserting motivating beliefs and supporting them with reasons. When this process is inconclusive—when the reasons available to me do not resolve the conflict—I need to move to the "critical level." There, I critically reexamine the motivations in conflict by asking myself: Do I value the outcome I expect to achieve if I pursue X? Do I value the outcome I expect to achieve if I pursue Y? When I allow myself to feel the "pull" of each, which do I desire more? I make this comparative assessment by attempting imaginatively to experience feeling X (which I expect to experience if I follow course of action X) and feeling Y (which I expect to experience if I follow course of action Y). Because I ask what I *would* feel and desire, the critical level of evaluative thinking might be called the "hypothetical" level. The feelings and desires I form through this imaginative thought process are "hypothetical" in the sense that they're not actual—they're what I would feel and desire if I were to make my decision in light of relevant information that up to this point has not influenced my decision.

4. Each person's effort to reach a personal judgment about a matter of public concern cannot be (prudently) separated from our collective effort to arrive at a public judgment. Given each individual's limited personal experience and information, a sound individual judgment requires consideration of others' beliefs, experiences, needs, sensitivities, reactions, and feelings. By listening to the views of others, I obtain information and the benefit of different perspectives that help me work toward a sound judgment about how to resolve conflicts between the things I care about. The process by which I form a personal judgment is—or should be—the same process by which, together with my fellow citizens, I work toward the formation of a public judgment. We arrive at personal judgments and a public judgment simultaneously.

5. This doesn't mean that when the process is complete we will have reached *consensus,* if by "consensus" we mean complete agreement. To some extent, individuals' personal judgments will (and should) differ from the public judgment we arrive at. (For more on this point, see chapter 9.) But because the two types of judgment are arrived at simultaneously through the same process, the participants will have created common ground upon which they can begin to build a shared judgment to which all can *assent.* (Again, see chapter 9.) The "mutual comprehension" required by practical politics permits us to transform an interpersonal political dispute into a shared, quasi-intrapersonal conflict. It does so by enabling us to create the common ground of mutually comprehended motivation, which in turn supplies the foundation for the construction of a shared, public judgment that everyone can assent to.

6. In many cases it may be unnecessary to reach people's ultimate levels of motivation (because they're readily able to comprehend the desirability for each other of the good things each seeks); in disagreements involving deep-rooted differences over priorities (as in the dispute over abortion) we typically will find it necessary to probe for the ultimate motivations underlying the conflict, to "drive beneath the surface" to find out what really moves us. Only at the level of fundamental human needs are we likely to find that we can understand and appreciate each other's perspective. The deeper we have to probe, however, the more we will have to ask of our capacity for sympathetic imagination.

7. The difficulty of answering the question of what we collectively should do when faced with a conflict owes much to an unstated assumption we make when posing it.

If we think of ourselves as unconnected individuals, we find it hard to see that the things we care about are connected. The perception of a conflict between values and interests, which is real enough, is exacerbated by our perception of each other as discrete and isolated from each other. This perception permits differences in priorities to overwhelm the recognition that we all are motivated by the same needs, and hence can value the same things. It obscures the potential help we can offer each other in sorting out what to do when priorities conflict.

8. This happens all the time. It happens whenever events bring two or more of my evaluative opinions into conflict. I believe it's good to reduce the amount of plastic I consume. But there are, or could be, situations in which it's at least as good not to do so (e.g., when it's important to save energy or when it's important to cut down on the use of paper to conserve our forests). We're often too attached to our opinions about what's good. One reason is our natural reluctance to alter our beliefs; we don't like change—we like stability and predictability. Another reason has to do with the basic human needs I discussed earlier. The beliefs we hold about what's good and bad, right and wrong, often fulfill a psychological need. It's difficult to give up the belief if it helps meet that need.

9. Speaking about the difficulty of devising a policy to cover all medical situations, John Nelson, of the American Medical Association, has said, "You can't get the ink dry on a protocol"—a prescribed method for handling a medical situation—"before you find yourself in the operating room faced with a circumstance you haven't thought of." Quoted in Joe Klein, "The Senator's Dilemma," *New Yorker,* January 5, 1998, 35.

10. An example that comes to mind is capital punishment. Abundant data exists from within the United States and from abroad that strongly suggests capital punishment has little deterrent value. Facts have little effect on people's opinion of capital punishment in large part, I believe, because although the terms of the public debate tend to focus on deterrence, the chief motivation underlying support for capital punishment is the (understandable) human wish for vengeance.

11. On this point see, for example, Bem, *Beliefs, Attitudes and Human Affairs.*

12. See D. N. Perkins, Richard Allen, and James Hafner, "Difficulties in Everyday Reasoning," in *Thinking: The Expanding Frontier,* ed. William Maxwell (Philadelphia: Franklin Institute Press, 1983), 177–89. All quotations from Perkins et al. in this chapter are from this source. For a thoughtful account of ethical reasoning in "everyday life," see Norma Haan, "An Interactional Morality of Everyday Life," in *Social Science as Moral Inquiry,* ed. Norma Haan et al. (New York: Columbia University Press, 1983), 218–44.

13. Textbook fallacies can serve a useful purpose if pointed out in a constructive spirit, that is, if used not to win an argument or defeat an opponent but to stimulate reflection and inquiry. For example, it would be helpful—in principle, at least—to object to fallacies of linguistic confusion (e.g., ambiguity and distinction without a difference), question-begging fallacies (e.g., circular reasoning and loaded or leading questions), unwarranted assumptions (e.g., the slippery slope and the fallacies of composition and division), fallacies of missing evidence (e.g., the fallacy of negative proof and the contrary-to-fact hypothesis), fallacies of irrelevance (e.g., missing the point and the genetic fallacy), irrelevant appeals (e.g., appeals to tradition, public opinion, or questionable authority), fallacies of diversion (e.g., straw men and red herrings), fallacies of deductive inference (e.g., an undistributed middle, denying the anteced-

ent, and affirming the consequent), and statistical fallacies (e.g., insufficient and un-representative samples).

14. One device in particular is an effective tool for dealing with mistakes in reasoning: the "absurd example" method. This method calls attention to a faulty pattern of reasoning without relying on technical terminology. It can be used on both formal fallacies (e.g., undistributed middle and affirming the consequent) and informal fallacies (e.g., the slippery slope). Offering another argument with the same form but with an obviously false conclusion—i.e., an absurd example—is generally more effective with people not schooled in formal logic than is resorting to the sort of argument that underpins most fallacies. Lewis Carroll provides a good illustration of the "absurd example" method in *Alice in Wonderland:*

> "You should say what you mean," the March Hare went on.
> "I do," Alice hastily replied; "at least—at least, I mean what I say—that's the same thing, you know."
> "Not the same thing a bit!" said the Hatter. "Why, you might just as well say that 'I see what I eat' is the same thing as 'I eat what I see!'"

15. I strongly recommend that one or two persons, preferably from outside the group, be given responsibility for facilitating the discussion. The facilitator(s) should not only be fair and even-handed, but should also be perceived to be fair and even-handed. They should be able to help keep the discussion focused and on track. They should help create and maintain a comfortable, "safe" environment. They should be able to draw people out. They should help clarify matters, draw useful distinctions, ask probing questions, and summarize accurately what people say. The more insight and empathy they bring to bear, and the more thoughtful, reflective, and informed they are, the better able they will be to foster a constructive and productive discussion.

### Chapter 8: Fourth Principle

1. On the rationality of cooperation, see Alfie Cohn, *No Contest: The Case Against Competition* (Boston: Houghton Mifflin, 1986). For scholarly discussions, see Michael Taylor, *The Possibility of Cooperation* (New York: Cambridge University Press, 1987), and Robert M. Axelrod, *The Evolution of Cooperation* (New York: Basic Books, 1984).

2. "Beating the System," *New Republic,* November 5, 1990, 7.

3. Garrett Hardin, "The Tragedy of the Commons," *Science* 162 (December 1968): 1243–48.

4. Some contemporary examples of rational individual decisions that collectively yield results that are in no one's interest: relying on private transportation leads to traffic congestion; building a house in open space leads to overdevelopment; supporting legislation that grants a tax break for a particular activity leads to a complex, loop-hole-ridden tax code that is unfair.

5. See Mancur Olson, *The Logic of Collective Action: Public Goods and the Theory of Groups* (New York: Schocken Books, 1971). See also the entries for "prisoner's dilemma," "game theory," and "social choice theory" in Audi, *Cambridge Dictionary of Philosophy.*

6. Axelrod, *Evolution of Cooperation.*

7. Robert Putnam, "Bowling Alone: America's Declining Social Capital," *Journal of Democracy* 6 (January 1995): 65–78, and idem, "The Strange Disappearance of Civic America," *American Prospect* 24 (Winter 1996): 34–48.

8. Bellah et al., *Habits of the Heart.*

9. "Ontological individualism" doesn't imply that individuals should, or even can, live in physical isolation from each other, having no contact and rejecting the advantages of social living. Rather, it implies that individuals can become fully human, can develop their characteristically human capacities without creating a society that actively respects, encourages, and fosters the development of these capacities.

10. Brent D. Ruben, *Communication and Human Behavior* (Englewood Cliffs, N.J.: Prentice-Hall, 1992), 323–24.

11. Beth B. Hess, Elizabeth W. Markson, and Peter J. Stein, *Sociology* (New York: Macmillan, 1982), 93.

12. Ibid. Specifically, a group has the following characteristics: (1) a distinctive set of social relationships among members; (2) interdependence among various individuals; (3) a feeling that the behavior of each member is relevant to other members; and (4) a sense of membership or "we" feeling.

13. As Hess, Markson, and Stein point out, groups should not be confused with *social categories,* "which are classifications of individuals who share one or more common characteristics but are not interacting. . . . Simple possession of an attribute or occupancy of a status does not make one member of a sociological group. Nor does awareness of similarity alone produce group membership. . . . The term *aggregate* should also be distinguished from *group.* . . . Aggregates are collections of individuals in one place. . . . Such a collection . . . does not constitute a group because there is no notion of interdependence . . . or sense that the behavior of each person has some relevance to others." (Ibid., 88.) For purposes of our discussion of civic infrastructure and cooperation, we are interested in groups, not social categories or aggregates.

14. Ibid., 87–88.

15. Ibid., 88, 90.

16. Ibid., 90.

17. Schwarzenbach, "On Civic Friendship."

18. Hess, Markson and Stein, *Sociology,* 95.

19. Schwarzenbach, "On Civic Friendship," 109.

20. Fisher and Ury, *Getting to YES.*

21. Roger Fisher and Scott Brown, *Getting Together: Building a Relationship That Gets to YES* (Boston: Houghton Mifflin, 1988), offers useful advice on how to get people talking to each other.

22. Bruno Bettelheim, "Punishment versus Discipline," *Atlantic Monthly,* November 1985, 51–59.

23. People resort to coercion for many reasons. They may feel it's futile to engage in discussion, that no amount of patient explanation of their concerns, needs, and fears will change our mind. Or they may think it places an unfair burden on them to have to persuade us to do what seems to them self-evidently right. Or they may simply be too fearful, too frustrated, or too angry to assume responsibility for themselves and to incur the psychic cost of having to restrain their emotions and undertake the laborious effort of working out their differences with us. In resorting to coercion, they fail to take personal responsibility for the dispute to which they are party. Rejecting responsibility, they feel justified in coercing. Failure to take responsibility stems from a

person's fear, anger, insecurity, lack of self-esteem and self-confidence, or personal unhappiness. Resort to coercion is most likely when people perceive a threat from another person or group to something they consider important and rightfully theirs: their "identity," values, rights, interests, privileges, freedom, control, or property.

24. On this point see, for example, Ury, *Getting Past NO: Negotiating with Difficult People.*

25. Friedman, "Healing Through Meeting," 33–35, 85–87.

26. It is not uncommon, of course, for people who lack the psychological resources and interpersonal skills for obtaining positive confirmation to seek it "negatively," by provoking hostile reactions that, in a perverse way, "confirm" their personhood. The remedy for such "negative confirmation," however, is positive confirmation.

27. Kemmis, *Community and the Politics of Place,* 70–73.

28. Ibid., 79.

29. Ibid., 64.

30. Ibid., 78.

31. Ibid., 117.

32. *Report of the Third Annual Trinidad–Las Animas County Community Convention* (Trinidad, Colo.: Las Animas County Forum, 1997).

33. Harry Boyte and Nancy Kari, *Building America: The Democratic Promise of Public Work* (Philadelphia: Temple University Press, 1996).

34. Here are some other examples of public goods created through public work: a council of neighborhoods, a river walk, a community center, a YMCA or YWCA, a new school district, an annual celebration or festival, a child-care cooperative, a community foundation, a youth baseball field, a neighborhood park, a soccer association.

35. Kemmis, *Community and the Politics of Place,* 113.

## Chapter 9: Public Judgment and Action

1. I've put quotation marks around the word "decision" here because I want to reserve this term for a conclusion that everyone can live with or go along with. In my view, if the conclusion that members of a community reach is not one that everyone can live with or go along with, the community has not made a genuine collective decision.

2. As I noted in chapter 1, mechanical procedures such as majority rule are not adequate for the purpose of making a collective judgment. Such devices do not permit us to deal intelligently, wisely, and fairly with competing values and with the interests people have in realizing those values. They can aggregate people's desires— add them up—but they can't integrate them. They can't reconcile the things that are important to people. An aggregation of people's desires—the results of a typical opinion poll, for example—is akin to Rousseau's notion of a "will of all." Rousseau contrasted the "will of all" with what he called the "general will." The concept of a public judgment, which I'm trying to articulate here, resembles the latter.

3. Despite the impressive and laudable efforts of writers such as Naomi Wolf ("Our Bodies, Our Souls," *New Republic,* October 16, 1995, 26–35), George McKenna ("On Abortion: A Lincolnian Position," *Atlantic Monthly,* September 1995, 51–68), Kristin Luker (*Abortion and the Politics of Motherhood* [Berkeley and Los Angeles: University of California Press, 1984]), and Jonathan Glover (*Causing Death and Saving Lives* [New York: Penguin, 1977]), there appears to be no logical (conceptual, theoretical,

philosophical) solution to the issue of abortion. The only possible solution is a (practical) political solution that depends crucially on comprehension and deliberation, which are glaringly absent from the current debate. Because we cannot predict the content of the judgment that an actual group of (comprehending, deliberating) citizens might reach, any hypothetical resolution—indeed, any actual resolution—that might be offered by way of illustration is bound to appear contrived, improbable, or unacceptable to nonparticipants.

4. For the sake of the present example, let's suppose that the participants have dealt with the question of when life begins, and hence the question of whether the fetus is a "life" in the morally relevant sense, by setting that question aside and focusing on the more important part of life for both the girl and the gestating fetus: the part that begins with and comes after a live birth. In the stated facts of the hypothetical case given in chapter 7, of course, there was a question whether the girl could survive delivery. But let us suppose that the participants considered this particular circumstance to be sufficiently rare that it need not figure decisively in their attempt to reach a shared judgment that might serve as the foundation for a general policy. Let us suppose they concluded that, in the vast majority of cases, survival of both mother and child would not be in doubt. Accordingly, they agreed that the more pressing question is whether it is possible and morally permissible to weigh the value of the (postdelivery) life of the gestating fetus against the value of the (postdelivery) life of the pregnant girl.

5. The kinds of cases under consideration here are those that, for adherents of $V_1$, involve the "innocent life of unborn children."

6. I assume here that, for adherents of $V_2$, the life of the fetus, because it is "potential" rather than "actual," does not have equal standing with the life of the mother.

7. As indicated in chapter 5, devices such as the council of neighborhoods, the Citizens' Jury™, and the citizens' advisory committee might also serve as useful vehicles for working toward a public judgment that will authorize and facilitate community action.

8. An effective but also manageable way to conduct this sort of weighted voting is to hand out self-adhesive dots that people can place next to the items on the list. For example, you might give participants six dots and tell them they may distribute them any way they like.

## Chapter 11: Leadership, Practical Politics, and Hope

1. Assembling and maintaining a numerical majority for the purpose of obtaining the authority to make binding decisions requires the skill to be responsive to the desires of as many individuals and groups as possible without upsetting others. It requires a knack for keeping peace between persons and groups, getting them to compromise so that a majority will form behind a particular policy stance or proposal. It requires adeptness at persuading people that their interests will be protected, their wishes respected, and their positions defended—even though it goes (literally) without saying, someone has to lose.

2. It does so by undermining the willingness of citizens to take personal responsibility for the difficult decisions that inevitably arise in our public life. Recall the analysis I offered in chapter 1: Suppose that group A and group B disagree over whether policy X (which A prefers) or policy B (which Y prefers) is the proper response to a particular problem. If A and B believe that their representative, R, has the authority to re-

solve the conflict between X and Y, they will be inclined to believe it is also R's *responsibility* to resolve it. Why? Because "ought implies can." We can't, A and B reason; therefore, we ought not. It doesn't occur to A and B that *they* might have a responsibility to choose between X and Y, because they believe they "can't" (in the sense of "are not authorized to") make that choice. Instead, they transfer their responsibility to R, and R accepts it. The result is that citizens are excused from the hard work of resolving conflicts themselves, and are licensed to press their demands untempered on the persons who represent them. Leadership becomes a matter of responsiveness to the opinions and preferences of the political "market."

3. In chapter 3 I described two putative alternatives to "consumerist politics," which I labeled the "service" and "protest" approaches to responding to matters of public concern. On the service approach, "professionals" (the service equivalent of producers) help "clients" meet their personal or social needs. On the protest approach, the counterparts of consumers and clients are "victims"—disempowered unfortunates whose injuries, suffering, or oppression cannot be alleviated without the aid of strong "advocates." Each of these approaches—consumerist politics and the service and protest alternatives to it—divides people into two basic categories: those who do things in response to public problems or needs, and those on whose behalf things are done.

4. McKnight, "Regenerating Community." See also his *The Careless Society.*

5. On the importance of such organizations in the life of a community, see Peter L. Berger and Richard John Neuhaus, *To Empower People: The Role of Mediating Structures in Public Policy* (Washington, D.C.: Enterprise Institute, 1977).

6. Charles W. Anderson, "Political Philosophy, Practical Reason, and Policy Analysis," in *Confronting Values in Policy Analysis: The Politics of Criteria,* ed. Frank Fischer and John Forester (Newbury Park, California: Sage, 1989), 34.

7. Douglas Torgerson, "Between Knowledge and Politics: Three Faces of Policy Analysis," *Policy Sciences* 19 (1986): 34.

8. Because problems such as crime, economic stagnation, ineffective education, and the like cannot be solved by any one person or group, they require a public response. Even when a "market solution" for a social problem is appropriate, no individual or group acting unilaterally can effect such a solution. Only the public can authorize and implement a market-based response. When markets are permitted to operate, they do so because, explicitly or implicitly, we agree that they should.

9. See the discussion of this in Harry Boyte, *Commonwealth: A Return to Citizen Politics* (New York: Free Press, 1989).

10. Schneider, "An Insider's View of the Election," 55–56.

11. Richard Flacks, *Making History: The Radical Tradition in American Life* (New York: Columbia University Press, 1988), 3.

12. James S. Fishkin, *Democracy and Deliberation* (New Haven: Yale University Press, 1991): 3.

# Index

**Michael K. Briand** is director of the Community Self-Leadership Project, a community civic-development consulting service in Denver, Colorado. He holds a Ph.D. in political philosophy from Johns Hopkins University.

Typeset in 9.5/13.25 Sabon
with Univers display
Designed by Evelyn C. Shapiro
Composed by Jim Proefrock
at the University of Illinois Press